Culúa

Dear Dorothy:

With very best wishes

Culúa

My other life in Mexico

SAMANTHA WOOD

BANTAM BOOKS
SYDNEY • AUCKLAND • TORONTO • NEW YORK • LONDON

CULÚA
A BANTAM BOOK

First published in Australia and New Zealand in 2003 by Bantam

National Library of Australia
Cataloguing-in-Publication Entry

Wood, Samantha.
  Culua.

  ISBN 1 86325 365 3.

  1. Wood, Samantha – Journey – Mexico.
  2. Mexico – Description and travel. I. Title.

917.2

Transworld Publishers,
a division of Random House Australia Pty Ltd
20 Alfred Street, Milsons Point, NSW 2061
http://www.randomhouse.com.au

Random House New Zealand Limited
18 Poland Road, Glenfield, Auckland

Transworld Publishers,
a division of The Random House Group Ltd
61-63 Uxbridge Road, London W5 5SA

Random House Inc
1745 Broadway, New York, New York 10036

Cover photograph courtesy Richard I'Anson/Lonely Planet Images
Cover and internal design by Darian Causby/Highway 51
Typeset by Midland Typesetters, Maryborough, Victoria
Printed and bound by Griffin Press, Netley, South Australia

10 9 8 7 6 5 4 3 2 1

For my parents, Maxim and Sara,
and my brother, Miguel, for everything.
A mi abuela, Rebeca, con amor.

Contents

Prologue

Seven years ago I made a decision that would change my life, although I didn't know it at the time. I'd go to Mexico: the country of my mother's birth, and a place, for me at least, of mystery and intrigue.

My decision wasn't entirely spontaneous. I had a month's annual leave from my job as a researcher at a newspaper and I wanted to do something different. Mexico, it seemed, was *quite* different from tranquil Melbourne. Why I chose there instead of, say, Paris – somewhere I had always wanted to go – was simple. In Mexico City I could stay with relatives, they would show me around, I might even pick up a few words of Spanish. What could be better? I was off on an adventure to a land oozing Latin rhythms, peopled by sensual women and macho men, the country where *mariachis* roam, singing their love songs and laments, a place of roasted iguana with black beans, bullfights and ancient pyramids. A place like no other.

What I knew of Mexico was gleaned from the snippets my mother had told me of her life before Australia, and from my memories of a trip there when I was nine. My mother had taken my brother and me to her country and we stayed with our grandparents in Mexico City. I was agape at the sight of beggars in the streets, men riding donkeys, and the enormous bags of pastries my grandfather brought home from the bakery every evening. At the age of twenty-five, sixteen years after that journey, I was back, ready to fill in the blanks created by a hazy childhood imagination. I was confident and expectant. I remember thinking I would get along because my mother is Mexican, as if, by maternal osmosis, acceptance and understanding would be immediate. But it didn't happen that way.

I was in for the shock of my life.

Chapter One

Land of the Culúa:
Into Mexico

I am exhausted and follow the other passengers down a long corridor. I do not ask for directions; the other travellers have a self-assured air which suggests *they* know where they are going. The skin on my arms is puckered with goose bumps in the cold air, but I don't care – I'm too excited to concern myself with trivialities.

Suddenly the corridor comes to an end and everyone stops. I find myself standing in a vast room with grey linoleum tiles and the faint odour of disinfectant. As if by prior arrangement the passengers quickly form two lines to await passport inspection – with the exception of a few stragglers at the back, myself included. Even through my jet-lagged eyes I find this scene amusing. In one line are the foreigners: white-skinned, passports in hand, orderly and standing at a respectable distance behind one another. In the other, the locals: dark complexions, passports nowhere to be seen and lolling, leaning or shoving impatiently.

My mind must be elsewhere, because I do not hear a woman talking to me. Even if I had, I wouldn't have understood her. It is only when I feel a rough tap – from a baton, not a hand – on my bare arm that I turn around. The uniformed official reproaches me in a loud voice while waving her instrument in the air. '¡Señorita!' Who, me? Responding to my O-shaped mouth she speaks faster and louder. Yells, to be more accurate. She is saying something about a line. And foreigners. *Usted. Fila. Extranjeros.* In desperation I join the dots. I have to because she is now inches from my face, her rapid speech sending flecks of saliva in my direction. *You!* What are you doing in this line? The one for foreigners. I hold up my passport and she looks at it before walking away, an expression of mild confusion darkening her brow. Welcome to Mexico . . .

I claim my baggage and make my way towards the exit. There are no automatic doors like those at Melbourne airport. No doors at all, just a long metal barrier separating travellers from a sea of waiting relatives. Before me a set of traffic lights. Green means go. Red? Haul your bags onto a steel bench for inspection by a customs official and about three hundred curious onlookers. I get a red light. A bored woman opens my case, takes everything out and then says, 'Okay.' What does she mean, okay? And was it really necessary to remove every last sock from my suitcase? I spend ten minutes trying to shut the lid before pulling the whole thing off the bench. I sit on it and pull the zipper shut.

I take a deep breath and keep moving and suddenly I am in the arrivals hall. It's an old building with brown tiles on the walls, like the ones you might find in an Australian suburban kitchen, circa 1970. It seems as if the building itself is resigned to its neglected, doleful state. I don't know what I was expecting but it wasn't this. It smells too, of ammonia, sweat, perfume and the dense throng of humanity surrounding me. I walk to the exit. What's one dirty airport? Why such trepidation? I have lived in London. Travelled around Europe and America alone. Could it be that this mystical country may not live up to my expectations? I bury the thought. I can do this, I say to myself. Yet as I approach the doors, I feel a knot in my stomach.

Finally I make it outside. My head, still troubled by my thoughts, is now assailed by an image that will be forever recorded in my memory. My view is of a concrete landscape. Cement buildings all in jagged rows, each vying to be bigger and uglier than the others. Construction sites. Cranes. Scaffolding. High-rises. Above me a concrete overpass weaves into the distance, blending with the sky, which is *exactly* the same colour as the buildings. It is as if the whole city has been spray-painted a dull grey. Of course, that's not the least of it. The noise is unbearable. Car horns blaring, tyres screeching, yelling, whistles, planes overhead, the voices of men, women and children all trying to be heard. An indecipherable language. A cacophony of sound set against a backdrop of grime and poverty. Mexico City is just *so* dirty.

My mother always spoke of her country in glowing terms, describing the quiet city where she had spent her childhood. It was a place where men travelled on horseback, children played stickball in the streets and women sat together on long homestead verandas, sipping *limonada*, lemonade, talking, laughing and whiling away the afternoons under a postcard blue sky. But now that I'm standing here all I can think is that I've been duped. I think of her words, *you have to make the best of what you've got*, and try to look for something redeeming. But the truth is, if I could change my 'unchangeable' ticket I would go straight back inside and head to Hawaii.

By the time I find the line for the official airport taxis, the initial bravado that propelled me through the United States has well and truly vanished. What seemed like a wonderful idea two weeks ago – a month in Mexico, *how exotic* – now looks like the ill-conceived, hastily made decision it was. I should have thought about what I was doing. Too late now.

A man is yelling at me. Still unable to shake off my exhaustion, I stand looking at him, watching his mouth contort into angry shapes. He comes over and grabs my elbow, pointing to a taxi. Now I am not just disappointed, shocked and tired but I'm also pissed off. 'Get off me,' I tell him. Seeing my annoyance his tone softens as he attempts a few words in English. You. Taxi. Miss. Huh, that's more like it. I'm barely out of the airport and already two complete strangers have yelled and manhandled me. Sort of. I thought Mexicans were supposed to be *kind* and *gentle*?

By this stage I just want to get to my grandmother's house. After nearly two hours in baggage claim and then customs my last reserves of energy are about to dry up. It is early morning and the sun has not yet managed to peek through the clouds. I am starting to feel a chill, standing here in a sleeveless top. Tropical Mexico. Singlet weather. It never occurred to me that it might be cold. Another misconception. Clearly I have to come to terms with my situation, and very soon, because I will be here for four weeks. As I get into the taxi, I cheer myself with the idea that things will get better when I get to my grandmother's apartment.

'*Colonia Narvarte*,' I tell the driver. '*¿Qué?*' he says. What? Instead of repeating myself I hand him the piece of paper with my grandmother's address. He nods before pulling into the traffic and narrowly missing a man crossing the road.

From the taxi window I can see more grey buildings, industrial sites and general disrepair. The view is one of unmitigated poverty. I have little time to take it all in because there is a more pressing matter at hand: the driver is trying to kill us. I want to tell him *not so fast* but the only part of that sentence I know is *rápido*. It is worth a try. '*Rápido*,' I say. '*Si señorita*,' he replies. But instead of slowing down he hammers it. I quickly realise my mistake. Now we are going to die. For the rest of the trip I hold onto whatever grip I can find in the back seat as the driver brakes within inches of the cars in front and changes lanes so fast I am thrown off balance.

After forty minutes we enter a residential area of tree-lined streets and even occasionally small parks, their stone benches tinted pastel blue by the pollution and the sun. This is the city where my mother grew up, I think, looking at the urban sprawl. I try to restore my flagging spirits, telling myself what a wonderful adventure I will have in a country so steeped in tradition and history, but the knot in my stomach hasn't loosened at all.

The taxi turns down a quiet, leafy side street and stops outside a three-storey apartment block rendered in tiles similar to those I saw at the airport, except these are green. After I pay the driver I find myself standing on the nature strip outside the apartment my grandmother shares with my aunt and her two children. Next door is a mechanic's yard, strewn with the wrecks of old cars and with hubcaps, tyres and fan belts hanging from nails on the wall. Just inside the gate a black dog is lying on the ground. He snarls when he sees me. To my surprise the street is empty. Somehow I had assumed it would be full of women and children going about their business. There is nothing left to do but ring the bell.

The security door is open so I go in and start to drag my awkward suitcase up the six flights of stairs. The last time I saw my grandmother I was nine years old. My grandmother had come to the airport to meet us. She was wearing a green dress. That is my only clear memory; other recollections are fuddled by the passage of time. I stop on the first landing to catch my breath. My heart is pounding and it is not just because I am puffed. What am I going to say to her? What *can* I say to her? I don't speak Spanish. She doesn't speak English. I can barely remember her. My initial doubts have now turned into full-blown terror. Coming here was a bad, bad idea.

Still, there is no going back now. I reach the top floor and see that the apartment door is open, and my grandmother and aunt are standing in the hallway. They haven't seen me yet. I hesitate. I'm not sure what to do next.

Suddenly a great commotion ensues. Arms waving. Talking loudly. That must be my cue? I walk over to my grandmother, who is now standing with her hands over her face, crying uncontrollably. I hug her. 'Don't cry,' my aunt says, 'your granddaughter is here now.' My Spanish is terrible but this much I understand.

They hustle me into the lounge room and I sit down on the sofa. I can't believe it. When did the beautiful girl I had seen in my mother's photos give way to the old woman before me? The grandmother I knew from old black and white photos had round eyes, pale skin and curly hair, a voluptuous figure in velvet stilettos and feminine dresses. An extraordinary beauty. Now she is tiny, grey and stooped. She is so changed, not a speck of her former self remains. Seeing her does not trigger any memories from that childhood trip sixteen years ago. I don't remember her. I simply don't remember *anything*. I do not know these people in front of me, even though I assumed we would bond immediately. I bubble with frustration at my inability to communicate, feeling cheated because in my fantasy of what Mexico was like it looked nothing like this. I want to scream at my grandmother: *Who are you?* My arrival moved her to tears yet I feel nothing. Just tired and ashamed.

In spite of my dark mood I am curious. As my grand-mother passes on her way to the kitchen I notice something I hadn't when I came in – her eyes. My eyes. Her features. My features. She is wearing my face. An older, wiser version, but there is no mistaking our physical similarities. The realisation sucks the breath from my chest and my shock must register because she smiles, comfortingly. In front of her sits the woman she once was; in front of me the woman I will be in fifty years. No wonder my mother wanted me to come to Mexico. *Don't you want to know where you come from?* Well, maybe I do. I grip the edge of the couch and turn away to look out the window, stunned.

The balcony door is slightly ajar. Outside, the noise is nearly as deafening as it was at the airport. I also recognise the same stench: stale cigarettes and body odour. It is, as I am soon to find out, the smell of pollution. My train of thought is interrupted by my aunt asking me a question. I can tell it's a question by the arch of her eyebrows, although I have no idea what she is saying. '*Comida*,' she says. Ah, I get it. Food. Come to think of it, I am starving. On the plane I had beans, rice and chicken. To my surprise it was delicious, or maybe I was just hungry.

I sit at the table. It is set with a line-up of Western condiments: mustard, tomato sauce, white bread. So far so good. My grandmother brings out a few dishes and then goes back to the kitchen, finally returning with something wrapped in a tea towel. Tortillas, I discover. My two cousins, six and eight years old, are now sitting next to me. They seem more interested in lunch than the stranger beside them. I take a tortilla and bite. They laugh before my grandmother shushes them. The older of the two pats me on the arm and takes a tortilla, puts a spoonful of beans in the middle and rolls it like a cigar. Eating lessons from a child. How much worse can this get? Looking at my cousins, I feel a pang of jealousy. I know it's ridiculous, but nevertheless it's there. Growing up on the other side of the world robbed me of my grandmother. Is it normal to ricochet from bewilderment to jealousy in a matter of seconds? I know these people are my relatives but I can't help feeling nervous, like a stranger who just barged in on a private occasion.

For the next five minutes I take my cues from the children. Everyone is talking too fast for me to follow. My cousins tug at my clothing, asking me things in what sounds like gobbledygook. All I understand is my name: '¡Samantita, Samantita!' I try to join the conversation but each pronouncement is a painful, laboured affair. In the end I just sit and eat.

After pasta, tortillas, beans and stew another plate is placed in front of me. I study its contents. Chicken. Definitely chicken. And brown stuff. My grandmother must catch my dubious expression because she points to the plate and says twice: *mole*. I remember reading about the origins of this spicy sauce. The nuns of a Puebla convent, told of the imminent arrival of the bishop, put together a lunch for him using all the ingredients they could find in the kitchen. Chocolate, onions, herbs, cinnamon, almonds, raisins, chile, tomatoes and peanuts. Some twenty ingredients and a national dish was born: *mole poblano*.

Everyone is chowing into it so I do the same. Immediately I regret my decision. It's awful. It tastes like mud pie. With stones. I swallow and feel it burning my gullet as it goes down. The aftertaste reminds me of the time I went riding on my bike with my brother and fell off, hitting the ground face first and eating a mouthful of dirt.

I take a sip of Coke.

The *mole* isn't bad, it is *disgusting*. I wonder whether one of my cousins put detergent in it when my grandmother wasn't looking. In the middle of this thought I realise my aunt is talking to me. She speaks slowly. 'Your grandmother has been preparing this for the last two days. It's her specialty.'

'Mmm,' I say. My grandmother and aunt both give me a strange look. Later I learn *mmm* has a sexual connotation in Spanish – somewhere along the lines of *hubba hubba* but infinitely more explicit. At the time I don't know that nor do I know the word for delicious. It's probably a good thing, as the lie would get stuck in my throat.

After spending the afternoon sitting on the couch in a bit of a daze, catching only snippets of the whirl of conversation around me, just after seven I decide to go to bed. My head is starting to bob as I try to stay awake. I'm sharing a room with my eight-year-old cousin, Julia, who is already asleep. From the lounge room I hear the muffled voices of my grandmother and aunt, the tone of their voices soothing even though I can't understand what they're saying. As I put my head on the pillow I listen to Julia's soft breathing. In the back of my mind is the idea that sleep will remove me, temporarily at least, from the nightmare I am in. I lie in bed for hours but despite my tiredness I can't sleep. Some four hours after going to bed I am about to drop into an exhausted sleep when the bed starts to shake, gently at first but then with great force. I sit bolt upright and think for a moment it might be an earthquake until I hear the beep of a horn and the rumble of a truck.

Tomorrow is another day, I say to myself. Things will get better. But as hard as I try to convince myself, the truth is that I absolutely detest this place. No amount of self-talk can change that. I see little of myself in these people. My own family are practically strangers. Their language is beyond me. It's noisy and polluted. I need clean air and blue sky. Where are the palm trees? Somehow I imagined Mexico City to be full of palm trees. Perhaps in my fantasy I had added elements of Mexico's tropical coastline to this cityscape. Or maybe I'm wishing I'd holidayed somewhere tropical.

The image of Mexico I had created in my mind before I got there was so far removed from reality it may as well have been modelled on a Speedy Gonzáles cartoon. I can still recall the Mexicans' confusion (or disgust, I can't be sure) upon discovering I didn't speak Spanish, because my appearance – hair, eyes, skin colour – marked me as not exactly Mexican, but somewhere in the ballpark. I felt acutely foreign. During my stay I was horrified by what I saw. Crime. Pollution. Poverty. Gritty reality. I couldn't see beyond the veneer of decay. I was doing what Mexicans call *seeing with your eyes shut*. It was all too much for me. I was out of my depth and desperate to leave.

After that fateful trip I returned to Australia, vowing never to return. But this magical country was not done with me yet. Nor I with Mexico. Something, perhaps a little voice from deep within, told me I had to try again. That there was more to Mexico than meets the eye.

In Mexico it is often said that there are no shades of grey. There is only black or white. Passion, love, hate, anger and joy are all felt strongly. If there is one expression that encapsulates my experiences in this ancient land, it is this: you love it *and* hate it, but you are never indifferent. It might be best described as a fiery relationship between two lovers but, all the same, it's one I can't get enough of.

Chapter Two

Breaking a Promise

The plane arrives in Mexico City at dawn. The cabin lights come on and an unruly queue forms in the aisle. I decide to wait until the line disperses; I don't want to be squashed between these tired and fed-up strangers. The other passengers are mostly Mexican. Men with blue-black hair and moustaches, women wearing floral shirts, heavy make-up and elaborate hairdos, children with big brown eyes and angelic faces. After no sleep I'm buzzing with the kind of exhaustion that makes you forget who you are. I close my eyes. But as people shuffle past, their sweet, singsong voices reach my ears and bring me back to life, sparking a recollection; a memory of a promise I'd made to myself after my previous visit fourteen months ago:

I'll never come back.

At the time I meant it. But it was a decision soon overcome by my love of travelling and curiosity about Mexico.

Which is why I now find myself sitting on this plane shrouded in fog – or smog, more likely – waiting to cross the threshold into this strange other world. Stragglers are beginning to dribble past so I take my bag from the overhead locker and follow them off the plane. Down the gangplank. Through customs. And into the arrivals hall. I'm back!

On this January morning the arrivals hall at Benito Juárez airport is just how I remember it: dank and depressing. I stand near an exit door and every few minutes I get blasted by the arctic current coming through the automatic doors. I don't move; somehow the cold is invigorating. Having been here before, I'm more or less prepared for what's on the other side of the glass doors. No more promises, I tell myself. Expect the unexpected.

Eventually my ride turns up. My uncle and his girlfriend are taking me to my grandmother's place in their car. A car! What a luxury. With no hair-raising taxi ride to contend with, I settle into the back seat. As we leave the airport I turn back to see it lit up, blinking blue and yellow against a still-dark backdrop.

I watch as the silhouette of the airport gets swallowed up by the surrounding buildings. And then it's gone. I sit back and think about why I have returned to a place I remember hating with a passion. I'm not sure why I'm here. The only thing I know for certain is that I don't want my abiding memory of Mexico to be a negative one. For me, one of the main attractions of Mexico is its mystery, and the knowledge that there *is* more to this place than I have seen so far. I want to peel back the layers of this country to find out what lies beneath. Sure, the thrill of adventure and the chance to embrace the unknown have played a part in my decision, but there is another less tangible motivation – *el destino*. Destiny has led me here.

This place offers me an escape from all that is familiar.

Here I can reinvent myself away from the influence of family, friends and home. I have left my job and bought an open ticket, so I have no idea how long I will stay. Leaving my job is a risk, financially at least, but it's one worth taking. Having worked at the *Herald Sun* since I was twenty-one, I'm ready for a change. And while the future may be uncertain, there is something seductive about not knowing what's going to happen next.

By the time we arrive at *Colonia Narvarte* the sky has turned crimson pink. In the early-morning traffic a sea of trucks, semi-trailers, old flatbed Fords, bakery and removal vans compete for space on the road with green and white taxis, all old Volkswagen beetles. Passengers jump from buses that haven't quite stopped. I watch this congestion soup in amazement and put on my sunglasses, even though there's no sun, so I can get a better look at the chaos.

The car makes another turn and I begin to recognise familiar sights. We make our way down a narrow laneway lined with bakeries, pizzerias and fruit shops. I open my window and as I lean back the aroma of baking pastries wafts under my nose. I make a mental note to come back once I'm settled in.

Finally we turn into *Calle Tajin*, my grandmother's street. We drive past low-rise buildings and empty office space. Houses with tiny garden plots – cacti, yuccas, roses, box hedges – arranged beautifully; manicured welcome mat lawns; toy gardens contained by steel fences. And then we pull up outside the green-tiled apartment block. To my delight, I climb the stairs not with a feeling of anxiety but one of eagerness. I'm looking forward to seeing my grandmother again. On this trip I've resolved to give myself time to get to know my family. Too much of my last visit was clouded with unrealistic expectations – expecting to bond *immediately* with my relatives. I'm determined not to make the same mistake again.

My uncle and his girlfriend are already on the landing outside the apartment. Pulling my suitcase behind him, my uncle leads us through the already open door. The house is silent.

'The children are at school and your aunt is at work,' my uncle says without prompting.

Suddenly my grandmother comes out of the kitchen. She is nodding and smiling.

'*Hola mijita*,' she says, embracing me. Hello daughter.

She greets me as though I was only here yesterday. And in a way I feel like I never left.

Soon I'm seated on the couch with a cup of coffee, watching a breakfast television show. My grandmother wanders back into the kitchen and my uncle and his girlfriend leave for work. I sit back and look around me. The scene is *exactly* the same but I feel different. More optimistic perhaps. I close my eyes, feeling warm inside.

It's late morning by the time I get out of the apartment. I make my way towards the shops I saw earlier in the day, at the same time staying close to home. I had discovered on my last visit that strolling around Mexico City can be a dangerous habit – with such a proliferation of identical grey buildings it's easy to get lost. After a few minutes I come across a tiny bakery. Inside, the aroma embraces me. I am in an Aladdin's Cave of pastry: the shelves are full of donuts – chocolate, strawberry, cinnamon, and jam, my favourite – croissants, cream buns, biscuits, and dozens of other variations on cream and butter. They also have distinctly Mexican treats. There are *orejas*, ear-shaped pastries made with butter and coated in sugar; *churros*, fried pastry fingers rolled in sugar; and another goody, whose name I do not know, that looks like a large communion wafer, folded over and held together with a squirt of caramel. This is my idea of heaven. Up to my eyeballs in gooey delights, I finally pick randomly and thank the woman behind the counter in halting Spanish.

I sit down on a bench on the corner of *Calle Tajin* and take the pastry from the bag. I've chosen something that looks like a piece of bread buttered on both sides, encrusted with sugar, and quite probably fried. I take a bite. It's delicious. Mexicans have a great love affair with pastries: they make them into a million shapes, sing songs about them and have special breads for national holidays. A country that celebrates cake. This is my kind of place.

Suddenly my reverie is interrupted by the arrival of a bus; I'm sitting at a bus stop. I wave the driver on with a sugar-coated hand. The bus screeches off into the traffic, leaving behind a cloud of exhaust fumes that head directly for me. I laugh in spite of myself. I left behind a funky St Kilda apartment and a Melbourne summer lying on the beach for this! Never mind that the apartment wasn't mine and I won't even leave the house without a hat. I've swapped it all for my very own cloud of diesel.

The smell of exhaust fumes, dust and cooking food stirs memories of my previous visit. I feel a knot of tension in my stomach but I ignore it; I refuse to give in to negative thoughts. If I'm going to stay in this country I have to find a new way of seeing the world. I need to put aside thoughts of Australia and the life I had there, to forget about how I do things back home. If I can do this, then I'll be on my way to finding beauty amid the bus fumes.

It takes a week to get over my jet lag. While my aunt is at work and my cousins at school I spend a lot of time watching television with my grandmother, our conversations limited by our mutual inability to speak each other's language. It would be nice to be able to talk with her; to get to know her a little better. And from this thought a seed is planted in my mind. I decide to enrol in language classes.

None of my extended family speak English and I am forced to communicate in Spanish, so this is a perfect opportunity. And unlike my previous visit, I saved for months before I came here so money for tuition won't be a problem.

Life here will be much easier when I can speak and understand Spanish. In any case, if I sit around doing nothing much longer my thoughts will start to rattle around my head like the tigers in the children's story that chase each other's tails until they all turn into butter.

On the recommendation of my aunt, who works as a psychology lecturer at the National Autonomous University of Mexico, I settle on the Teaching Centre for Foreigners, which is part of the University's arts faculty and is also the oldest language school in Mexico City. When I call they ask me to come in to sit a 'competency' test. *¿Qué miedo?* How scary? Not at all, they tell me. It is just to see what level of proficiency you possess. Now I'm getting excited. In my mind I'm already at the top of the class. Fluency is only weeks away. In no time I'm going to have this language business covered.

The National Autonomous University is a sprawling campus situated south of Mexico City. It is enormous. This fact is brought home to me one afternoon when I try to walk around the entire campus, a circuit that takes me just under two hours. There are some 270,000 students, and to get an idea of how large a university has to be to accommodate so many *estudiantes* you only have to begin with the Faculty of Medicine, which is larger in scale than Melbourne University as a whole.

Although I live on the same side of the city as the university, it still takes me an hour to get there by *colectivo* – one of the rickety buses that fan across the city like arteries, pumping out passengers to the far reaches of this metropolis and every stop in between. For the first week I catch the bus heading to Copilco feeling like a bigger version of Paddington Bear as I clutch a piece of paper on which my aunt has written my address, phone number, destination and a couple of handy phrases: '*Ústed me puede decir cuando lleguemos a . . .*', and '*La que sigue por favor*' – 'Can you tell me when we arrive at (insert destination)', and 'Next stop please'.

After a couple of weeks I begin to notice a certain *colectivo* etiquette, as though each passenger has a role in a well-rehearsed play: men disperse to allow women passengers on first; they also hang – effortlessly, it seems – from the stairwells; bus fares are passed through a dozen hands to the driver and then the process is repeated with the change; strangers hold your bag and your children. I'm fascinated by this considerate behaviour. What are the chances of ten strangers passing your fare to the guy next to the ticket machine on a Melbourne tram? And then passing back the change? The trip itself soon becomes almost as interesting as the classes.

The Spanish lessons are the highlight of my day; they are also an exercise in humility. (Despite my initial confidence, I'm in level one, only one step above the can't-even-say-hello Spanish virgins.) There are twenty students in the class: an American married to a Mexican girl; a German with an accent so strong that the first time I hear him speak I feel like I've been thumped with an anvil; a Swiss who shows great promise with Spanish; fourteen Koreans; one Chinese girl; a Japanese guy, Yoshio; and myself. Together we make up the sorriest bunch of students to ever open a textbook.

For the Asian students, the chances of getting their tongues around the rolling 'rr's and double 'll's that appear so often in Spanish are slim, not only because these letters do not exist in their language but because this is another *alphabet* for them. The rest of us at least have the benefit of familiarity with the Western alphabet, although we still don't often outshine our Asian counterparts. It's true I have mastered the double *ll*, as in *¿cómo te llamas?* (pronounced 'yamas'), but anything with more than one 'r' is beyond me.

The rolling 'rr' is so named for the 'rolling' sound that comes from the back of the throat when these two consonants are pronounced together. When a Spanish-speaker rolls their 'rr's' it has a lovely, singsong quality. But for us, it's not so easy. Our teacher reassures us this is a common problem for many foreign students. When it comes to some of the simplest words like *perro*, dog, I fall over my pronunciation every time. Instead of pronouncing each 'r' with a gentle roll I emit a sound that resembles 'aargh'. It seems you have either got it or you haven't – and I certainly haven't. I just can't seem to get my throat to raise the right sound. The problem is rectified to an extent by adding a suffix, and so my neighbour's little dog is a lovely *perrito*, and his other dog, a big one, is a *perrote*. Although they all have the rolled 'rr', for some reason it seems easier to pronounce a word where the emphasis is on vowels: perrote, perrito, and not consonants. But what will I do when I meet someone with a medium-sized dog?

What surprises me the most during the six-week course is how little of the language I actually know. Somehow I had convinced myself that because of my genetic bloodline I would grasp it in no time – which I suppose is a bit like saying you know how to perform brain surgery because your dad is a neurosurgeon. My mother had attempted to teach her language to my brother and me when we were little, but we weren't interested. It was bad enough looking like a wog – dark skin, thick black hair, *foreign* parents – without sounding like one too. For my part, whenever she tried, I covered my ears and hummed until she walked away.

And now here I am paying for the privilege. I can picture my mother grinning smugly as I tell her about the classes over the phone. The irony is not lost on me.

At the end of the course, even though I'm still speaking in the present tense all the time – I'm yet to master past or future conjugations – I pay for the next course. The six-week semesters are very expensive (four hundred American dollars) and will leave me with little money, but I'm undeterred. I don't want to miss this opportunity. Learning another language is such a rewarding experience, and even though my progress is painful, I feel a sense of achievement. There is another, perhaps more significant reason, one I have been dwelling on since I arrived in Mexico: it is time. Time, I think, to embrace my heritage.

'*¿Te puedo ayudar?*'

I'm standing in the doorway of the kitchen, watching my grandmother struggle with a heavy earthenware dish. My offer of help is met by a dismissal. If you want to help, I am told, you can go and sit down. The table is set for lunch and my cousins are already seated. I hover, not sure if I should obey this directive or try again. I make one more attempt. Can I put the dishes on the table? The tortillas? A voice sings out in reply.

'*¡No! ¡Qué no!!!*'

Far from being pleased by my persistent attempts, my grandmother is annoyed. I slink away. In Mexico, after being shooed from the kitchen about, oh, a zillion times, I have discovered that a woman's kitchen is her domain. Pitching in, as my friends do when they come around for dinner in Melbourne, is an alien concept here. I can't help feeling uncomfortable with this social code. Why should my grandmother do all the work? A seventy-eight-year-old woman shouldn't be waiting on me. But what I see as the norm, she sees as interference. Rather than start a cross-cultural war, I sit down and shut the hell up.

Atop a white tablecloth is an assortment of earthenware dishes. I peek at their contents, and even though I wasn't allowed to help, at least I can now tell what all the dishes are: black beans with *chorizo* (Spanish sausage); *caldo de pollo* (chicken broth with rice and lemon); and *albondigas* (meatballs) for my cousins. There is a platter of *nopales* – strips cut from the nopal plant, a type of cactus that tastes somewhere between raw green capsicum and what I imagine grass would taste like – and a stack of tortillas made from blue corn, wrapped in a white cloth embroidered around the edges.

On my previous visit I had been shocked by the amount of food that appeared on the table every lunchtime. I'd hoped the table was a sturdy one because it had to be, straining as it was under the weight of plate after plate of beans, rice, bread, tortillas, chicken, beef, potato salad, more beans, jelly, pastries and Coke. One day I had tried to ask my grandmother about it. '*Abuelita*, the food . . .' I said, pausing to put together the rest of the sentence in my head. I didn't get the rest out before she answered me.

'Yes, I know,' she said solemnly. 'I didn't make much today.' I was stunned. It looked like the Mexican army was coming over for lunch. But after dining with other relatives and, on a couple of occasions, teachers from the Teaching Centre for Foreigners, I have begun to notice a pattern: everybody here eats like this. Mexicans have *very* big appetites. And the words I once read in a Mexican travel guide now begin to make sense: *food is the greatest expression of love*. At this rate I'm going to be loved to death.

I begin with a bowl of soup, lingering over every mouthful. The chicken is light and tender, the broth has just the right balance of lemon and salt, and the rice is soft but not too soft. The exquisite flavours mingle in my mouth. After the soup I reach for a tortilla and spoon in a small amount of beans before rolling it cigar-like to eat it, as my cousins so memorably showed me. Well, I'm satisfied. The beans are the perfect ending to a delicious meal. I sit back and thank my grandmother for all the effort she has gone to. But there will be no getting out of lunch so easily. My grandmother puts down her fork.

'Just wait,' she says, 'I'll get the rest.'

'Oh,' I reply. 'There's more?'

My grandmother laughs; she thinks I'm joking. The next course is a plate of *sopes* – a kind of small thick tortilla, filled with melted, stringy Oaxaca cheese, lettuce, mashed kidney beans and onions. Their tantalising smell wafts under my nose as if the little blighters are daring me to eat them. Well, okay, if you insist. I pick one up and take a bite. Delicious. Divine. Better than heaven. My grandmother has come back to the table with her own *sopes*, four of them crowded onto her plate. My aunt looks shocked. '¡*Mamá!*' she says. 'Look how many you've got!' I begin to laugh. My grandmother puts a finger to her lips and chuckles too. 'Shh,' she says, 'don't tell anyone.' We all laugh. Maybe the guidebook was right: happiness is a many-course meal among family.

Of course, I have the good fortune to have a grandmother who is an extraordinary cook. My grandmother could make a piece of cardboard taste like haute cuisine; cooking is a skill she has spent a lifetime perfecting. When my great-grandfather was killed during the Mexican Revolution, my great-grandmother Julia put her culinary skills to use by opening a restaurant in a marketplace, and the youngest of her daughters, my grandmother Rebeca, learned to cook while watching her mother at work.

Like all women of her time, my grandmother has spent her life cooking and feeding first her siblings, and then an extended family of aunts, uncles and children. When she was married at the age of fifteen she took charge of cooking for her husband and *his* family. This is the only life she knows. Still, I can't help thinking this is rather unfair. I'm not suggesting anything radical involving brassieres and matches, just *a load shared is a load halved*. That's all. Yet as I sip from a cup of *café de olla* – an earthy coffee infused in a clay jar with cinnamon and dark chocolate – I remind myself that my way of doing things isn't necessarily better just because it's what I'm used to. And I remember the resolution I made on the day I arrived: *find a new way of seeing*. From now on I'm not going to insist on helping with lunch. I'm going to enjoy the pampering and make the most of the grandmother I have been separated from by geography and almost a lifetime of years.

I finish my coffee and accept a refill. As I sit alone at the dining table, a feeling comes over me, one I can't quite put my finger on. Happiness? Contentment? I'm not sure. It is something more subtle. It's the same feeling I had as a child when, at the crack of dawn on Christmas day, my brother and I would show our presents to our parents while they sat on the couch smiling and yawning. It's happiness and comfort and safety. All of the above and something more – *it's love*. I sip the coffee and listen to the sounds of children's voices coming from the lounge room.

By the time I finish my second Spanish course I have been in Mexico City for nearly four months. I would like to keep studying but as I've spent nearly all my savings it won't be that simple. If I want to stay in Mexico I will have to work. Either way, I will have to extend my visa, and this detail will prove to be the clincher.

I go to the immigration office in Polanco, a glittery suburb of beemers and Bentleys, office towers and designer boutiques. Armed with my passport and nine photocopies of my original tourist visa I arrive at the fifth-floor office hoping to obtain the all-important extension stamp. The woman behind the counter is amiable and cooperative.

'Yes, you can extend your visa as many times as you like.'

I can't believe what I'm hearing. I had heard nightmare stories about Mexican bureaucracy from other students. I hadn't expected it to be this easy. This sounds more than promising. I hand over the documentation, smiling. The woman scans the documents, then looks up and smiles. 'No problem,' she says. Just what I want to hear.

'Leave these with us. They should be ready soon.'

'How soon?' I ask, imagining I might be able to return in a couple of days to pay and pick up my passport.

'Oh, probably June.'

This is *not* what I want to hear. June is two months away. Maybe I misheard her.

'June?'

'Yes.' She smiles again.

I explain my predicament and how I would need the stamp by the end of the week, and would she be so kind as to speed up the process. The woman is not unhelpful – at least, she's still smiling. Then it's her turn. She tells me the situation is *afuera de mis manos*, out of her hands. She has a point. Like that of many other countries, Mexican bureaucracy is notoriously slow. But the difference here is that anything this side of next year is considered *soon*. I'd always thought the expression *mañana* land (tomorrow land), coined by the Americans, was mean-spirited and untrue. But now? Americans see their neighbours as lazy and unmotivated. The Mexicans think Americans are stressed-out control freaks. Is that how I'm behaving? Like an uptight *gringa*? I wonder how long I will need to live in Mexico before I become so lackadaisical about life that *everything* can be put off until tomorrow!

'Of course, there is another way,' the woman says.

She beckons me with a finger and I lean over the counter conspiratorially.

'You can always pay a *coyote*.'

Oh. I hadn't thought of that.

In this country, the only way to get anything done in a hurry is to pay a bribe. Technically it's illegal but, as with many things in Mexico, the definition of legal is vague and open to interpretation. In other words, for a price anything is possible. As it happens the only way to get anything done at immigration is to bribe a *coyote*, a hustler in the art of speeding up paperwork. *For a fee.* I am tempted; it would mean I would be given another visa in no time. On the other hand, the fee – exorbitant bordering on obscene – is always hiked up because, as most Mexicans know, foreigners are too trusting for their own good. I decide against it – I don't have the money. And even if I did, I wouldn't be confident of my negotiating skills. I'm pretty sure I would be 'negotiated' out of my remaining funds in no time.

In the end I decide to go home. Returning to Australia, organising a long-stay visa at the Mexican embassy in Melbourne, and working to save money seems a much more sensible option than putting my trust – and money – in the hands of a stranger. I can always come back to Mexico.

It is early afternoon by the time I get home. My grandmother, who is sitting on the couch, looks up when I come in. 'Quick, hurry up! It's starting.' I drop my bag and bound into the room.

For months we have been watching a soap opera that has captivated the nation. *Mirada de Mujer*: The Look of a

Woman. The entire country is transfixed by the steamy goings-on of a middle-class housewife, Maríinés, her husband Ignacio and her lover Andrés. While the affairs, backstabbing, lies and deceit go against Mexico's traditional Catholic sensibilities, it seems the nation can't get enough of this show. At two o'clock every afternoon television sets all over Mexico go on and power stations report electricity surges as they struggle to cope with the extra demand. The usually sober evening news bulletins have special polls on this phenomenon. Should Maríinés stay with Ignacio? She shouldn't. Is Andrés committed to this relationship? He is. Am I going to cope in Australia without my daily fix of melodrama? Probably not.

As today's show begins, Maríinés is having her hair done at the beauty salon. Marí has caused *un escándalo verdadero*, a real scandal, by leaving Ignacio (a philandering schmuck) for the young buck Andrés (a sexy *papacito* with a nice bum). Traditional Mexico is up in arms. A woman does not behave like this! A Mexican woman! A respectable mother of three children! Oh, the outrage. At the moment the other women at the *salón de belleza*, who have heard rumours about Marí's new man, are giving her the third degree. 'So tell us about your gentleman friend?' they ask. Snigger. The protagonist doesn't miss a beat. 'Oh, there's nothing to tell. I'm just in it for the sex.' Gasp! The self-righteous tormentors are lost for words. One of the women jerks back so violently that a false nail dislodges from her bejewelled hand and scuds across the floor.

I laugh and then glance at my grandmother, worried she might be offended by all this sex talk; far from it, she is as amused as I am.

While all this melodrama might seem far-fetched, the truth is that it's a fairly accurate representation of Mexican society. It pokes fun (in an over-the-top way) at traditional

Mexican mores – in other words the Ten Commandments – while also reinforcing its moral clause: *love is all that matters*. And in Mexico love is a *big* deal. Mexicans love God. And the Virgin Mary. They love their families. And given the number of soap operas on TV on any day of the week (around twelve), they are in love with the idea of romantic love. The paradox, however, is that in this country of dedicated romantics, infidelity is rife. The Mexican man's right to cheat on his spouse is almost a constitutional right. Perhaps that's why this soap is so popular; it's thumbing its nose at patriarchal society by empowering its female lead with sexuality and opinions of her own.

But the best thing by far about this show is that for one hour every afternoon my grandmother and I are bonded by a common interest. Our struggles to communicate with her non-existent English and my bumbling Spanish are forgotten. Right now it's just me, her, and a bevy of big-haired women and angry-looking men. Maybe that's why I so studiously watch her reactions. I don't want her going off in a huff. It's not just a TV show, it represents something more: a chance for us to connect. If I lamented not having her around when I was young – 'Why don't I have a grandma?' I asked my mother – then these afternoons together help to make up for it.

When the ads come on, I turn to my grandmother. I have to tell her I am leaving. After what happened at the immigration office this afternoon, I can no longer put it off. My departure is imminent. The moment is tinged with sadness, and I'm all too aware that afternoons like these are coming to an end. It is a feeling of future time lost. Yet my grandmother doesn't seem upset. Nor does she say what I expect to hear. Not *you should stay* or *have a think about it* but something else entirely.

'You'll be back,' she says.

I look at her but I do not respond. She continues speaking in a slow, measured voice.

'Mexico is in your blood.'

A pause.

'You can't deny who you are.'

I nod but still don't say anything. I turn to look out the window. Outside, the sky is translucent grey. A dog stands on the very edge of a roof across the road; a four-legged tightrope walker. Washing blows in the breeze. As I survey the mottled landscape I think that in less than a week I will be back in Australia. I wonder if I will think of this place when I return to the other side of the world. When I am standing on the beach at dusk, watching the autumn sunset.

I do not register the importance of my grandmother's words. But it will not be long before I discover how inextricably linked I am to this country, and then I will begin to understand the resonance of this parting advice.

Chapter Three

Bringing Light to the Dead

By the time I return to Mexico, a year and a half has passed in the blink of an eye. This trip hasn't been planned. My grandmother has been unwell and this provides the impetus for my visit. She is diabetic and, although her condition is not considered life-threatening, I realise that her time is limited and I need to see her. I am young and my time is my own; I decide to stay here for a while, at least until my grandmother's health improves.

Of course, there are other factors. At home, as the months rolled by, I could not get Mexico out of my head. The idea of returning was always at the back of my mind. And perhaps that was why I saved so diligently for the past eighteen months. I have no idea how long I'm going to stay. Maybe one month, maybe two? I'll wait and see. But these are not my only reasons for coming here. I feel *compelled* to return, as though unseen forces have conspired to bring me back. There is something about Mexico that I can't get enough of; something indefinable, mysterious. And within me an overwhelming sensation that I have come home.

Amid the airport crowds I'm struck by the familiarity of the place. As I walk towards the exit, the sound of *boleros*, Mexican love songs, coming from a nearby radio carries me into the street, their plaintive, acoustic rhythm filling me with contagious joy.

My first week passes in a fog of exhaustion. During that time I relax on the couch, enjoying my grandmother's company while my cousins are at school. I had been concerned about her health but now that I'm here I see she is strong and in good spirits. Indeed, she still gets out of bed at dawn and is a bundle of energy. Her appearance doesn't give any hint of her illness. On the contrary, if it were not for the blood sugar and blood pressure medications on top of the fridge, you would find it hard to believe she is unwell. Perhaps the most telling indication of diabetes is the black bruising on her shins, a result of poor circulation.

On most mornings I have breakfast with my grand-mother, my aunt and the kids. When the family leaves for the day I move to the couch, where my grandmother joins me to watch breakfast television. With its thick cushions and wide armrests, this couch is the perfect place to relax. My grandmother's presence beside me is a comforting one; I feel right at home. I think the feeling is mutual. The entire family seem to accept my presence as though I have always lived here.

When I'm over my jet lag I begin to take regular walks around the Narvarte district. Early mornings, when traffic is sparse, are the best time of the day to take in the cool, ghostly beauty of this area. Late October heralds the begin-ning of winter but it is a cool season only in name.

The brisk mornings give way to an emerging sun that peeks through the blanket of pollution and leaves slanted rays of sunlight on the ground. Around the corner from my grandmother's apartment, the cedar trees that line *Avenida Ángel de la Raza* have shed their leaves, carpeting the footpath in golden brown. I have to resist the urge to jump into the piles of swept-up leaves.

Towards the end of my second week in Mexico, I begin to explore further afield. It's part of my plan to get to know this city brick by brick. On previous visits I'd gone to some of the famous tourist sites, but for the most part I stuck to a well-worn path. Home. School. Downtown. It was a familiar beat guaranteed to stop me getting lost and, inadvertently, from discovering anything new.

On a cool Sunday morning I walk to the bakery to buy a donut for breakfast (it's a habit I've picked up since I arrived here, to try every pastry in the shop – today it's donuts) before taking myself to Coyoacán, a nearby suburb of beautiful churches, seventeenth-century façades, cobbled plazas and colonial buildings that have been converted into museums. It seems appropriate that my explorations should begin in one of the oldest *colonias* in Mexico City and the first place the Spanish conqueror Hernan Cortés set up home with his mistress, Malinche, after his defeat of the Aztecs in 1524. Malinalli, as she was known, was the interpreter for the Spaniards, an Aztec woman who fell in love with the power and fervour of the seemingly omnipotent Cortés and, in the process, betrayed her countrymen. It was to Coyoacán that she came after the sacking of the city of Tenochtitlan, to be hidden behind the adobe walls of her lover's residence, rejected by her people and eventually discarded by the Spanish. In Mexico, to call someone a *malinchista* is the worst insult imaginable.

As I wait for the bus under a canopy of naked branches I see a young guy running across the road. I turn to look down the road for any signs of the bus but I'm distracted by the blurred figure I can still see out of the corner of my eye. The boy is now standing in front of me, out of breath.

'*Disculpe señorita*,' he says.

'Yes?' I reply, wondering what he is going to ask me.

'Do you know if this bus goes to Coyoacán?'

For a moment I'm confused. I grimace. What's he asking me for? I turn around to see if he's addressing someone else, another *señorita* perhaps. Nope. It's me. He's asking *me* for directions. I smile, uncertain. Up to now he's assumed I'm Mexican but as soon as I speak he'll know I'm not. And suddenly I'm feeling very embarrassed. If I look Mexican, I think to myself, then I should speak like one too. This thought rattles around my head as the boy waits for a reply. I should answer but I just stand there, mute. I hope he doesn't ask me anything else because I'll have to respond and then the ruse will be up. By the time I spit out a reply the moon will have waned and the bus will be long gone. Finally, I reply.

'*Perdón. No sé.*' Sorry, I don't know. It's an outright lie and I'm ashamed to say it, but in my absurd thinking I want to use as few words as possible so he doesn't catch my accent. I know this bus goes to Coyoacán because that's where I'm headed. I suppose I could always nod or point, but I can't bring myself to do that either. I just continue to smile at him.

'Well, thanks anyway.'

The boy says something else I don't quite catch and then he turns and walks away. I watch him disappear down the street and then I feel bad because he's gone and will miss the bus. But what's most surprising about this exchange is that being asked the bus schedule by a stranger who thinks

I'm a local makes me feel immensely proud. I'm energised by the encounter. Jubilant, in fact.

I'm still smiling as I mull over *exactly* why I'm so thrilled about being mistaken for a Mexican. Even though I have what a Greek–Australian friend describes as a 'multipurpose' ethnicity that could pass as Italian, Brazilian, Portuguese and – remember, we're talking first impressions – Maori, I've never really considered myself particularly Mexican-looking. I'd always assumed that with my genetic mix of nationalities – Mexican mother, English father – my features were too ambiguous to be easily defined. But an innocuous question from a stranger has touched me and I think this highlights a deeper need, one that for many mixed-race children is at the core of identity. In my mind I keep coming back to the same thought: *I want to look Mexican because I want to fit in.* I smile at the irony. Growing up in Australia I wanted the opposite – to *not* look like a Mexican to fit in.

My thoughts are interrupted by the rattle of a wheezy engine. The bus pulls up and I clamber on. I hand over my fare and tell the driver where I want to go.

'Coyoacán, please.'

'*¿Qué?*'

He doesn't understand me at all and I'm sure I can sense the impatient eyes of the other passengers on me. Feeling self-conscious, I laugh nervously. We can't go anywhere until I pay and I can't pay until the driver works out where I want to go. Short of writing it down I don't know how this is going to be accomplished. Right now we're Dumb and Dumber. Curly and Mo. At this rate we could be here all afternoon. I try again.

'Co-yo-a-cán,' I say, enunciating every single vowel.

'Ah, Coyoacán! Why didn't you say so?'

'I did,' I reply.

'Oh, really? I didn't understand your accent.'

I sit down at the back of the bus and watch cars and trees, buses and pedestrians whiz by. The landscape is a blur of grey interspersed with flashes of pink and blue, yellow and green buildings. Thinking of the exchange with the driver, I smile wryly. I'm a foreigner again. My buoyant Mexican-girl-at-the-bus-stop fantasy has disappeared into a cloud of exhaust fumes.

The bus leaves me in front of *Viveros de Coyoacán*, a large park with a meandering river, where teenagers play soccer and locals feed peanuts to the resident squirrels. I walk through the park towards the main plaza. Along the cobbled streets I pass eighteenth-century compounds with ornate iron gates. Once home to Spanish noblemen, the cool stone buildings are now private residences patrolled by security guards. Somewhere around here lives the author and Nobel laureate, Carlos Fuentes, in what he calls his own air-conditioned 'biosphere'. As luck would have it, today many of the gates are open, offering me a glimpse of the beauty of these secluded havens – courtyards with tiled fountains, surrounded by tropical gardens of hibiscus and frangipani, elephant ferns and date palms.

Although my original plan had been to spend the after-noon at the Frida Kahlo museum, as I come to the outskirts of the plaza I am distracted by the music coming from the *mercado de Coyoacán*, the marketplace. I recognise the *salsa* music. It's the same music our teacher played us in the Spanish classes I attended on my previous visit to Mexico. 'The words aren't important,' she'd said. 'Just feel the soul of the music.' Now, standing under a red awning at a side entrance to the market, listening to the exuberant music, I understand what she was getting at. I'm entranced, as though the rhythm has cast a spell over me, and before I know it I'm standing inside the market, taking in the sounds, sights and smells.

In front of me is a stall selling blankets. It's an incongruous sight in a tropical country, even more so because the thick woollen blankets have Caribbean designs: palm trees and cocktail glasses. There are vendors selling socks, handmade sandals, jeans, running shoes and T-shirts – Guess, Gap, Tommy Hilfiger, Nike. All high quality fakes. Further along are stalls selling lace doilies, embroidered tablecloths and smaller cloths for wrapping tortillas. Bright papier-mâché *piñatas* sway in the faint breeze: traditional donkeys hang alongside Pokemon, Bart Simpson, Barney the dinosaur and a variety of farm animals. The smell of roasting meat is coming from the other side of the market but for the moment I am content to wander through the *artesanías*, looking at the handmade crafts and other odds and ends. There are people everywhere and I feel a heady excitement as I look around me. *This* is Mexico: radiant colour, music, noise, textures and shapes.

The scene is even more colourful than usual today because, instead of the usual sawdust covering the concrete floors, beneath my feet is a carpet of bright orange petals. As I pass through the motley collection of stalls, I occasionally have to shake the petals of marigold and chrysanthemum from my sneakers. The flowers are called *cempasúchil* – the flowers of the dead. My last visit had coincided with Day of the Dead celebrations, and I remember all the garlands of *cempasúchil* hanging above the doorways of the apartments in my grandmother's building. Fortunately, I have returned to Mexico in time for the festivities. Today is the first of November, the beginning of the two-day *fiesta*.

Towards the end of October, Mexicans begin to prepare for *el Día de los Muertos*, the Day of the Dead, when the departed are celebrated. On the first and second of November the *difuntos*, the spirits of the dead, come back to earth, guided by the candles and floral tributes laid out for them. Since my arrival I have watched the preparations for this day with fascination. There are shrines in shop windows, outside train stations and on the dashboards of buses; altars and offerings in churches, restaurants and cafés. The city is awash with flowers and candles. Incantations. And *pan de muerto*, bread of the dead, in the bakeries.

As I wander I begin to notice shrines, some small, others elaborate, set up among the stalls. I remember how as a child, on certain anniversaries, I would watch from my mother's bedroom doorway as she placed candles in front of photographs of dead relatives. She would leave them burning for an hour, always careful not to let candle wax drip onto her embroidered doilies. When I asked what she was doing the answer was always the same: 'I'm bringing light to the dead.'

I guess to some people these traditions might seem morbid and, indeed, on my previous visit some of my class-mates had wondered at the strangeness of it all, but most of us found Mexico's unique view of life and death bewitching. For me there is a gentle beauty to this tradition. The way I see it, the Day of the Dead is not a celebration of death but rather a celebration of life, a way of keeping alive the memory of those who are no longer with us. Recalling my mother's rituals as I walk among the *ofrendas*, floral offer-ings and family shrines, makes me feel like I am part of the mysterious tableaux of Mexican society. The thought comforts me as I squeeze through a cluster of people milling around a stall. The stallholder catches my eye.

'¡*Señorita*, *cómpreme una calavera!*' Miss, buy a skull!

I don't quite understand what she means until I look at the table in front of me: an array of skulls, skeletons and bones, all made of sugar. I had heard of the *alfenique*, sugar offerings for the Day of the Dead, but I had never seen them up close. There are pop-up skeletons and skulls that come in all sizes, from tiny to coconut-sized, decorated with coloured flowers like the ones on wedding cakes, with tin-foil eyes and sugar ears, noses and teeth. There is a selection of marzipan treats: men lying in coffins, complete with white kerchief and little pink hands crossed over their breasts; *mariachis* with guitars; skeleton women riding bicycles; donkeys; dogs; lambs; and miniature plates of food. The attention to detail is extraordinary. Next to these are sugar bones in different sizes and, to the back of the display, the *pièce de résistance*: skulls with names written across their foreheads. Before I can laugh at the bizarre delight of it all, the vendor asks me what I would like.

I ask for a *calavera* – a skull – one of the large ones.

'Do you want your name on it?' she asks.

It's usual for *calaveras* to come with *nombres*, or names, written on them. Sometimes it's the name of the dead person, the sugar skull taking pride of place in the shrine, alongside flowers and food offerings. On other occasions, you can request your own name. I'm mad about the idea of having a personalised skull. I nod vigorously.

'Sure. Won't take a minute.'

I watch a man pipe icing letters onto the big skull: *SAMANTITA*. Perhaps because I want to be open to all that is new, or maybe because watching my mother's candle-lighting rituals has given me some understanding, the whole experience of the marketplace and the Day of the Dead seems somehow comforting and familiar. A subtle shift has occurred within me.

It is late afternoon by the time I leave the market. A whole afternoon has passed without me even realising it. The museum will have to wait for another day. As I stand waiting for the bus I open the paper bag with the *calavera* inside. I should keep it as a kitsch souvenir of Mexico. But then again, maybe it will go off. I decide to eat it. I savour the almost sickly sweet taste, untroubled by the weirdness of eating a head with my name on it.

When I return to the apartment I notice the front door is ajar. I look over at the washing basins on the other side of the landing to see if my grandmother is there, but no-one is around and the air seems eerily still. I gently push open the front door.

In the hallway candles line the windowsill; there must be at least twenty of them. They flicker in the breeze. My grandmother is standing in the hallway, holding in her hand a candle in a plastic cup, chanting softly. Standing behind her is my aunt, also holding a candle and chanting. The curtain rod is adorned with garlands of orange flowers, like fragrant, living tinsel – more *cempasúchil*. The usually drab hallway, with its scuffed and crayon-covered walls and tired lace curtains, now looks romantic and serene.

'Oh, sorry. I didn't mean to interrupt,' I say.

Although in the middle of what seems to be a very solemn ritual, my grandmother looks up and smiles.

'It's all right, daughter. Come in.'

In the lounge room, there are more candles; the long, skinny ones that are supposed to burn for ten hours. They sit on top of the refrigerator, in between the bills, house keys, jars of pens and a dish full of broken trinkets. On the television. Everywhere. On the bureau there is a *Virgen de Guadalupe*, the Mexican version of the Virgin Mary, the fluorescent picture enclosed in a glass case and lit up by a tiny bulb at its base. To love the virgin is a patriotic duty; she is national pride and Catholic fervour all rolled into one. Every schoolchild knows how she appeared to Juan Diego, a poor Indian, on a barren hill in 1531, and the peasant looked at this brown-skinned woman who spoke to him in his own language as she called him 'my son' and told him she was the Virgin Mary, the mother of Jesus Christ. For the Indians she would come to represent a new beginning: she did not look Spanish and so gave hope to the displaced people in this new world, and she had appeared to an Indian and not to a Spaniard, so in this new Mexico she was *theirs*. But on the other hand, to those with Spanish blood, she was Catholic. All that is good. A mother. It isn't hard to see why the Virgin is as Mexican as tortillas and *mariachis*.

This room is large and airy; its stone walls, linoleum floor and line of windows overlooking the street usually keep it cool, even in this climate. Except today. The heat from the candles is stifling.

My aunt and grandmother are now walking up behind me. I step out of the way as they go to each corner of the room, still chanting. I don't know what to make of this ritual. What does it all mean? I sit in an armchair and look up at a photograph of my grandfather, who died in 1984 at the age of fifty-eight. A tealight candle burns in front of the photograph.

My grandmother has gone into the kitchen, and when she comes back she is carrying two cups of *café de olla*. I move over to the couch so we can sit together. She turns on the television and puts the sound on mute; pictures skip across the screen, distorted and alien without words to lend them validity. I see my opportunity to ask about the chanting and she tells me it is to protect the departed souls from evil spirits that might impede their journey back to earth to collect their *ofrendas*.

Eager to know more, I venture another question. 'And what about the candles?'

'Listen carefully,' she says, putting her cup on the armrest. 'The dead come back to earth every year.' She is speaking slowly and patiently, happy to have a captive audience. 'They come to see what we have been doing while they were away.' I nod. 'You must make an altar with offerings of all the things they loved when they were alive – to show them your love. The candles light their path.'

I hang on to my grandmother's words, taking in every detail. Somehow her stories go beyond the gritty, noisy and polluted Mexico that I see. After all, my grandmother has seen all the changes. She remembers the old, sleepy *capital* of her youth and is slightly bemused by the sprawling metropolis it is today. She is familiar with its traditions and its beliefs; its superstition and soul. To listen to her explain this particular custom is to find the source of understanding. I begin to see my mother's candle-lighting ritual as more than just a matter of tradition. Perhaps it is a way of keeping alive a connection, not just with dead relatives, but with her mother, who instilled in her this particular brand of Mexican mysticism.

'You probably think we're crazy,' she says, then turns to the television. I look at the screen too. The picture shows a reporter standing in a graveyard, surrounded by families: grandparents and children, mothers and babies, their heads bowed in prayer. The camera pans across the burial ground; one grave after another carpeted in orange flowers and more candles. The scene is surreal: behind the reporter a man dressed as an eight-foot skeleton, replete with turn-of-the-century dress, ambles past.

'What's with the giant skeleton?' I ask.

'That's *La Catrina*,' my grandmother replies.

'Oh, of course,' I say, none the wiser as to how this man in his skeleton suit and big pink dress fits in the mystical scheme of things. I take our coffee mugs back to the kitchen and the candles in the kitchen blow out as I walk past them.

'I didn't blow them out,' I tell my grandmother defiantly

as I sit back down, thinking that this might be bad luck.

'I know you didn't,' she says, looking smug. 'Your grandfather just wants to say hello.'

I enjoy the idea that family are here with us; the spirit of my long-departed grandfather hovering nearby. It may be a strange feeling but it is not unpleasant. I turn to see my grandmother next to me; her eyes are shut. As I sit watching the mute television I think of my decision to come here, my conviction that this was meant to be. And I remember something my grandmother had said to me the other day. I can't even recall what we were talking about. 'Don't think. *Feel*,' she had said, patting her heart for emphasis. In other words, use your heart and not your head. Be guided by instinct. Not a bad rule for living. It is, I realise, the reason I am here.

Chapter Four

Ghosts from the Past

Not long after the Day of the Dead, I am standing in front of the mirror in my grandmother's apartment, studying a small gold frame on the shelf below. The face I do not know – a pale woman with black hair pulled back tightly – but the expression is familiar, a strong gaze, fierce and determined, betraying no hint of what its owner is thinking. My grandmother shuffles past on her way to the bedroom, a pile of washing folded neatly in her arms. 'That's my mother, Julia,' she says.

She is full of surprises. My grandmother hardly ever speaks of her mother, and when she does it is as if she were talking about a stranger. 'That woman was really hard,' she would say. 'She went through too much.'

My mother always said my grandmother was the world's greatest storyteller, that you just had to get her at the right time. Ask her a question at an inopportune moment and you would get: 'Who cares! Leave the *difunta* alone.' Let the dead rest in peace. But my grandma had her reasons for keeping things to herself. She kept her past closely guarded, its secrets safe. There were five children in the Gonzáles family – my grandmother Rebeca, Carmen, Concepción, Soledad, and their only brother, Juan – and they all grew up in the shadow of the Mexican Revolution. 'You just watch what you say to people,' their mother Julia would tell them. 'One wrong word and it's you hanging from a tree.' Discretion was the difference between life and death. Julia's advice stayed with my grandmother all her life.

I grew up with stories of my family. My mother would sit on the end of my bed at night and talk for hours about her father and her grandfather, her cousins and everybody else. She even spoke about her beloved grandmother, Sara, but those stories always ended in tears because she loved her so much that when Sara died it was as if her world had come to an end. I thought I knew these people pretty well, and what I didn't know about them I could ask and my grandmother would fill in the blanks. But the problem is that she is not like my mother. She doesn't offer up snippets of information willingly. She will tell you a story and, just when you think you are about to discover some magnificent secret of the past, she will stop and say, 'Enough of this, I'm tired. They were all fools anyway.'

I am sitting on the couch watching *Good Morning Mexico* when my grandmother walks over and says, 'I might sit down for a minute.' For a woman who rises at dawn and does not stop until late evening, this is a rare occurrence. I venture a question: 'So what about your father?' I have to take a chance. I only have a small window of opportunity before my aunt comes home from the supermarket with my cousins and my grandmother will swing into action in the kitchen.

Her father, she tells me, was one of those men who went to war with their own instruments. In those days they didn't have any money so they made weapons out of anything they could find – blocks of wood with scythes taped to the ends became bayonets – and off they went.

'He was a stupid man,' my grandmother says. She is looking away from me and her voice is mellow and calm, so much so that for a moment I imagine the ghosts of the past no longer haunt her, but I know this is not true. Time has not healed painful memories, it has just numbed them. I feel guilty, like an interloper prying for information when it isn't really any of my business. But I know my grandmother: if she wants to talk she will, and if not, well, you can stand on your head all day but not a word will pass her lips.

My great-grandfather Juan Gonzáles was born in the late 1800s. He was a boy of seventeen when the Mexican Revolution began, and he wasted little time in joining the revolutionary army of General Francisco 'Pancho' Villa.

'He was brave,' I venture.

'He wasn't brave,' my grandmother scoffs, 'running off like that. All he did was end up dead.'

His reputation for bravery did not come from the blood of the Aztecs but from his adventurous father, a man of resolute character and big dreams who had arrived here on a Spanish galleon and made his home in the Mexican desert. An irascible man with capable hands and a sharp mind, Juan's father worked hard and adopted his new *patria* completely: he bought land, stepped out in tailored suits and was by all accounts a gentleman among gentlemen. Juan's mother was wooed by the adventurer, marrying him soon after they met and giving birth to many children, all hardworking, serious and determined. Her sons could have lived their lives as gentlemen of fortune but instead they chose to fight with their countrymen. 'Fools, every single one of them,' my grandmother says. A madness mixed with a fervent nationalistic pride had been instilled in them by their father. They became soldiers of the Revolution, untempered by the folly of emotion or a sentimental heart.

It is enough to say that, like all men of the time, Juan was impetuous and proud, a man with a heart for the Revolution and his *patria*, but little room for sentiment towards his young wife, my great-grandmother Julia. She in turn was a capable *soldadera*, one of the many women who, with a gun slung over one shoulder and a frypan over the other, followed their husbands, marching silently alongside the mounted soldiers into war. Juan and Julia, still barely out of their teens, travelled across the countryside, following their legendary leader.

Much later the Gonzáles located themselves near the capital, not far from the deserted *haciendas* and sprawling gardens of the former aristocracy. 'You see, that is how it all started,' my grandmother says. 'The rich just took and took and never gave anything back until one day the poor people just said enough.' The *federales* and the rebels rode into town and took everything from the land owners, giving them the choice of handing over all they had or facing the firing squads. In the midst of all this, Julia gave birth to five children in quick succession, the youngest being my grandmother, Rebeca. Her arrival was marked by the departure of her father, who rode back into the dying breaths of a war that had limped on for eleven long years. Although he had risen quickly to the rank of *coronel*, it wasn't enough to save him. Nobody could explain how he died, but he was found with a fist-sized bullet hole in his chest.

My grandmother's life was set to be shaped by her father's death. Juan Gonzáles became the intangible caesura in the family's lives. In that time, when a widow was treated as a pariah, Julia steeled her resolve for the sake of her children and her dead husband. Without sentiment, she went to work, opening her own restaurant. Doña Julia became well respected, due in no small part to her culinary skills. 'How she could cook!' my grandmother exclaims. 'Just the smell was enough to bring men in from miles around.'

'Did she teach you to cook?' I ask.

'No, child,' she says. 'There are some things you just know how to do.'

The Gonzáles children all grew to be proud and hot-tempered. My grandmother's sister Carmen became the town's main source of gossip with her acid tongue and her penchant for exaggeration; Soledad, a gentler character, in her old age wears food-stained dresses and applies her lipstick liberally all over her face because she can't see, yet stubbornly refuses offers of help from others. '¡Caramba! I can do it myself,' she grumbles. Now in her nineties, Soledad still speaks of her youngest sister as the baby of the family and reminisces about how it was true Rebeca really had known her departed husband, Alfredo, all her life. He was my grandmother's best friend in primary school, a little boy she met when she was only five years old.

This is where my grandfather enters the story, as the youngest of twenty-two children, with a fierce demeanour and, like his fourteen brothers, dark skin, a strong build and an Aztec nose. My grandmother, the little girl whose beauty was unquestionable even at such an early age, shared her lunch every day with Alfredo and resolutely refused to acknowledge anyone but him. 'My mother would get so upset because I was giving my lunch away,' she says. 'And to make it worse I was giving it to that *Indito*.'

A decade later, when love had gestated quietly for so many years, the childhood sweethearts spent the night together. In a time when appearances were everything, Rebeca snuck out to visit my grandfather without an escort. She would soon pay dearly for what she saw as an innocent oversight: 'Oh, they all carried on when they found out, but nothing happened. We spent the *whole* night talking.' My grandmother turns to me with a mischievous grin and I imagine this is how she looked when she was a naive and inquisitive fourteen-year-old.

The next day the families came looking for their young charges and announced they would be wed as soon as possible in an effort to salvage Rebeca's tattered reputation. Alfredo was arrested for carnal knowledge and spent two days in the local prison; my grandmother was quickly sequestered behind the walls of the family home. Like all young women of the time, she had been warned of the precious nature of a woman's virtue. But it was too late for regrets, the damage was already done.

My grandmother was married on the eve of her fifteenth birthday. She stood at the altar clutching a bouquet of gladioli and wearing a black mantilla on her head that matched her black wedding dress. The bride's sombre outfit was worn out of respect for her mother, who had died a month before the wedding. Carried away by the romance of the story, I ask my grandmother if she was in love, but she just turns to me with a bemused, you-have-so-much-to-learn expression. 'Love didn't have anything to do with it,' she sighs. 'We got married because we had to. If you made your bed you had to lie in it.'

With the ink of her marriage certificate barely dry, my grandmother found she was pregnant with twins, but it wasn't meant to be and she lost them. In keeping with Aztec tradition, Rebeca's stillborn children were not given Christian names but named after months in the Aztec calendar: 'That way my babies would be devoted to the ancestors who would take them to the other side.' At the age of twenty, she gave birth to a little girl – my mother, Sara. My mother's sister Julieta and brother Alfredo were born fifteen and sixteen years later.

My grandmother has been talking for nearly an hour. It is just like my mother says – it's all about timing. An hour of my grandmother's time is precious because you have to fight tooth and nail for it, jumping up and down and pleading for her attention while competing with her other interests, including, but not limited to, hanging out the washing, soaking the black beans, talking to the door-to-door salesmen, curing her favourite clay pots for cooking, and doing washing in the new washing machine her son bought her, which she was initially skeptical about but now loves. She handwashed everything up until the age of seventy-six.

As if to prove my point, I hear a key in the door. My aunt and cousins are back from the supermarket, and I watch as my grandmother swings into full-time grandma mode. There will be no more trips down memory lane today.

Chapter Five

Frogs for Diego

'Watch this. I can get it in without looking.'

My classmate Jean looks confident. My other classmate, Kumi, sits across from me eating Japanese prawn crackers. She looks at him, unconvinced. 'Just watch,' he says. He gets up from the bench and goes to the far corner of the room, where he turns to face the wall and then throws his polystyrene cup over his head. It flies across the room, hits the wall and lands right in the middle of the bin. 'I hate you,' I tell him. He smirks. The wall behind the bin is covered in a brown stain that looks like paint splatter. My contribution to coffee cup basketball.

After six weeks in Mexico, I've enrolled in a two-month Spanish course at the Mexico Academy, a language school on Insurgentes Avenue, one of the city's major thoroughfares. The college is a converted turn-of-the-century bluestone house with large shuttered windows, climbing vines and manicured gardens of elephant ferns, frangipani, hibiscus and wild roses that are now blooming in rich reds and a fuchsia pink that I associate with Mexico. I am here because my friend Tadeshi, who had been in my level one class at the National University, was still in Mexico City when I came back, and he suggested I join him at the Mexico Academy, where the classes were smaller, one teacher to five students, as well as being much cheaper and more centrally located than the University. Although I felt I hadn't achieved much, I must have learnt something at the University because when I went for the entrance exam at the college I was told my grammar was sound and I had a good ear for the language. They would be recommending me for placement in level four.

This time around, everything is different. Where previously I had been in a class with nineteen other students, now I have only two classmates. Before I was frustrated and impatient to learn, now I'm allowing myself to enjoy the experience, even though I wonder if my head is going to explode from the concentration – mixed with pollution – that seems to give me a headache each night.

Now, as we wait for our teacher to arrive, Kumi gets up to have her shot at the bin. She misses by a mile. Her throw, however, is not without merit – the cup clears the open door and lands in the hall. I'm impressed. Jean starts to laugh.

'*Merde!* You're worse than her,' he says, as he pelts me with a scrunched-up piece of paper.

'Well, I'm small,' Kumi protests.

Although our Spanish is limited, after a fortnight of classes the three of us have developed a strong rapport. To an outsider it might even appear as though we have been friends for life. It is probably telling of our status as foreigners that we are drawn together by our unfamiliarity with this place far from home. In any case, we make an unlikely trio.

Kumi is Japanese, tiny, with a beautiful, sweet face and a cheeky smile. We met on the first day of classes when she came and sat next to me. I instantly liked her. Kumi is warm, friendly and open. She is in Mexico because she felt like a change. 'This place is very different to Japan,' she says. It sure is.

Several weeks earlier, on the day of enrolment, Jean had come over to introduce himself. Tall, gangly and relaxed, he looked far from the stereotype of the uptight Parisian. 'Am I Jean?' he said in Spanish as he held out his hand. 'Um,' I replied, 'I don't know. Are you Jean?'

'Yeah, that's what I said.'

We shook hands, the lanky Frenchman still unaware his conjugation of the verb *to be* meant he was asking me who he was instead of telling me. After a short conversation he'd told me his girlfriend, a scientist, was doing a field study in Mexico and, rather than be separated from her, he'd decided to come along. He studies Spanish in the mornings and takes a marketing course at a business college in the afternoons. I soon meet his girlfriend when she comes to the college one afternoon. Sandrine is gentle, sweet and fiercely intelligent and we connect immediately.

Finally our *maestro* arrives. Rogerio Mastretta is a tall man in his late sixties with a white beard and kind eyes, who bears more than a passing resemblance to the lovely Sean Connery. He is a founder of the college, revered not only among his colleagues but throughout the country for his skills as a master linguist. He has been teaching Spanish for forty years and has the knack of inspiring confidence in every student he meets. I like Rogerio a lot and enjoy his classes immensely, not just for the way he makes learning gratifying but also for teaching me the things I really need to know, such as how to deliver polite but deadly replies to sleazy men in the street: *¿Qué no tienes madre en casa?*

¡Maleducado! Uneducated man, don't you have a mother at home?

'Good morning, my little chickens,' Rogerio says.

'Hello Chief,' Jean says. He used to call him *Hohe-hee-hoo*, the guttural pronunciation of Rogerio spilling out of his mouth like a violent crime. Now it's just 'Chief'. Rogerio doesn't mind. He calls his student Professor Jean, and has even drawn him a complex diagram of the voice box and diaphragm to demonstrate the difficulties Anglo-Saxons and, to a lesser extent, the Gallic have with the dreaded rolling 'rr' – or, in Jean's case, any word with 'r' in it. *Ferrocarril*, train; *perro*, dog – this word is still my nemesis; *cigarrillo*, cigarette. My continuing problems with this pronunciation technique often leave me feeling defeated but under Rogerio's tutelage my Spanish, and that of his other charges, begins to take shape. He tells us to be patient. 'Rome wasn't built in a day,' he says with a wink.

Over time I begin to see these hiccups for what they really are: challenges to be faced and, eventually, overcome. Once I come to this rather simple realisation, everything changes. I begin to make progress. Perhaps my ear is becoming more attuned to the language. Perhaps it is the impromptu singalongs to Cuban *salsa* classics. My favourite is the song about the guy who sets fire to his house: *Se quedo dormido . . . y no apagó la vela*. He fell asleep and didn't blow out the candle, the song goes, every note infused with rhythm and life. I now recognise the rise and fall of mellifluous sentences that not so long ago were completely alien to me. I don't dwell on the reasons for my improvement; I'm too busy enjoying myself.

But I do know the real reason for this exuberance. My progress may be slow and measured but it's a step towards fitting in. What's more, by mastering the language I will learn more about Mexico and this, in turn, will lead me to a greater understanding of what makes these passionate people tick. It is as though they can reveal their secrets to me: *to understand them is to understand me*, I tell myself. Of course, I don't expect to get to the core of Mexican identity – that could only come from a lifetime here. But there is one thing I'm sure of: Mexico plays a big part in who I am. It's something I've always known, deep down at least. And my mother knew it too. *Don't you want to know where you come from?* she'd said to me before my very first visit. Well, I did and I still do. And that is why I'm here. These language classes are an enjoyable diversion but, more importantly, they offer me a key to understanding this magical land and my place in it.

In the afternoon I catch the train to La Noria, on the southern outskirts of the city. By now the cool December morning has worked itself into something more substantial. The sun is fierce and I'm suffering under the weight of a woollen cardigan, heavy coat and scarf. I unpeel myself from layers of clothing and leave the station.

The Dolores Olmedo museum sits in the midst of this derelict suburb of dusty, unmade roads and empty factories. I've come here because it keeps appearing on the list of 'must see' places in the city and my curiosity has been piqued. This museum is a relic of old Mexico, a sleepy, romantic land of painters, poets and artisans, who seem to have been swallowed up by the present-day monster that is Mexico City. But I've discovered that beauty does prevail – you just have to know where to look for it.

I approach the heavy wooden gates of the entrance hesitantly. This place doesn't look like a museum; surrounded by high walls, it's reminiscent of the grand, heavily guarded residences of Coyoacán. A small door is cut into one of the gates. After checking the address I've ripped from the newspaper, I walk up to the entrance and push on the door. It doesn't budge. I'm puzzled. This is definitely the right place. I try again, leaning against the door with all my weight. The door still doesn't move, but I do – backwards.

I step back and chew on my bottom lip for a moment. And then I see the sign under the door handle, a small gold plate that flickers as it catches rays of sun. Just like the bumbling student in Gary Larson's 'Midvale School for the Gifted' cartoon, I'm pushing with all my might on a door that says, quite plainly, PULL. I laugh and pull on the handle, and this time the door opens. I step inside and the heavy portal clangs shut behind me. What I see when I look up is something that makes me gasp. Before me is an extraordinary sight: serenity as pure as a painted landscape, a startling contrast to the tired world outside.

I'm in Paradise.

Surrounded by imposing stone walls covered in creepers with violet flowers is a garden that goes on forever: manicured lawns, box hedges and tropical plants, with peacocks and ducks meandering across the lawn. An expansive walkway leads towards a colonial building with tall windows and walls tiled in Moroccan mosaics. A peacock screams and its haunting call echoes through the garden; the sweet aroma of frangipani lingers under my nose; even the smell of rotting garbage from the street has dropped away.

The gardens of Olmedo have cast their spell over me.

It takes me a few minutes to adjust and then I notice in front of me a wrought-iron gate with two frog sculptures adorning the gate posts. I move closer to get a better look.

'They're for Diego.'

The voice startles me. I turn to see who it belongs to. A small woman in a blue uniform stands with her hands clasped in front of her. She pulls a pamphlet from her pocket and hands it to me; it's about the museum. On the cover of the brochure is a picture of an exquisitely beautiful woman, the museum's namesake, Dolores 'Lola' Olmedo, who bought the property as a private residence in 1962, and opened it to the public as a museum in 1994. When I look up the woman is still standing in front of me, her face open and patient. She begins to speak again.

'The frogs,' she says, pointing at the sculptures. 'They're for Diego.'

Diego. The name itself is enough to inspire reverence. No surname needed. It is like the rising of the sun. The movement of the tides. A name guaranteed to make every Mexican chest puff out with pride. I know who she's referring to but I decide to check anyway – there might be another famous Mexican Diego I don't know about.

'Diego Rivera?' I ask. 'The painter?'

'Yes, yes,' she says, looking thrilled. She obviously wasn't expecting me to know who she was talking about. I have passed the test. She smiles and then walks away. I turn back to get another look at the polished green sentinels glistening in the sun. I'm not sure why she seems surprised. The man in question is Mexican muralist Diego Rivera – sometimes nicknamed the 'Frog-Man' – and it is impossible to be ignorant of Diego for long in Mexico. I had already seen his giant murals at the University and at the National Palace in the old district. His works are larger than life, and they are everywhere.

Undoubtedly one of the greatest painters in Mexican history, Rivera made a name for himself by creating large-scale murals of bloody conquests, peasant uprisings and daily life among the marginalised of Mexican society. But it was his romantic exploits that secured his infamy in this conservative nation. In his lifetime he managed to seduce about nine billion women, give or take a million: young, old, Mexican, foreign, it seems few were immune to his charms. He also married four times, including twice to troubled genius and fellow painter Frida Kahlo. The patron of this museum, Dolores Olmedo, was another of Rivera's lovers.

Of course, none of this would seem astonishing except for one particular detail. Rivera was – not just by my account – a hideously ugly man. I flick through the museum pamphlet and come across his photograph. In the picture I see a man with mountains of flesh and bulging eyes that would make a cane toad proud – hence the frogs on the gate. Diego had a face that could blow off a manhole cover. It's said he was a man of great charisma – and he would have to be, because looking at this guy my first instinct would be to run for my life.

I put the brochure in my pocket and walk towards the turnstiles.

'Enjoy yourself,' the woman behind the counter calls out.

'Thank you,' I reply.

I already know I'm going to. As soon as I stepped into the garden I felt I had crossed a portal into another world, one where birds of paradise drink the honey nectar of the gods and where a kaleidoscope of yellow, purple, orange, red and pink flowers grow alongside tropical ferns, defying the polluted sky that lets the sun through only in bursts. Whoever said Mexico was a mystical country obviously had this place in mind. I feel so fortunate to be here, as though I'm in a waking dream bursting with sublime beauty.

I walk along the smooth, reflective cobblestones towards the first gallery, watching as the resident *xoloescuintles*, a breed of Mexican hairless dog, chase a peacock around the lawn. Just as the footpath widens into a courtyard with bubbling fountains, I look into the garden at another surreal sight. Amid façades and overflowing vines a man in blue overalls is leaning against a broom. Nothing strange about that. But in front of him sit a gaggle of ducks. Three rows of them, all nestled in the grass, one behind the other, evenly spaced and facing the broom man. It is a sight so unique in its strangeness that it belongs in a Dali painting. I linger for a moment and then climb the stone steps from the courtyard to the gallery entrance.

I begin in a room with vaulted ceilings and floor-to-ceiling windows that are only inches wide. Sunlight streams in, leaving patterned slivers of light and dark on the marble floor. There are Rivera portraits of beautiful women in traditional costume, still lifes, urban landscapes and pre-Hispanic arte-facts: bowls, religious icons, hunting instruments, and *talavera*, handpainted pottery used in traditional cooking. I'm overwhelmed by a childish awe and stand agape as other visitors move respectfully around the hushed room, the clacking of their soft footsteps the only sound that can be heard.

As I study a painting a guard approaches. I think he is going to tell me off for standing too close to the velvet rope barrier, but quite the opposite happens. He leans in and takes my arm, gently turning me towards the room's centre-piece. He points to a canvas of a woman in a *huipil*, a traditional cotton blouse and skirt with elaborately embroidered flowers; she is holding up one side of her skirt in a curtsy pose.

'Dolores Olmedo,' he says. 'When she was young.'

'She was beautiful,' I reply.

'Oh yes, *una joya*.' A jewel.

The guard is eager to chat. I figure that standing around a museum all day must be pretty dull; the silence is deafening and, for a nation of people who love to talk, this must be hell. But he perks up as we chat quietly. He looks back at the painting, his eyes now bright and his face animated.

'You know, she still lives here,' he says.

'No way! She must be a hundred years old,' I whisper.

'Nah,' he replies, 'she's been dead for years, she just won't lie down.'

I try not to laugh, picturing in my mind a creaky old woman in a rocking chair by a window. (In months to come an artist friend will bring me back to the museum for an exhibition opening attended by the famed Dolores Olmedo. I'm at the bar when I see a tiny old lady with dyed black hair and red lipstick shuffle past. It's her. The crowd fawns. She waves. And then she is gone.)

From here I enter a long, darkened corridor hung with small canvases. Children peer from under long lashes, a seated woman cradles a child, another holds hands with an enormous man. One canvas depicts a bloody, stabbed body lying on a bed. *Unos cuantos piquitos*: but it was just a few nips, the banner reads. This is the room devoted to Rivera's wife, Frida Kahlo, probably the most important female painter in Mexican history.

It strikes me as odd that Kahlo's work would be housed in the museum of a woman who spent many years competing with the artist for the affection of her spouse. But as I make my way through the museum I notice that not only do Frida's canvases appear everywhere, but they actually outnumber those of Rivera. Here it seems the sisterhood is alive and well. There are also drawings by Rivera's first wife, Russian painter Angelina Beloff. Rivals in love. Allies in art. This contradiction makes me smile. An attendant sees me and smiles back.

After the first two gallery rooms I start to tire. Although my plan had been to spend hours combing through the museum, now that I'm here I realise this isn't going to happen. There are seven galleries in total and I'm no hero. All this culture is exhausting work. What I really need now is coffee. I happen to look out the window at the sun-drenched garden, and this hastens my decision not to waste another moment indoors. The marvellous paintings of Rivera and Kahlo can wait for another day. I walk outside into the golden sun.

It's getting really hot now. Heat shimmers off the cobblestones; rising vapour lingers like fog and it takes a moment for my eyes to adjust to the light. I've emerged in a courtyard café with outdoor tables scattered haphazardly among the ferns. I order coffee and sit down at a table in the shade. The stones are set on an incline so I position my chair at an angle – putting my feet up on the slope that has now conveniently become a footrest. Peacocks wander past. One stops at my feet and fans out its tail so I get a close look at nature's own artwork. It peers over the table but, seeing nothing of interest, it glides away. The area has a secret-garden quality to it and at any moment I expect to see fairies spring from behind the stone pillars. I fan myself with a serviette and watch another cluster of peacocks posture and shriek.

A little voice interrupts my contemplation. I turn to see a small boy leaning against the table, his chin cupped in his hands. He has thick brown hair, caramel skin and luminous brown eyes. When he smiles I notice he is missing a tooth. Mexicans are very friendly and have no problem starting a conversation with a stranger, and children are especially at ease. This one is now studying me intently.

'Hello, I'm Raul,' he says.

And before I can reply he fires another question at me.

'Are you English?'

I laugh. I don't know how he has surmised that I'm not a local but I like the keen intelligence in his eyes.

'Australian.'

'Oh.' His face is blank. For many Mexicans, Australia is a place so remote it might as well be outer space. 'Don't go anywhere, okay?' he says. I nod and watch as he runs away only to return minutes later with a scrapbook and pencil. For the next ten minutes we go over his English homework. *Mary left her pencil in the garden.* And other useful phrases: *My house has a red roof.* Even my Spanish comes under scrutiny. 'What's this called?' he asks, holding up his pencil.

'*Es una pluma*,' I reply confidently.

'No, silly, it's not a *pluma*, it's a *lápiz*!'

The kid's got me there. We both laugh at my dumbness. Then with the same ease that marked his arrival, Raul picks up his stuff and fishes from his pocket a handful of lollies that he plonks on the table as my reward. And then he's gone. 'Thank you,' I call out to the furtive figure disappearing down the footpath.

It's now almost four-thirty and I finish my second coffee as I watch a steady stream of visitors pass by. A lengthening shadow creeps across the lawn. In half an hour the museum will close and I will have to leave. But I don't want to go. I'm anchored by this beauty and the feeling of liberation. That I can spend an entire lazy afternoon peering at paintings, sipping coffee that smells of earth and tastes like heaven, and resting my feet on charcoal-coloured cobblestones in a tropical garden feels wonderful. Indulgent, even. Finally I gather my things and make a reluctant move. The trees come to life as a flock of birds rises in a collective screech before sweeping noisily across the languid sky.

From the food stalls just outside La Noria station, the odour of roasting meat, corn tortillas and chile so pungent it makes my eyes water mixes with smells of dog poo, dust and petrol. I negotiate my way around a body lying on the ground, covered in a green and red striped blanket. A beggar child runs up to me and tugs at my arm. He is dressed in rags and has dusty black hair but, just like the boy at the museum, has the most beautiful brown eyes.

'¿*Pesos, señorita?*' I shake my head. I know I only have a train ticket home but I check anyway. It's then I come across the caramels in my pocket. Raul's present. I hand them over and the child rewards me with an enormous grin. I smile too and walk into the station.

The train arrives to take me back into Mexico City. As I sit in the air-conditioned carriage, lulled by its gentle rocking motion, a vague feeling of guilt ripples in my chest. Raul's extraordinary generosity in sharing his lollies with a complete stranger has touched me deeply. I feel sorry for the beggars at the station, knowing that only a few hundred metres away is a Garden of Eden where the peacocks eat better than them.

From my window I watch as spanking new hypermarkets and fast food restaurants flash past. Mexico is a country of such violent extremes; the disparity between poverty and wealth is unsettling. But most of the time I just feel confused. Perhaps it's because I haven't had much first-hand experience with such grim reality. How often have I seen amputees with gangrenous limbs outside train stations in Melbourne? Never. How can I deal with such jarring realities? This country is a living, breathing contradiction. I want to be part of it, but to move ahead I need to find some answers, a way of processing and comprehending what I see. I decide to go to the voice of wisdom. The big cheese.

My grandmother.

In the evening as we sit in front of the television I put this conundrum to her. She mulls over it for a while before speaking.

'There are degrees to everything,' she says. 'The world is not a fair place but you will find your way. You will understand.'

Oh. Her lips purse and she nods, then turns towards the sound of a child crying. I watch her shuffle away. Sitting alone on the sofa, I contemplate my grandmother's words. I understand what she is saying, or at least I think I do. She accepts that some people have a lot and others have nothing. There is a certain degree of resignation in this pragmatism and it's something I will come to see as uniquely Mexican.

Over time I will come to recognise the relationships that exist between different sectors of the community. Train commuters slip change into the palms of the beggars outside the stations, policemen in patrol cars slow down to throw their sandwiches to street urchins, vendors leave food aside for the homeless to collect when they are ready. It may be one of the most important lessons Mexico teaches me: that amid great suffering is great humanity. *There are degrees to everything.*

That night as I lie in bed, listening to the sounds of this crazy, chaotic city coming in through the open window, a sense of hopefulness settles on me like a fine mist. Mexico, a land of such endless mystery, is slowly beginning to reveal her secrets to me. I close my eyes, feeling optimistic.

Chapter Six

Pieces of the Puzzle

I'm sitting on the steps outside the French House in the suburb of Roma, waiting for the library to reopen after lunch. The complex is the newest public library in Mexico City, built by the French government on the site of their original consulate, which was razed during the massive earthquake that devastated Mexico City in 1985. It sits amid manicured lawns, dwarf palms, slate walkways and a café with stainless steel tables that glint in the sun. The perimeter is flanked by the remaining walls of earthquake-damaged buildings. Metal rods curl around foundation slabs standing at obtuse angles, like a concrete stack of cards.

Across the road there are abandoned allotments, car parks and derelict building sites. It's a rough part of town, even with Mexico City's main avenue, *Paseo de la Reforma*, just around the corner. Directly in front of me is an empty lot, fenced with sheets of corrugated steel painted bright blue.

Between the gaps in the fence I can see crater-like holes in the ground and piles of rubble: twisted steel and chunks of cement with valiant tufts of grass poking through. Years after the earthquake that razed entire city blocks and killed thousands, many areas have been preserved as they were. Buildings lean together for support. Engineers are worried a cleanup will do more harm than good, risking a domino effect. And so the worst affected areas, like this one, are frozen in time, snapshots of the past. Not a pebble has been moved. I muse over the effort required to do nothing. It is a miracle of corruption and inaction. I gaze at the blue fence, running my fingers over the smooth surface of the imported marble beneath me.

'*¿Lista?*'

I turn towards the voice. '*¿Perdón?*' My voice is muffled because I have a cardigan on my head, trying to protect myself from the sun that washes the sky in a perpetual grey haze and makes my eyes water. I stand up and stuff the cardigan back into my bag, self-consciously patting down my hair. The security guard smiles as he unlocks the gate.

'*¿Lista?*' he says again, more as a statement than a question. Ready? Lunch is over.

In the marble foyer of the French House, artwork hangs from the mahogany wall behind the reception desk and light filters through ornate window panes. The entire area is pristine – polished to mirror the impeccable style of its creators. The air smells purified and silence bounces off cool stone walls. I register and go upstairs to the reading room.

I unpack my books – grammar and exercises, dictionaries and Mexican idioms – but they remain unopened for the moment. I have been reading about the history of Mexico. The library has an extensive collection of reference books and it is this trail I am following. One that is leading me towards unexpected discoveries.

I walk to the other side of the room where there are archives going right back to the Spanish conquest. I look up to the very top shelf and spy the books I am interested in – ancient Mexican history. Pulling across a stepladder on wheels, a finicky construction that skids across the polished floor, I hang on to the bookcase tightly in case the steps disappear from under me.

It's a strange sensation to be standing in this place where the stories of the past are held between gilded pages. I feel as if I am being seduced by history; drawn into a web of intrigue. Lately I see a change in my attitude. Just as I sense a growing maturity – and a desire to use my time wisely in Mexico – there is also something inside me that tells me I'm ready to look at myself, not just in relation to my family, but as part of the bigger picture. I have to look at the past to understand my future. This thought occupies my mind as I pull a book from the shelf and try to get off the ladder with one foot hooked around the bottom step to stop it moving.

I take the heavy volume back to the table. It tells the stories of the Aztec scholars who, rather than simply watch their culture be destroyed by the invading Spaniards, decided to record history for future generations. The book includes illustrations of the original Náhuatl manuscripts: bold representations in brown and ochre, the colours of the earth. I look at the hieroglyphic letters on the page and think of these scholars, trying to grasp the reality of their world disappearing before their eyes, putting down on paper what they knew, what their fathers taught them, their past and that of their ancestors. How do you represent a culture in words alone? And how much of the Aztecs' oral history was lost in the translation from voice and song into documented evidence?

I trace ancient maps of Mexico with my finger, taking

in places like the Isthmus of Tehuantepec, Pontonchan, Xicalango and Tenochtitlan, the site of the Aztecs' final defeat by the Spaniards. I read on, discovering new words, but I'm unable to master the difficult pronunciation and the complex stacking of vowels and syllables.

I discover that the word *Aztec* means 'the people of heron place'. This name was given to the Culúa-Mexica – pronounced 'coolwah mesheeka' – a nomadic tribe who arrived in the valley of Mexico in the early thirteenth century. The Culúa were the bully boys of history: an ancient version of a neighbour who trashes your house, kicks your dog, eats all your food, steals your wife and sets the place on fire when he leaves. They arrived one day in the valley of Mexico and set up camp alongside the two hundred or so already established tribes of the region. But the Nahua-speaking locals were horrified by the newcomers who, in ritual sacrifices, skinned their enemies and wore their skins as capes. The locals named them *Aztecas*, Aztecs, an ugly word meant as a slur against the Culúas' rootless existence and barbaric ways.

Sticks and stones. The Culúa reacted by riding roughshod over the neighbours. By the time the Spanish army arrived in 1519, the nomads had founded the city of Tenochtitlan and subjugated all the tribes in the valley of Mexico. Barbarians or not, they were supreme rulers. The Spanish general, Hernan Cortés, had expected to find a Mexican empire under the hegemony of one man, the emperor Moctezuma, leader of the Culúa-Mexica. What he found instead were countless tribes, some allied, others at war, linked only by their hatred of the Culúa.

In time Cortés would take advantage of the animosity towards the Culúa-Mexica by forging an alliance with their enemies. The conquest of Tenochtitlan, with the aid of one hundred and fifty thousand allies, was swift and absolute; disease, hunger and poor sanitation did the rest. The Culúa once again became a people with no place or identity. After the conquest, the remaining tribes of Mexico – linked loosely by a common language, Náhuatl – were collectively classified as Culúa-Mexica; no differentiation was made between the Culúa, Texcocans or Tlaxcaltecas. In the 1800s a historian renamed them *Aztecas*, a term as inaccurate as Apache for all native Americans. The slur was now recorded, for one and all.

My thoughts linger on the Culúa-Mexica. What were their weaknesses? I have read of their bravery and fortitude, but I can find nothing of their fears. The fears of men whose superstitious beliefs led them to hold aloft to the moon the still-beating hearts of their victims to appease the gods, convinced darkness was a punishment sated only by blood. But of human frailties – love, passion and jealousy – there is little available. I need more than names, dates and places. What good is history to me if I can't get to the core of discovery? Sometimes I feel the truth is a bandy-legged piglet that is always running from me.

I gaze out the window, through the black-bordered diamond insets of the window pane, which fit together like pieces of a puzzle. The thought brings back a long-forgotten memory. When I was nine years old, on my very first trip to Mexico, my grandfather gave me a map of Mexico. It was made of rubber and the pieces pulled apart like a jigsaw puzzle. He bought it from a street vendor and told me to study it well. I remember I thought it was shaped like a turnip. In my mind it was a distant land, a faraway place. History is like that, I think. Pieces slotted into place until a picture forms. And for me a picture *is* starting to form: as I fit together the pieces of the puzzle, of the past, I start to see who I am.

I look back at the book, thinking of this world of warriors, fierce battles and history steeped in blood. How much time have I wasted rejecting this culture? And how much more will I learn as I delve further into the past? I study the ancient faces of the Culúa-Mexica with their chocolate-coloured skin, hooked noses and elongated fore-heads, and in them I see my ancestors. Perhaps what fasci-nates me so much about this history is that I really want to be part of something: I want to belong. If the past influences my future then surely it has an abiding effect on the present; by learning today what happened yesterday I can own a little piece of history. I can take it all in and make it part of me.

'Here, let me help you.' I am returning the book to its shelf but someone has moved the steps. I can't quite reach and fear that the heavy tome will crash down on my head. A man comes to my aid. 'No, I can do it,' I reply. I don't want to look useless, even though I think I already do.

'I insist,' he says, taking the book from my outstretched arms. He stands on his toes and slots it back into place before stepping down and clapping his hands together, whether to congratulate himself on a job well done or to remove dust from his palms, I can't tell. 'Thank you so much,' I say. He bows slightly. '*A sus ordenes*,' he says. At your service. He has white-grey hair and coppery brown skin, a hooked nose and a taut mouth, just like my grand-father, but in a thinner, softer face.

I'm thinking about this peculiarity as I sit down again. I seem to recognise my grandfather's face in many other men: the dark skin, the brooding aspect and his distinctly Aztec appearance. I stare, incredulous, at men who could be his twin, in the street, on the train, everywhere. *It's not him*, I say to myself. But still they manage to stop me in my tracks. I often wonder if the spirit of my long-dead grandfather is checking up on me; the prodigal granddaughter returned.

As I sit here, picturing him in my mind, I think about how I have, inadvertently, become custodian of the past; the one person who can represent, from stories handed down, the lives of those who came before me. Perhaps it is because others want to forget. I know memories of bad things and difficult times still have the power to reach out from the past and hurt those still living: my mother and grandmother, in particular. I hold on to the stories of my grandfather's adultery, his wanton indifference to his wife's suffering; his dreams of futher education, crushed because men didn't study, they worked. Maybe I am the keeper of family history and all its secrets because these stories do not have the power to hurt me so acutely.

A memory stirs in my imagination. I'm thirteen years old and at home during the school holidays. I'm bored. Nothing to do, nothing on television. I pull a bag of photos from the cupboard and sit on the floor to look through them. One catches my eye. It's my grandfather as a young man, riding a horse and wearing a cowboy hat. He rides a dun-coloured horse and his hand is raised, half in salute, I guess. He looks confident and very young.

I smile at the recollection. Memory has such an appetite for details. The early days of my grandfather's life, the tales told about him, related to me by my mother, are now sharpening in my mind, and suddenly I am washed away by a torrent of thoughts from the past.

By the end of the 1920s, the Revolution in Mexico had finally ended – there were skirmishes among different factions but these were more from personal vendetta than political conviction. The country was in tatters: industry suffered, jobs were scarce and schools were closed. My grandfather, Alfredo Rodríguez, managed to complete seven years of school, but he was the only one of his siblings to do so.

'Your great-grandfather, Odon, thought education made people lazy,' my mother said.

I'm picturing her on the couch all those years ago, on the afternoon of the discovery of the photographs. She is contemplative, relaxed, talking between sips of coffee. I'm half-listening, invoking my teenage prerogative to be sullen and moody.

As a young man, Alfredo worked on Odon's farm with his brothers: men with gnarled hands, sinewy shoulders and muscled bodies. Alfredo eerily resembled his mother, doña Sara, the great matriarch who lorded over the family with decisions that were never questioned. Alfredo and his brothers, those same men who slung dead cows over their shoulders with ease, beat other men unconscious for minor altercations, and found willing lovers in spite of their gruesome appearances, were reduced to shuffling unease whenever their mother found reason to berate them.

Doña Sara wanted Alfredo to finish high school, but this time Odon had the final word. Alfredo would be a farmer, and the subject of education would never be brought up again.

After he dropped out of school and after he married my grandmother when he was sixteen, Alfredo went to work full-time on the farm. His mother said nothing. Not a word more about school, or the indiscretion – spending the night alone with his teenage girlfriend – that forced him to marry. What could she say? By the time he was twenty-five, my grandfather had been married for nearly ten years and was father to a child, my mother Sara.

My mother was born looking like a wrinkled monkey, with a shock of black hair to match a dark, uneven skin tone. Over the next few days her colour did not change as was hoped, and it became obvious her features were pure *Azteca*. For whatever reason, Alfredo took one look at his firstborn and rejected her outright.

'My grandmother Sara was there when I was born,' my mother said. 'She always said I was a gift to my mother, to make up for her losing two babies before me, although she was probably the only person who thought that. The rest of them, they couldn't stand me, they would have sent me back if they could.' From that moment on, doña Sara never wavered in her devotion to her granddaughter, who was named after her and looked so like her. As she grew, my mother was insulted, ignored and humiliated by her family, and set apart from her cousins, who were all blessed with the pale complexions and fair hair favoured by society. But doña Sara would fly to her defence like a lioness, mercilessly bringing justice to all those who dared to insult her favourite granddaughter.

I remember my mother's face when she told me these stories: she is standing in the kitchen chopping vegetables, while I sit at the bench watching. The tone of her voice softer than usual, contemplative, sad. Back then they were just stories, but now I see that it was a determination on her part to instil in us doña Sara's legacy. From her my mother did not just inherit her appearance, but also an extraordinary faith in God that doña Sara, in her wisdom, knew would sustain her granddaughter long after she herself was gone. Doña Sara's faith was centred around a combination of Catholic dogma and pre-Hispanic ritual: respect for the dead, raising altars to the ancestors and the lighting of candles were as important as the Ten Commandments. For doña Sara, pagan rituals were part of who she was: not a *mestizo* but a descendant of the Aztecs, with her aquiline nose, shiny black hair, copper skin and lilting speech.

It was well known that doña Sara had a direct line of communication to the dead, but she kept her psychic abilities to herself. Her sons were not so discreet, and took great pleasure in scandalising the family at the dinner table with preposterous stories: they would say that the currents of air in the kitchen were the spirits of dead family members begging to be forgiven for past indiscretions; and that the musty odour surrounding the barns was not that of the animals but rather the spirits of the Revolution's dead, whose remains had rotted unburied in the yard.

During the war many people left buried gold and valuables in heavy iron caskets throughout the countryside, often being shot in the process by *banditos* keen to get their hands on the booty. The bodies would simply be pushed into the trunk by the robbers as, in their haste to get away from the approaching *rurales*, rural police, they would grab a handful of coins. It was believed that if you lived near one of these trunks, at some stage you would be visited by the spirit of the deceased to let you know of its whereabouts. My grandfather and his brothers spent many evenings in macho one-upmanship, regaling each other with tales of the ghostly apparitions they had seen hovering near the house.

Eventually the temptation grew too strong and they went searching for the treasure. The brothers were all strong men: tall, bad-tempered and with faces only the most forgiving of mothers could love. They had come face to face with wild animals that threatened their lives, been involved in brawls where only their brute strength saved them, and lived for weeks at a time in the jungle, but when it came to the intangible, they had no defence whatsoever, as they were soon to find out.

Doña Sara knew exactly what they were getting themselves into. She sat in her rocking chair in the kitchen, surrounded by the gathered wives and children, waiting patiently for their return. 'She warned them on their way out the door,' my mother said. 'She said, *If you invite the dead, they will come*. But they didn't listen.' Her sons would pay for their meddling. 'Well, they came back and they were all white and shaking and they couldn't speak.' My mother always laughed at that part of the story, her face crinkling up at the very idea – the stupidity of it all. 'They thought they were so clever.'

According to legend, the few men who did find treasure became increasingly nervous and preoccupied, constantly looking over their shoulders until finally being driven insane by apparitions only they could see. My mother remembers this night and many more to come, when the children who caught snatches of the story began to wet themselves because they were too afraid to go to the toilet outside. Doña Sara told the men off for frightening the children. *Now look what you have done.* The brothers never again went looking for treasure, the dinner table bantering stopped and the events of that night remained a secret, shut firmly behind lips as tightly sealed as the lids on the elusive iron caskets.

Men did not express their feelings in those days. Instead they drank. A lot. Alfredo and his brothers frequented the *pulqueria*, a bar where the only drink sold was *pulque*, an unrefined extract from the agave plant. This was a place where a respectable woman would never loiter. Women of virtue never stepped out after dark, let alone to enter a cantina; apart from the obvious danger, it would mean her respectability would be stripped as fast as it took to take a swig of *pulque*.

In the evenings my great-grandmother Sara always sat in that same rocking chair in the kitchen, dozing off with her *rebozo*, a knitted shawl, wrapped around her shoulders. But suddenly one night she was up and heading out the door before anyone could ask where she was going. And along with her she took her favourite grandchild, my mother.

Telling me this story many years later, my mother was still amused by the memory of this woman who she loved so much. I can picture her sparkling eyes and remember the warm flush on her cheeks, and in spite of the distance that separates us, I can almost imagine she is here with me, sitting across the communal table in this monument to French architecture.

'By the time we got to the *pulqueria* she was all red and puffing and *so* angry,' she told me. Arriving at the cantina, Sara gave one peso to a child outside, telling him to get her son. 'She was smart enough, she wasn't going in. Instead she gave those boys a message: *you tell him that if he doesn't come out right now I'm going in.*'

Soon enough the inebriated son staggered out the door, keen to avoid the embarrassment of being dragged out of a bar by his mother. It was quite a rash move on Sara's part, but such was the respect accorded her that no-one ever criticised the action. Indeed, her sons' wives, including my grandmother, would never have attempted such a thing and thereafter, whenever their husbands had spent too long at the *pulqueria*, they would come to the matriarch and ask her to bring them home.

Here it was, in this magical country, that these men and women lived and died, I think, looking around the silent reading room. My family's story says a lot about Mexico, much more than I could ever hope to learn from books in the library. As I linger on the precipice between past and present, I have a surreal sense that I am not alone. It is as if the very act of remembering invites the departed, and those separated by distance, into the here and now. I can still see my mother telling me these stories some fifteen years ago, sitting on the couch, driving me home from school, standing at the kitchen bench; so too, she can still remember her beleaguered uncles and her father staggering home from the pub, trailed by the gaggle of dogs that followed doña Sara everywhere.

Outside the window the light has changed. The street lights have been turned on, bathing the street in an orange glow. I hadn't even noticed the blanket of evening approaching, entirely losing my sense of time as this melding of history and the voices from the past overtook me. I throw my books in my bag and leave the library, suddenly starving. As I shut the door behind me I feel the cool evening breeze on my face. I walk across the courtyard towards the gate and into the deserted street. In two weeks my parents and brother will be here, and I look forward to sharing my experiences with them, and talking about all I have learnt of our shared ancestors.

Chapter Seven

México Verdadero

In late December my family arrive in Mexico for a holiday. The trip is a long overdue one since my parents
haven't seen my grandmother in fifteen years. I go to meet
them at the airport and, after a speed-of-light taxi ride, we
arrive at *Colonia Narvarte*. The reunion is a noisy one.
There's a lot of hugs and kisses and smiling amid a babble
in two different languages. The children are overexcited, my
grandma is overwhelmed and the rest of us are just trying
to take it all in.

Immediately, we are ushered into the dining room where
a celebratory lunch awaits.

As the main meal of *enchiladas rojas* is served, my
mother leans across to her sister, who is across the table.

'Pass the salt, please,' she says.

'*¿Qué?*'

'Pass the salt.' She doesn't even realise her mistake.

Thinking she is going to repeat herself for a third time, I tug at her sleeve.

'¡Má! You're speaking in English!'

My aunt thinks this is hilarious. 'Who can't even remember how to speak their own language?' she teases. Smiling, my mother reaches for the salt.

'Little sister, you might have a point. I can't even remember how to say salt.'

A few days later, after visits from a dizzying number of cousins, aunts, uncles, nieces and nephews, we leave for a holiday in Chiapas. As we descend the staircase outside my grandmother's apartment, she leans over the railing and calls out to my mother.

'If it's cold, make sure you wear a jumper.'

'Yes mamá.'

I laugh. So much for being not answerable to anyone. In the family pecking order my grandmother has the final say. My mother turns to me and smiles.

'It's like I never left.'

In tropical southern Mexico, it seems that roads are an afterthought. The bitumen is crumbling, pock-marked with holes you could lose a cow in. An old man in a straw hat walks along the roadside, trailing a bullock behind him and lazily slicing at the humid air with the machete in his other hand. He tips his hat and smiles as we pass. Our tour bus drives past enormous palms and lush earth. In the middle distance the verdant mountains seem to be closing in, drawing us into a tropical embrace. The air is teeming with the calls of dusk: the haunting call of a macaw, the screech of a spider monkey, like a little girl screaming.

Approaching the town of Palenque on the cusp of a clear evening, with the air fragrant from rain and nature, I feel alive, my every sense awakened. A soft breeze is coming through the open window and it is cool on my face. Our tour guide, Antonio, is standing at the front of the bus, giving us a short history of the place where we will spend the next three days. Palenque is home to the world-famous eighth-century Mayan ruins that lay hidden in overgrown jungle for centuries. In 1784, following rumours of an ancient city lost in the Chiapan jungle, the mayor of the nearby town of Santo Domingo del Palenque, José Antonio Calderon, accompanied by Antonio Bernaconi, an Italian architect, went looking for the ruins. Two years later Calderon, joined by the Spanish army captain, Don Antonio del Río, and a group of Chol-speaking Mayan labourers, returned to Palenque, hacked through the dense foliage and 'unearthed' the mystical city.

This place is *México verdadero*, our guide says. The real Mexico. 'So watch out for the snakes,' he adds as an after-thought. Up ahead our hotel gleams like a shiny obelisk, out of place in this sleepy village where pigs rustle by the roadside and Indian children play marbles in the dirt, surrounded by a gaggle of mangy dogs.

Minutes later, the bus pulls into the hotel car park and the engine shuts down with a shudder. We get out, followed by the others in our tour group. My brother, Miguel, punches me in the arm and I lose my balance, falling into a garden bed. I start to giggle. My parents stand nearby, smiling. None of us speak of our excitement but it's there all the same, bubbling just beneath the surface. We are in the jungle and none of us can quite believe it. I guess we can't comprehend either how we've managed to all end up in the same place, at the same time. My brother, on secondment to the Home Office, has come from England, my parents from Australia. And now, here we are, four days before Christmas, together again.

We walk into the hotel and stand in a huddle in the foyer. The building is sparkling and new. The ochre tiles beneath my feet lead to garden beds of tropical ferns and giant *macetas*, terracotta urns. In the middle of the garden a pool that has been lit from within glows eerie and turquoise. Next to it a hut with a thatched roof and cream-rendered walls, surrounded by foliage, looks like a Balinese temple. And in the distance the mountains overlook the village, their imposing trees throwing a cool blanket over the heat of the afternoon. It begins to rain in sheets. I'm still trying to take it all in when my brother comes over to stand next to me. As I stare, overwhelmed, he sums up my feelings with his typical understated eloquence.

'Bloody hell,' he says.

Apart from the spectacular scenery, this place has an unrushed, earthy appeal. Antonio tells me the region is basically unchanged – apart from a couple of flashy hotels – since tourists started visiting the ruins en masse in the 1960s. Villagers do good business selling postcards, T-shirts and soft drinks to the tourists, but this is supplementary income. Their main income is derived from farming and coffee production, using methods unchanged since the time of their Mayan ancestors. There is something refreshing about the locals' weary indifference to the tourist dollar. An internet café down the road seems to be the only concession to modernity. My brother goes there and comes back laughing as he tells us about the donkey that followed him down the street.

Later we watch the rain coming down in stops and starts from under the thatched canopy of the hotel restaurant. The air is so rich I could get drunk on the smell. Looking at my family as we sit down to dinner, it seems they are as captivated with this place as I am – this beautiful hotel, the magnificent gardens and landscape and the pure evening air. This fairytale land.

The restaurant is starting to fill with other people and a

group of musicians play traditional music of the region on a *marimba*, a kind of wooden xylophone. It's wonderful to be here with my family, to slot myself back into this nucleus comprising brother and parents. My kin. I hadn't realised how much I'd missed them. It dawns upon me that this is the first time in two months I have felt completely at ease in this country. Utterly relaxed. It is as though I have finally let go of the coil of tension that I have been vaguely aware of since my arrival in Mexico City. But that's how life is in the *capital*; you are always on your guard, aware. Here it's different. In this place I can enjoy the heady liberation of being in the countryside. I'm on a high: tired and happy. Glasses are raised and a toast is made. 'To us,' we say.

As we sip white wine an anguished cry comes from the garden.

'*¡Déjeme cabrón!*' Get away from me, asshole!

I put down my wine and turn towards the strange, high-pitched voice. And then there is a bloodcurdling cry. It sounds like someone is being attacked in the garden. But nobody takes any notice. Away from the light of the pool the garden is pitch black. I peer into the inky night but I can't see anything. Maybe I'm imagining things; the sweet air must be playing havoc with my head. I turn to my dad.

'Did you hear that?' I ask.

'No. What?'

My dad probably isn't the right person to ask. Years of rifle practice during his national service with the British army have left him deaf as a post. He can't even hear the alarm going off on his watch. I shrug and pick up my glass again. The next cry is louder, more insistent. Okay, that I heard. Something terrible is happening in paradise.

'*Get away from meeee!*'

I look back into the garden.

'*Asshole!!!*'

While I am imagining the worst, the waiter comes over with our meals. 'Don't worry,' he says. 'It's not what you think.' Clearly he is amused by the ripples of interest the mysterious screecher has caused.

After putting down the plates he points towards a bush in the garden, not far from where I'm sitting. 'Out there,' he says. I squint and see a form rustling in the leaves. An intruder perhaps? In the darkness it takes shape. As if on cue, a parrot moves into the light filtering from the restaurant. He's now hopping among the leaves, pecking here and there, looking adorable, all fluffy green, orange and red feathers. Butter wouldn't melt in his mouth, this clever little bird that swears like a wharfie.

'Someone taught him those words and now he won't shut up,' the waiter says. 'We like him.'

Visions begin to form of the parrot insulting wealthy foreign tourists, who smile at him, blissfully ignorant that he is telling them in pitch-perfect Spanish to '*Piss off, idiot*'. Bird with attitude. I like him too.

The waiter leaves with a slight bow and a surreptitious wink at me. We turn our attention back to our meals. We all inadvertently ordered the same dish, *bacalao*, local codfish cooked in a sauce of sherry with parsley, onion, tomatoes, green olives and garlic. We have also ordered prawns with tomato *salsa* and lemon. Palenque is not far from the coast of the Yucatan peninsula so all the *mariscos* are fresh from the sea this morning. In the middle of the table there is a pile of tortillas and bowls of sliced onion, avocado and black beans.

My *bacalao* is delicious. I chew slowly, savouring the gritty texture of the cod and crunching its brittle skin in my teeth. I wash it down with a sip of wine, cool and sweet, as the taste of garlic lingers on my palate. The dinner lasts into the late evening, our conversation punctuated by the sounds of birds, howler monkeys and jaguars reaching across an ancient plateau.

After dinner my brother disappears and my parents make their way to the poolside where they sit together on a banana lounge. I walk across the grass to my room, taking in the fresh smell of earth dampened by rain.

I sit on the patio outside my garden-view room and look over at my parents. They haven't moved. Fate has brought us here – together. Over the years we have all come and gone, my mother to see her mother, my previous visits, even my brother squeezed in a short trip some years back. The lure of the country is strong for my family. It seems we can't stay away. Maybe now that we are here together, we can share some of our fascination with Mexico; an intrigue that up to this point has been a singular experience.

There is one exception. My father. He hasn't set foot in Mexico in over thirty years. The last time he was here, he was a young man.

Maxim Wood had joined a group of friends who emigrated to Australia for ten pounds back in 1964. After four years in Australia he took a trip to Mexico City to see the Olympic Games. He hadn't gone looking for a wife, far from it. But, nevertheless, there she was one afternoon, sitting with her girlfriends in a popular bar, waiting politely for the moment she could blow this joint full of *gringos*.

My father had just turned thirty-three, was thin and nervous with big grey-green eyes, and could not speak one solitary word of Spanish, but he singled out the most aloof girl of the group of friends, and made his way to her side. He asked the only one of the girls who spoke English to interpret his request: to ask my mother on a date. She was not impressed. She had no business with a foreigner and told her friend she wouldn't be going anywhere with him, especially since she couldn't even say hello in English.

But my father insisted, and when my mother's friend offered her services as interpreter, she reluctantly agreed.

The next day the three of them met at the entrance to the Museum of Anthropology, where my mother's friend immediately grabbed my father by the arm and led him away, leaving my mother to trail behind them. But her plans to muscle in on the Englishman were quashed as he took every available opportunity to glance in my mother's direction. The day after that, he took my mother to watch an athletics event at the Olympic stadium – just the two of them and a bilingual dictionary. Two weeks later he proposed in faltering Spanish.

My mother accepted; she knew in her heart that this was the man for her. A fortune teller had once predicted this fate: 'One day,' she had said, 'you will marry a foreign man.' My father returned to Australia to save for the wedding, and they were married a year later in Mexico City.

Separated by oceans from their relatives in England and Mexico, my parents made their home in Australia. The quiet Englishman and his passionate Mexican wife. An odd couple, he as white as she was dark. Beans and rice, people said. My mother struggled in the early days. They lived at Wilson's Promontory, a windswept coastal town outside of Melbourne. The cold made her hair fall out; she couldn't speak English and was *very* lonely. A year later my brother was born, and then I followed. We moved to England for a few years, where my mother learned English at night school. Then we returned to Australia, and when they moved into their house in Sorrento they knew they were finally home. That was almost three decades ago.

'Your family,' my grandmother often says, 'are not just people. They are as much a part of you as your own limbs. Without them you are incomplete.' I look out at this perfect vista as her words nestle in my brain, potent and truthful.

Maybe that's why being here together is so important. Because now I am whole again.

That night I sleep heavily and wake at dawn, feeling refreshed. Outside, the world beyond the glass door is already awake; filled with life, colour and sound. I dress quickly and walk into the garden, where my bare feet squish into the dewy grass.

Heavy mist shrouds the entrance to the Palenque ruins. Our bus driver, José, drops us off in the car park and leaves immediately, telling us he cannot stay because snakes often crawl into the warm engines of the waiting buses, rendering them useless. I'd read about the *víboras* at the library. These snakes are often more than five feet long, the most common being the Nawiaka, whose venom can kill within an hour. José waves and then he is gone, carefully manoeuvring his vehicle back along the narrow road out of this lush valley.

We walk under a canopy of trees as a melody of birdsong heralds our arrival. There are fourteen of us in this tour group but nobody speaks. As we enter the tropical jungle, the only sound we make is the crunching of leaves under our feet. Feeling light-headed, I realise I have been holding my breath since we stepped onto this path. I'm bubbling over with awe and anticipation.

The path comes to an end. We are now standing at the edge of a clearing. Antonio walks a few paces in front of us and then turns around. He is beaming. He raises his arm and leaves it there, suspended midair, looking like a frozen traffic cop.

'This, my dear people,' he says, 'is *Palenque*.'

Antonio's arm-raising gesture must have been a sign for God to cue the sun because suddenly the vast landscape is bathed in golden sunlight. This beauty is so exquisite it renders me mute. I look at the others, and I imagine that my face bears the same expression of rapt amazement. This strange *mezcla* of people – a Mexican family with their two adult children, a Mexican woman with her two grandchildren, a honeymooning Spanish couple, and us – we are all speechless. All of us in our own private communion with the spectacle before us; not quite sure if what we are seeing could possibly be real.

Palenque is a collection of pyramid-like buildings surrounded by grassy plazas. The site extends two kilometres into the jungle and has more than two hundred structures, different in size and complexity, each adapted to this environment. Beyond the immediate perimeter there are mountains and valleys covered in thick vegetation. During the time of the Maya, the city was known as *Lakam Ha*, or Big Water, for its many rivers, waterfalls and streams. The horizon is cloaked in great clouds of *niebla*, heavy fog. Everything about this place is dazzling and mystical.

Directly in front of us is the Temple of the Inscriptions, with images of Mayan deities rendered on stucco interior walls, and a place where archaeological interpretations of the inscriptions have revealed names of important figures and governors, dates of births, marriages, military conquests, alliances and rituals of this extraordinary culture. The hieroglyphics show the depth of the Mayan understanding of astronomy, architecture, mathematics and writing. Lives have been recorded on these *tableros*, stone tablets. The Temple of the Inscriptions is also where the emerald-and-jade-encrusted mask of the eighth-century King Pakal was discovered in a crypt. The stately palaces, temples, altars, deities, sculptures and immense stonework bear testimony to the achievements of the Maya. I breathe deeply, trying to take it all in. I'm standing before one of the greatest monuments to Mayan culture in all of Mesoamerica.

We walk over to the temple and our motley group stops to rest on the steps. Squinting in the bright sun, I look over to the Great Palace across the plaza. The stone building is four storeys high and was built by Pakal's son, Hok, somewhere around 721 AD. I try to picture the city as it was. What happened to the Maya? Why was Palenque abandoned? I return my attention to Antonio, who is now telling us how the physical characteristics of this race have changed little since their epoch of glory. To demonstrate his point he calls over a Mayan boy who is selling necklaces.

'Look at these features. Have you ever seen such a beautiful physicality?'

Antonio has a point. The boy *is* beautiful. He has a strong hooked nose and an elongated face, a flattened forehead and copper-coloured skin. Individually such features probably wouldn't work but as a whole they are impressive. He reminds me of a miniature version of the marble busts of the great Roman generals I saw once in a London museum. Nor is it hard to imagine that with a tunic, sandals and headdress this small child could have been plucked straight out of history. I close my eyes and feel the delicious warmth of the sun on my face. In this place I can feel the presence of the ancestors, their spirits that live on in the opaque black eyes of this child. Yet it is a cruel irony to see the race that created this ancient city and once ruled here are now so reduced in power and status, selling trinkets to foreigners.

We stroll through the Temple of the Inscriptions, where elaborate hallways bring us to the next plaza. I'm standing on a ledge just above the grass when I look up to see a film crew clambering down the steps, encumbered with tripods, cameras, reels and pulleys. They are young guys, laughing and talking, relaxed, not looking where they're going. I shudder. Maybe it's because I'm so clumsy that I see the potential for disaster everywhere. The steps look steep and very slippery. It's not hard to imagine how Mexico's original inhabitants *really* came to an end. Forget pestilence or invasion, *my* theory is far more interesting. The natives fell to their deaths trying to negotiate these killer steps while drunk on *pulque*.

By now I'm getting hot so I step off the ledge and head towards the Temple of the Sun. I haven't walked five steps when the predicted accident happens. I don't see it, I just hear the scream, and a loud crack.

'*¡Puta madre!*' (Too obscene to translate.)

One of the camera crew is lying at the bottom of the steps, clutching his ankle and writhing in agony. '*¡Diablos!*' someone exclaims, exasperated by this unexpected turn of events. Nobody seems too worried about the injured man. As it happens one of our tour group is a doctor. He goes over to investigate. My mum, who had gone on ahead, comes over to stand next to me.

'What happened?' she asks.

'He fell,' I reply. 'I think he broke something.'

She chews on her lip for a moment. 'Yeah, I knew that was going to happen.'

The doctor, who had been crouching down to examine the patient, now gets up and wipes his hands on his jeans. 'Yup, it's broken,' he says to the guy on the ground. And then he walks away. I can't believe it. What about an ambulance? The rest of the film crew pick up his equipment and start walking away. From what I gather they are not impressed with him.

Torn between total disbelief and sympathy, I'm almost tempted to laugh. Reading my shock, my mum tries to explain what we have just witnessed. 'That's how it is here. Men get no sympathy. They probably think he deserves it for not being more careful.' And as if to back up her words, the oldest of the film crew, a man in a *Goodies* T-shirt and khaki shorts, steps over the guy and walks off. 'Dickhead,' he says, loud and clear.

The rest of my group are already climbing the Sun Temple and they call me over. I join them, holding tightly to the chain that ascends, almost vertical, to the top step. Halfway up I stop for a breather. I turn around and sit on a narrow step so I can look out at the view, a postcard landscape of blue, green and grey. I breathe in deeply and as I get up again I notice a small figure in the distance – it's the injured cameraman hobbling back to the car park. I continue climbing on my hands and knees and collapse exhausted, as though I have been shot with a tranquilliser dart, at the top of the pyramid. Nearly everyone at the ruins seems to be gathered on this rather thin wedge of rock. I smile and rest my cheek on a cool stone base.

When I catch my breath, I get up and the film crew invite me to join them for a photograph. There's a lot of laughter and noise. We are all slightly drunk with this place. Someone calls out, 'This is hell! I want to go back to Mexico City,' and we all burst into raucous laughter. There's a click and an image is recorded. Back on terra firma, I think that in years to come someone will be going through an album and come across a photograph of ten burly, blokey men and one woman in denim overalls with rosy cheeks and a mass of gravity-defying hair. A moment frozen in time, in a paradise of man and nature.

Two hours later we return to the hotel, exhausted by all the climbing and walking but thrilled by what we have seen. I am euphoric. I have walked in the footsteps of the ancestors, breathed the air they once inhaled and stood on their *tierra*, their land. This holiday has allowed me to see parts of Mexico I would not normally see; to enjoy the myriad contrasts that make up this country. It is an experience I will never forget.

Chapter Eight

The Old City:
Relics of Tenochtitlan

After returning to Mexico City, our holiday together comes to an end. Two weeks have passed in the blink of an eye. Their trip has been a whirlwind of long lunches at my grandmother's apartment, breakfasts with the entire clan at Sanborn's, a restaurant that serves thick pancakes with butter and honey, or going to my cousins' primary school so my mother can tell their wide-eyed classmates about *cocodrilos*, crocodiles, and other scary Australian animals. Oddly enough, on this trip I felt like I knew more about Mexico than my mum, because so much time has passed since she'd last been. Our roles were reversed. I was showing *her* the sights while she shook her head, saying, 'It has changed so much. I don't remember *any* of this.'

Even some of the words I used were unfamiliar to her: '¡*Guacala!*' I said after eating something stale. 'What are you saying?' she asked. 'Yuck,' I replied. 'Huh? Never heard that word before.' A new lexicon has emerged in her absence.

Two weeks have flown by and everyone has to go back to work, my brother back to England. I wave off my family at the airport and, seeing them depart, have a sudden urge to go with them. When they are gone I catch a bus home, feeling like the loneliest person alive. Even the streets are deserted. During the Christmas–New Year period most of Mexico's residents escape to the coast for holidays in Acapulco and Cancún. Strangely, those who have stayed behind are nowhere to be seen.

My head aches and my eyes are stinging as my body tries to reacclimatise to the smog of Mexico City. I know I have to be patient, but it is still a shock to come from a sparse country landscape where roads are for cows to this one. Sunglasses and cocktails by the pool one day, weaving like a Spanish matador through traffic the next. I go to my room and flop on my bed, lying there for the next few hours, inert as a flat battery.

Several weeks earlier, in mid-December, my classmate Jean had taken me aside to ask me something. Did I want to move into an apartment near *Paseo de la Reforma* with him and his girlfriend? They had a spare room and I could have it if I wanted it. Having already decided I wanted to stay in Mexico, I had been thinking seriously about where I wanted to live. Conditions were cramped at my grandmother's place – I had been sharing a room with my cousin Julia. Studying, too, was proving difficult with two small cousins.

Although my grandmother made me breakfast every day, and fussed over me constantly, it was too much. I had lived away from home since I was eighteen, and I was used to coming and going as I pleased. I knew my grandmother would be upset, but for my own sanity, I needed to live with people my own age, and to have my own room again.

When I finally resolved to leave, I tried to soften the blow by telling my grandmother I was moving in with friends, but she would have none of it. 'Women don't live alone,' she said. 'They should be at home with their families – where they are safe.' I nodded and said nothing. I couldn't explain to her how things are different now, and there was definitely no way I could tell her I was moving in with an unmarried couple.

My grandmother's health had improved and this was the impetus I needed to move out. When I left, I told her I would visit often. But despite my reassurances, I knew she was upset. This was more than just a difference of opinions – it was cultural. My grandmother could not understand my desire for a place on my own. For my part, I couldn't understand why women in Mexico have to be so cosseted. In time I will understand this dichotomy better. But at the moment my actions seem incomprehensible to my grandmother in a country where family is sacred, and where women are not independent.

And that is how I now find myself staring out my bedroom window at the ornate grey tiles of the building on the other side of this apartment complex. A sparrow settles on the windowsill and I watch him peck at the crumbs of a forgotten donut.

Our flat is in a complex of thirty-two apartments, in a building hidden behind a heavy iron gate that leads into a wide cobbled pathway separating the two wings of the apartment complex. Originally built in 1898 as the home of a high-ranking politician, this place oozes charm, with garden beds of tropical plants, elaborate cornices on the outside walls and nineteenth-century brickwork. In fact, I was so captivated by the building when Jean brought me here one afternoon that I said yes to moving in without ever setting foot inside.

The apartment is on the second floor at the end of the walkway, where a brick perimeter wall protects the building from the street, the added benefit being that the sound of noisy traffic is muffled. Most of the apartments are occupied by foreigners who keep to themselves, so the place has an almost deserted feel. It reminds me of a secret garden, complete with butterflies and hummingbirds.

The entrance opens onto a large living area with a brick fireplace – a strange thing to have in a tropical country. A beautiful gilded mirror hangs above the mantel, sunlight spills through tall shuttered windows and the high ceilings give the apartment a sense of spaciousness. On this level are the main bedroom and a small kitchen that is almost entirely dominated by a large bench. Above me there are exposed wooden beams. It is all very rustic. A large window next to the kitchen sink opens onto the courtyard – the perfect spot for breakfast.

A spiral staircase in the corner of the lounge room leads to my bedroom on the mezzanine level. On one side of the 'bedroom' is a wall of shelves. Directly underneath is an odd window at floor level, as though the architect responsible for converting the building into flats only realised when it was too late that the window was in the wrong place. On the other side of the bed, behind a wooden door painted with swirling stems and delicate yellow flowers, is an ensuite. My own bathroom! And then there's the balustrade overlooking the lounge room. The layout is open plan and airy, and from the moment I stepped inside I felt right at home.

If Narvarte, the leafy suburb where my grandmother lives, was considered suburban Mexico City, then this area, San Rafael, can be classed as downtown. We are smack bang in the middle of the city. The museums, restaurants and bars, and Chapultepec Park, Mexico City's equivalent to the Botanic Gardens, are only a stone's throw away.

The vibrancy of this city is within my reach and I can almost feel its energy settle on my skin.

In the afternoon I pop out to the supermarket. When I return with a shopping bag full of crusty bread rolls, Gouda cheese and two bottles of the dubiously named red wine Bull's Blood, I'm sweating under the fierce sun. At the gate, our *portero* or porter, Roberto, is washing down the footpath. I side-step a puddle of suds and say hello. He puts the broom next to the bucket and wipes his hands on his trousers.

'You okay?' he asks.

'Sure,' I reply, puffing.

Roberto and I talk a lot. His job is to open the gate and so most of the time he doesn't have much to do. He passes the time by chatting with the tenants. He speaks with an easy familiarity and, even though I've known him for only a short while, he is someone I instinctively trust.

Roberto is a small man with chocolate-coloured skin. His hair is jet black so that when the sun shines it looks almost blue. He comes from an Indian family and lives in the basement in a converted boiler room with a single bed, a bedside table and a globe hanging from a cable in the ceiling. He's a kind soul who at my age has the eyes of someone much older; someone who has suffered greatly. Across his face is a scar that runs from temple to chin. The subject of how he got his scar comes up in passing one day, and he tells me the story without pity or *what ifs*. A friend, high on drugs, took offence at Roberto asking him to repay a loan and slashed him with a broken bottle. For a debt of forty pesos, or about six Australian dollars, Roberto has suffered more than two years of operations to repair the damaged nerves in his face, and will spend the rest of his life in chronic pain.

We talk briefly. I'd love to stay and chat but the cheese in my bag might turn in the heat.

In the evening Sandrine prepares dinner. Outside, the light is fading and I feel a soft breeze against my face as I sit in front of the open window. The apartment smells of *ratatouille* bubbling on the stove and the wine is breathing – although for fifteen pesos (about two dollars) I don't expect much. Jean has taken charge of the pasta. Both refuse my offers of help.

'Just relax,' Sandrine says. 'I've got it all under control.'

Sprawled on the floor, we enjoy a dinner of *ratatouille*, spaghetti and crusty rolls. Later, we drink the red wine and smoke cigars, talking and laughing until the early hours of the morning. I'm glad I moved in with Jean and Sandrine. My instinct was right: this was a good decision.

The beginning of a new year in a different apartment also signifies more than just a change of environment. It is as if the decision to strike out on my own, away from the cocoon of family, is representative of my changing feelings towards Mexico. My trip away has lit a fire within me. It has renewed my determination to really discover the soul of this country – not just by travelling but by being part of this city, by integrating myself into Mexican life. At the age of twenty-eight I no longer want to be unsure of who I am. And Mexico is the place where I'm going to take my journey of discovery. I'm not going to run any more.

This fire isn't going to go out and with that comes a realisation. Mexico, the name that once belonged to a tribe of great warriors, a land as ancient as the sun, is my spiritual home. If there's anything I know with certainty, it is this.

By mid-January Mexico City springs back to life. In the *Zócalo*, the old district, tired-looking office workers crowd the footpaths. Executives stop to have their shoes polished by the *boleros*. Newspaper vendors vie for attention with a man in an apron who is selling roasted chestnuts in paper cones. The smell is delicious. For a while the city was almost empty, but now as I watch the traffic rumbling along, I find it hard to recall the deserted streets of a fortnight ago.

It is early morning and I am standing across the road from the *Plaza de la Constitución*, the city square. On the first day of the new semester at the Mexico Academy I'm on an excursion to the *Templo Mayor* or Great Temple – Aztec ruins on the other side of the *Zócalo*, in the heart of the city. With me are my classmates Jean and Kumi, some students from another class, and their teacher, Carmen, who is acting as our guide. We are waiting for a break in the traffic so we can cross the road. (In this city traffic stops for no man, although once I saw a line of cars banked up and waiting patiently as a chicken crossed the road. It wasn't one of those crazy dreams where Winston Churchill is in your kitchen – naked – cooking pancakes. It happened. I pinched myself really hard just to make sure.)

In front of us the large square has been cut into segments of light and dark by the shadow of the maturing sun. In this part of town all the laneways and avenues lead to the plaza. The *Zócalo* is buzzing with energy. Music blasts from loudspeakers, pedicabs pass by carrying tourists, taxis and kombi vans compete for passengers. Strolling vendors are selling everything from cigarettes and chewing gum to papier-mâché marionettes and brightly coloured fans that spin like windmills in the breeze. In the middle of the plaza, crowds are milling around the Mexican flag. The air has a carnival atmosphere. Carmen turns to us, suddenly serious.

'Remember,' she says, 'when the traffic whistle sounds you have to *run* across the road.'

The lights have changed and the others are already on the other side of the road. Carmen calls out something that I don't catch. I'm not really listening; too much is going on.

On my left is the domed magnificence of the Metropolitan Cathedral, the oldest church in Latin America, sparkling as bursts of sunlight bounce off its ornate cream walls. Directly in front of me is the National Palace, the seat of government, an imposing stone backdrop set in bold against a patchwork blue-gold sky.

The old district is full of startling discoveries; the beauty of its man-made creations is awe-inspiring. These buildings are as wondrous as anything nature could create. Sometimes man gets it so right. I love this place. I love the eclectic mix of culture, history and people. Even though I think I know this city well – although three months by anyone's standards isn't a long time – I still sometimes find myself dazzled. This city is a monument to creativity. Being here is like standing at the entrance to a maze, where each pathway leads to a new adventure.

My reverie is interrupted by a loud voice.

'*¡Samantita!*'

Jean is calling me from the other side of the road. He waves a lanky arm in my direction.

'*¡Apúrate por el amor de Dios!*' For the love of God, hurry up!

I laugh. For someone who didn't know a word of the language when he arrived, Jean's Spanish is coming along in leaps and bounds. I run across the road. My reply, when I catch up to him, is also impressively articulate.

Finally we enter the Great Temple, where we find ourselves standing on a raised steel platform that stops tourists walking all over the ruins of this Aztec sacrificial ground, which was discovered in the late 1970s during excavations for the underground railway. Below me I can see skulls carved in relief on stone walls. This is a temple devoted to death. Information boards explain how each skull represents a human sacrifice; those people whose still-beating hearts were once held aloft to the moon by Aztec priests to appease the Gods of Darkness. There are thousands of elaborately carved heads, some with tongues lolling, others with wild eyes and fierce expressions. Further along is a line of smaller carvings. Are these for the child sacrifices? I don't ask. I don't want to know.

Before the arrival of the Spanish conquerors in 1519, the Aztecs were the greatest civilisation on earth; at the time, their population numbered two hundred thousand people, and the population of the whole *Valle de México* has been estimated at 1.5 million. In the city of Tenochtitlan (now Mexico City) they built temples and pyramids, aqueducts and complex irrigation systems. Awed Spanish scribes recorded that *brujos* or witch doctors performed dentistry, and they marvelled at the jewellery the Aztecs carved from gold and precious stones such as onyx and jade. I'm now standing above a structure the *Aztecas* built; fascinated by this race and, thinking of their violent sacrifices, a little horrified as well, and wanting to soak up every fragment of their history.

The ruins' complex architecture and stone carvings are intricate in detail and rich in history. The Great Temple is another example of modern Mexico's dedication to keeping the past alive; great care has been taken in preserving it. Yet at the same time the idea that each of these carvings represents a once-living person is a little unnerving and it is a thought I do not linger on.

I follow the rest of the group along the platform that loops around the ruins. The friezes continue around the corner, where there are more examples of the engineering prowess of the Aztecs: stone water vessels that I mistake for coffins, and an intricate network of stone pipes used to carry water to different parts of the temple. The site extends eastward but excavations had to be stopped when it was discovered the only way to unearth more ruins would involve knocking down the National Palace, Carmen explains. Past and present intertwined.

For a long time I stand studying the ruins, wondering what this place must have been like during the reign of the Aztecs. I imagine men with copper-coloured skin, wearing peacock-feather headdresses, jade and gold neckplates, and flowing robes layered with the stunning green and turquoise feathers of the revered *quetzal* bird. Women in long cotton tunics carry clay urns filled with water. Laughing children play with their hairless *xoloescuintle* dogs in marketplaces where straw crunches under sandalled feet. The air is redolent with the smell of dry, gritty earth, as if I am breathing in the past.

The platform has grown crowded and the air is now thick under this covered walkway. The sun is peeking through cracks where the corrugated iron roofing sheets do not meet, and the slivers of light create magical prisms on the stone ruins. Jean is standing nearby. He calls out, '*¡Oye Samantita!*' I look over to see his rubbery face contorted into a grimace of impressive ugliness: eyes crossed and chin jutting out. 'Who am I?' he asks. I suppress a laugh – it feels like we're in a mausoleum, for goodness sake! As stupid faces go it's a good one, but perhaps it's more of an indication of my discomfort with the gruesome nature of the exhibits that I find it utterly hilarious. I think it might be time to leave.

Carmen must read our minds. 'Ready to go?' she asks. We all nod.

'Come on then,' she says. 'I have something to show you.'

We cross the road to the *Museo de San Ildefonso*, another monument to colonial architecture and home to a number of murals by Diego Rivera and his equally famous contemporaries José Clemente Orozco and David Alfaro Siqueiros. We've only just begun to scratch the surface of this old city, and I feel like I'm losing myself in another world. An old man wheels a rickety barrow past us, his face as ancient as the sun. And now, as if by way of invitation, the sixteenth-century building shimmers gelato yellow and cream in the sunlight.

Inside, the foyer is cool and dark. Carmen stops us and points upwards. 'Look,' she says. On the ceiling angels float among gilded domes, holding trumpets and enveloped in golden wings. *Vé las nubes.* 'Look at the clouds,' says Kumi. Marshmallow clouds, I think. And naked women with voluminous breasts and thighs. These murals are a homage to femininity and beauty. To me, Rivera has admirably captured the essence of womanhood – that beyond round-ness and supple skin, beneath the veneer of beauty, at the core of female identity is an inner strength that marks women as the lifeblood of humanity.

Though I think I could stand here, on this very spot, for the rest of my life, Carmen has other plans. From here we are hustled up a couple of flights of stairs to the third-floor landing. There doesn't seem to be much to look at up here. In the far corner is an empty café. The ceiling has ornate framework around frosted glass panes that are partially covered by ugly plastic cladding; the concrete walls are unpainted and neglected. As with most colonial buildings, the landing is rimmed by a stone balustrade that looks down on an internal courtyard. Kumi turns to me and shrugs. She doesn't know why we're here either.

Carmen walks to a corner where the path begins to dip. We follow. 'Look down,' she says. And we do. Beneath our feet the floor slopes dramatically. It has been painted a salmon colour and the sheen of the paint combined with the muted light coming through the ceiling gives it a sense of movement; it seems to be flowing like a river, away from us.

Despite its austere beauty, the *Museo de San Ildefonso*, like many other buildings in the old district, is succumbing to what Mexicans call the 'Spanish Curse'. Quite literally, it is sinking. When the Spaniards conquered Tenochtitlan in 1524 they wasted no time in destroying the temples and the pyramids and draining the causeways and canals of *Lago de Texcoco*, the lake that surrounded the Aztec city. In years to come, more water was drained from underground viaducts. Although there were concerns about subsidence from city engineers and planners, other water supply options were not implemented. And now the grand old buildings of the area – museums, churches, quaint homes with iron balcony railings and ornate doorways – are slowly but surely disappearing downwards.

Suddenly Carmen – who isn't much older than me – runs along the landing, arms raised for balance, and skids along the length of the walkway until she gets to the other corner. After getting over our initial shock, we all burst out laughing. Our supposedly serious *maestra* has gone completely bonkers. She comes back with a huge grin on her face. 'Now it's your turn,' she says. Six faces look stunned.

'Won't we get in trouble?' someone asks.

'No way,' she replies. 'Look at the sign.' *Pista rally*, says the sign on the wall. Floor racing. On it is a cartoon of a man skidding gleefully across the floor. I have to laugh at the incongruity of it all. It seems a uniquely Mexican approach to problem solving: *ingenuity in the face of adversity*. The building is sinking. Oh well. Let's have some fun while it's still standing. And where else would this be allowed? Go-cart racing at the Louvre? Not likely.

'Aiyoooo,' screams Kumi as she scuds across the slippery floor. Then it's my turn. I parrot Kumi's gleeful bellow:

'*Aiyooooo!*' The others join in. Admittedly, it's a childish pleasure, but it is the perfect antidote to the imposing artwork downstairs and the morbid ruins across the road. Pretty soon we are all racing each other down the slope, laughing and shoving like a bunch of ten-year-olds.

When a museum attendant suddenly appears on the landing, we all stop and turn towards her. Caught in the act. She smiles, reassuring. 'Don't stop because of me.' I'm still catching my breath when the young woman strikes up a conversation. She tells me the *pista rally* has become so popular that even wheelchair visitors use it. I envisage some hapless person hurtling towards a wall at a hundred miles an hour.

'Isn't that dangerous?' I ask.

'They don't let go of the wheelchair,' she replies, laughing.

'Oh. Of course.' I knew that.

As we leave the museum I feel elated. This city of endless discoveries never ceases to surprise me. On one side, the artwork and the ruins, precious remnants of a cherished past. On the other, the staff of a museum encouraging, *insisting*, that patrons enjoy themselves by indulging in childish pursuits. It all seems so contradictory. And that is Mexico in one word. I don't think I'll ever really make sense of this place. But maybe that isn't the point. What matters is that I'm here. As we pass under a vaulted archway into the street, I think how fortunate I am to experience a world so different to the one I know. I'm still smiling as we walk towards our destination, a café on *Calle Tacuba* that serves traditional Mexican food so delicious it attracts diners from all over the world.

Because it is the middle of the day, the streets are crammed with people. We negotiate our way through them and arrive at Café de Tacuba armed with a reservation and empty stomachs. Inside the restaurant a crowd has formed;

it's one o'clock and at least twenty people are waiting to be seated. A hostess behind a lectern calls out: '*¿La mexicanita y los gringos?*' I chuckle. It sounds like a song title. The little Mexican girl and the foreigners. That would be us. Carmen's hand shoots up. The woman smiles and makes a gesture with her thumb and forefinger – *espérame tantito*, wait a moment, it says.

A group rise from a bench near the door and in an instant the seven of us are crammed together on a seat designed for four. As we wait a group of *mariachis* enter through a side door, singing a *corrido*, a Mexican ballad. Their voices are strong and harmonious as they sing '*El quisiera perder la vida a ser reunido con su amada.*' He wants to die so he can be reunited with his beloved. The words are heartbreaking but the music is soaring and sweet. Crowded tables of people turn to watch them sing. Another musician moves between the tables garnishing tips in an upturned hat. It doesn't matter how often I hear *mariachi* music – and it's played *everywhere* – without fail, I'm moved by its romantic senti-ments. It has an honesty that I see as Mexican, an irresistible heart-on-your-sleeve approach to life.

While we wait for the hostess to return, I lean my head against the wall. Everything about this place is typically Mexican, without being forced. Above our heads hangs a *piñata*, behind it a leadlight window whose reflected light creates multicoloured patterns on the floor. The ceiling has exposed wooden beams and the walls are painted with flourishes of flowers, birds and Grecian urns.

As more diners sandwich together in the doorway, we are led to our table. Before we have even opened the menus, Carmen orders drinks all round. 'Beers for everyone!' she says. 'And some cocktails.' The Sol beer arrives in bottles with a wedge of lime in the neck. On the table are baskets of bread, *totopos* (corn chips) and crackers, along with the accompaniments served here with every meal: *guacamole*, mashed avocado with lemon juice and chile powder; *salsa rojo* and *verde*, red and green chile sauce; and bite-sized pieces of *chicharrón*, fried pork skin, with sliced onion and lemon wedges. Before our eyes is a veritable banquet and we haven't even ordered yet. The waiter then reappears with a tray of *margaritas*, a potent cocktail of lemon, tequila and crushed ice, served in a salt-rimmed glass.

It is then we discover a problem. The Korean girl who hasn't said much all morning – although she did join in at the *pista rally* – now speaks up. '*Perdón. No tomo*,' she says. Er, sorry, I don't drink. 'Me neither,' adds the Japanese guy at the table. A shake of the head from the other Korean student. Kumi smiles, apologetic. In front of us there are seven beers and seven cocktails. 'No problem,' Carmen says. 'We'll drink them.' She nods at Jean and I. What? Well, okay. We raise our glasses. '*¡Salud!*' After the second glass I'm feeling woozy; the third makes me feel ill. 'I need an ambulance,' I say. The others laugh, thinking I'm joking. In this country leaving food on a plate or dregs in a glass is considered a grave social insult, akin to insulting somebody's mother – a most serious crime. I drink up. Over the course of the meal, the three of us drain every last glass.

The main meal arrives and they are plates of gargantuan proportions. Apart from Carmen, we all look slightly stunned. '*¡Híjole!*' says the Japanese student, signalling his surprise in perfect Mexican slang. Of course I know about voracious Mexican appetites but I'm still shocked when my *plato principal* is placed in front of me. Lunch is *chiles en nogada*, two large chiles stuffed with apples, peaches, raisins, onions, tomatoes and pork, and smothered in a walnut, cheese and sherry sauce. '*¡Vaya!*' I say to Carmen after my first mouthful. Get out of here! I continue to be amazed by the taste of food here; the pleasure of savouring a new dish in a country where traditional cooking is considered an art form. The chiles are exquisite; the blend of sweet and savoury mingles on my tongue. 'Good, huh,' she replies. I nod. The rich smell, the textures, the changing flavours as I chew. It is sensory overload.

Chatting to Carmen over lunch, the conversation flows freely. Dressed in a black tunic, striped green and red stockings and lace-up army boots, and wearing her hair in a chic bob, she is far from the stereotypically conservative *mexicana*. In Mexico, women are bound by tradition, much more so than men. A good woman does not smoke, drink, wear jeans (a sign of Western corruption) or swear. Right now, except for the jeans, Carmen is doing all of the above. Her liberal ways and direct manner are a breath of fresh air. She is lively and entertaining company. Now she tells me of her travels around the world, including a stint in Paris, where she lived for six months.

'I caused such an outrage when I did that.' She laughs.

'Why?' I ask, wondering naively what could be wrong with something as enriching as travel. She takes a drag on her cigarette before answering.

'Mexico is a *very* traditional society. Women don't travel. Hell, men don't even want them to *work*. Sure, they say we should be educated and have careers, but when they come home and find there's no dinner on the table, well, that's another matter entirely.'

It's an observation I've heard from many women in Mexico, invariably delivered with a tone of resignation. I feel vaguely guilty thinking of all the choices I've had in life, educational and otherwise. Carmen stubs out her cigarette and blows a smoke ring above her head.

'You broke the mould,' I say.

She smiles wryly. 'It's hard but it's not impossible.'

We talk some more. I'm keen to learn more about Mexican women, particularly from the perspective of someone in the know. And now here's my chance to ask her about something that has had me baffled for some time.

'Why do Mexican women wear so much make-up?' I ask.

Being confronted on the bus by a middle-aged woman who tells me I should be wearing make-up because a woman *should not leave home without her face on* – her exact words – leaves me speechless. Perhaps it's my casual, sometimes scruffy, Australian attitude to dress, but I just can't pick up this habit, nor do I understand where it's coming from. I've noticed that, almost without exception, all Mexican women wear thick, cabaret-style make-up. It seems a shame, given their natural beauty – large brown eyes, shiny black hair, caramel skin and cupid's-bow lips. To me they are the epitome of gorgeous but it seems they would not agree.

Carmen laughs and lights another cigarette. Obviously she has been asked this question before.

'Mexican women don't feel good enough,' she says.

'I don't understand.' I'd thought this make-up mask was habitual; it never occurred to me that it might be a manifestation of a deeper insecurity. I wait for her reply.

'It's simple really. We look at our *gringa* neighbours and we think if we were whiter and prettier and thinner, then we would be happy. Everyone here is so ashamed of being dark, so women wear lots of make-up because they think it makes them look more Western.'

Carmen's words are a shock. In a nation whose greatest assets are its rich culture and the strength of its people, it comes as a surprise to hear that Mexicans, especially its beautiful women, want to emulate their Anglo-Saxon neighbours. But I don't get much of a chance to mull over this cultural anomaly because someone interrupts and the conversation takes another turn.

Now the *mariachis* are back. They stop at the next table to play a request, '*Paloma Querida*'. Beloved Dove. *For you I will pluck the stars from the sky.* Ah, the heartbreaking romance of it all! Our chatter, punctuated by the sound of a violin and the haunting lyrics, skips ahead as glasses are drained, and soon we are laughing as Jean's attempt to sing along is met with a hail of crackers and scrunched-up serviettes.

After three hours we leave the restaurant. We are all in high spirits. The excursion and the long lunch have both been enjoyable. For me there is a sense of having shared my fascination for this city. And my chat with Carmen has given me some insight into the complexities of Mexican culture and it is something I appreciate. As we stumble en masse into the bright afternoon sunlight, I'm feeling full and decidedly queasy. We say our goodbyes. Jean and I leave the others and walk towards the metro to catch the train home. 'How are you feeling?' I ask as we sit on the cold platform tiles at the station. '*Spectacular*,' he says in French. I turn away and when I look back he is sound asleep, head resting against the wall, mouth open.

Chapter Nine

Come and Dance, Little One

'*¿Á donde vas mamacita?*'

I'm standing at the back door of the bus waiting for it to slow down so I can get off. It's Thursday night and that means dancing at a local Cuban bar with my flatmates and friends from the college. I'm wearing a coat and a scarf over my favourite dress in an attempt to ward off sleazy men, but my Arctic attire doesn't have the desired effect. Three men have surrounded me and I'm getting nervous. 'Where are you going, baby?' they ask. I shoot one an angry look but to no avail. A harsh stare is about as much use in dealing with a sex-starved Mexican man as a donkey in the Melbourne Cup. And with pretty butterfly clips in my hair and glitter on my eyelids I reckon I probably look anything but mean. Luckily for me, the bus slows and I jump off while it is still moving.

'Hey baby, come back!' they scream after me. 'Why don't

we all go somewhere quiet together?' I run across the road in my strappy sandals, leaving them gesticulating from the bus windows.

When I enter the bar, I see my flatmate Sandrine waving at me from the other side of the room. Mamá Rumba is already crowded. The red, yellow and green lights from the stage are creating patterns on everyone's faces in a kaleidoscope of cellophane colours. The band are playing bongos, drums and trumpets. '*Las mujeres bellas son el fruto de rico sabor*', they sing. Beautiful women are a fruit of exquisite taste. The men sing of love and heartache, their rich voices rising gracefully above the din created by a room full of people all talking at the same time. The soulful music creates an atmosphere of exuberance in the room; it lingers in the air like an aurora of fairy dust.

The sound of my name being called draws my attention away from the music, and I spot my friend Tadeshi standing at our table across the room. He waves to me excitedly, cups his hands around his mouth and yells over the din.

'Hurry up before the others drink all the beer!' He looks seriously concerned about this possibility.

Just thinking about getting over to my friends has me worried. The place is packed. Or, as my teacher Rogerio would say, *atascado*. Chockers. I tuck in my elbows and dive in. There are people all around me, pushing and shoving. Or are they dancing? I can't be sure. Women in tight dresses and heavy make-up sip demurely from tumblers of rum and Coke, as though they are at Ladies' Day at the races and not in the middle of a sweaty fracas. A group of men in black shirts stand in a huddle, heads bowed and deep in conversation, until a pretty girl walks past and they all lift their gazes. '*¡Hola!*' they chorus. Eventually, I make it to the table.

I peel off my coat and scarf and eye off the fried cheese balls on the table, but before I can sit down Jean's friend Octavio is standing next to me. He grabs my hand and leads me back into the moshpit.

'*Ven a bailar, chiquita.*' Come and dance, little one. I laugh. *Little one*. What's with this expression? In the past few months I've heard it countless times and always thought it rather odd. Not that I mind – it sure beats being called *big one*. Yet it seems strange that everyone, from friends to complete strangers, calls me by this familiar diminutive. Then again, even my Mexican nickname *Samantita* means 'Little Samantha'. In this country terms of endearment are as popular as the Virgin Mary. I like these names – they offer a warm embrace, a congenial familiarity that is quintessentially Mexican. And it helps too when you can't remember someone's name.

Right now, however, I feel anything but little. In my heels I'm nudging five-foot-nine and towering over most of the Mexican blokes in the room. I feel a bit like Gulliver surrounded by the Lilliputians in *Gulliver's Travels*. Admittedly, it's Gulliver as you've never seen him before – in a sexy black dress that I don't remember being *this* tight (I'm going to have to cut back on the donuts and Nutella sandwiches) and killer heels, but a giant all the same.

Octavio finds us a spot in the middle of the dance floor. He pulls me to his chest and I close my eyes as he rocks me gently to and fro. The music is growing louder, more people crowd onto the dance floor and the temperature rises. But right now nothing else matters. At this very moment, on this very spot, it's just the two of us swaying to the music.

The upbeat *salsa* tempo gets right into my bones and fills me with an inexplicable joy; it embraces me with warmth and unbridled enthusiasm. This music goes back to the African slaves brought to Cuba to work on the sugar plantations. It started as a way to colour their bleak world; a world of hardship and suffering became tropical blue. Such is the power of great music, I think. Cymbals and an acoustic guitar fill the air and the sound carries me away. Having completely immersed ourselves in the music we are both perspiring profusely when the song comes to an end. It's time for a drink.

Back at the table, more nibbles have arrived. The platters of *bocaditos* – little mouthfuls, the Mexican version of the Spanish *tapas* – are laid out in front of us. There are deep-fried potatoes with mayonnaise and chile powder; crumbed rice and cheese balls (my favourites); and *mariquitas*, plantain chips – a Cuban delicacy made from a relative of the banana. Squeezing onto a chair with Sandrine, I notice the fried potatoes are within reach. I take one and pop it into my mouth. It crunches between my teeth, the creamy mayonnaise coating my tongue. I wash it down with the glass of beer that miraculously appears before me, and then do the same with the plantain chips and a rice and cheese ball. Satisfied, I notice my glass is empty. Around the table other furrowed brows contemplate drained glasses.

'More beer?' Do I even need to ask?

'Yes, please,' happy voices chorus. Many beers. Two hands. This could be interesting.

I look in the general direction of the bar but I can't even see it. Again I struggle through the crowd, my every step accompanied by an 'excuse me' as I forge a path through a seemingly impenetrable wall of backs. I push through a group of people only to discover my right foot is suspended midair behind me – pinned by a cluster of men's legs. I yank it free and lose my balance so that I fall backwards, only to be righted again by the bodies around me. Very classy! But I'm on a mission now. And because I'm dying for another drink I drop all ladylike pretences and charge through the scrum.

Finally, I make it to the bar. A young guy in a Cuban shirt with slicked-back hair turns to me as I squeeze in next to him. He has a friendly, open face and his teeth are glowing Colgate white under the neon lights. Right now he's smiling a cool dude grin. His eyes are sparkling and I warm to him instantly, thinking, as I look at him, that he has eyes that make you want to talk – or maybe it's just the lighting.

'Hey,' he says, bursting the bubble of mutual, unspeaking admiration.

'Hey.'

'Nice dress.' He says it in such a way-to-go fashion that I have to laugh.

'Yeah, thanks.'

After paying for his drinks he turns to me again.

'Tell me something,' he says.

I nod.

'Mexican or Cuban?'

'¿Qué opinas?' I reply. What do you think? I'm interested to hear his answer. From our short conversation – punctuated by the very loud music – I don't know if he's picked up my accent, although I would like to think my looks are passably Mexican.

'Mexican, of course. It's your eyes.'

He smiles and then grabs four glasses of beer, raising them aloft as he lurches into the crowd. I watch as he weaves through the revellers, beer sloshing furiously onto their heads with every step.

I'm smiling too, amused. How does a complete stranger pick the elements of Mexicanness in me? What gives me away? And how do other people really see me? I am not Cuban and some would argue that I'm not very Mexican either. I am a *mezcla*, a mixture of two different cultures. My mother is Mexican, my father is English; his grandparents were Welsh and hers were *mestizo*: half-Spanish, half-Aztec. No wonder I sometimes feel confused: I'm a veritable United Nations. Since I arrived there have been a few incidents of semi-mistaken culture, if not identity: people asking for directions, or wondering what part of Mexico I'm from. Like the conversation I just had, every one of these encounters makes me feel good. It's nice to hear I look Mexican. And it's nice because, for a fleeting moment, *I am Mexican*. And that sense of belonging – even if it isn't entirely accurate – makes me feel happy.

The barman comes over and instead of ordering beers I ask for ten *mojitos* – rum with soda, sugar and mint leaves. As drinks go, the *mojito* is a killer, sweet and bubbly with only a hint of alcohol. You drink it and feel fine. That is, until you stand up and realise you are indeed *very* drunk. But in Mexico any excuse for a party will do, and tonight's festive atmosphere calls for an equally festive concoction. The barman reappears to ask me if I want lots of mint leaves. 'Oh yes,' I reply, knowing that the more mint in the mix, the stronger the brew. As I wait for the drinks, I turn and lean against the bar, surveying the crowd.

The predominantly male crowd is made up of men in tight shirts, sharp suits and shiny two-tone gangster shoes. Interspersed among them are clusters of women, all with thick, curly black hair, large brown eyes and coffee-coloured skin. I look around the room at the other women who remind me so much of myself. As a child in Australia my identity was confused; these very features made me different, yet indefinable. And I carried that dislocation into adulthood.

But here . . .

I'm suddenly struck by the realisation that there is nothing, physically at least, to distinguish me from these women. I'm one of the crowd. I have to laugh. It amuses me to think I spent years feeling like an outcast when in fact there were legions of big-haired doppelgängers running around Mexico. I'd bet the same goes for the Chinese, Lebanese, Greek and Italian–Australian kids. We are not alone! The idea of blending in fills me with the same euphoria as does the music; it is a liberating sensation.

My observations are interrupted by the return of the barman. I pay for the drinks and pick up the tray that I carefully carry back to the table.

I stay at Mamá Rumba until five in the morning, dancing with my friends and losing myself in the music. Our group is still having fun but the crowd has dispersed dramatically and at this hour the human landscape is looking rather woeful: the band went home ages ago so couples are slow dancing to recorded music; bar staff are yawning; and patrons – bleary-eyed, drunk and tired – are sipping from warm glasses of beer and puffing on cigar stubs.

After one too many *mojitos*, I end up outside the entrance, buying a hot dog from a street vendor. The hot dog perks me up. I'm feeling energetic again and decide, instead of going back inside, I might just walk home. *What a marvellous idea!* My alcohol-soaked brain tells me the fresh air will do me good. I leave without saying goodbye to my friends, barely registering the danger because my senses took leave of me somewhere around my fourth drink. Wrapped in my coat and scarf I leave behind the bright lights of the bar and head down the street to *Avenida Insurgentes*, where I turn right in the direction of home.

I stride purposefully along the deserted footpath, passing rows of shopfronts, clustered together under white plastic awnings and secured by brightly coloured steel grilles. On a street corner stands a lone *mariachi*, a rambling troubadour dressed in a green velvet suit adorned with gold bells on the trousers and matching buttons on the jacket pockets. Lost in thought, he draws on a cigarette as he paces back and forth, the spurs on his boots marking his steps with resonant clinks. I have no idea what he's doing here. Is he waiting for a taxi? Where's the rest of the band? He greets me as I walk past. '*Buenos días*,' he says. 'Oh, good morning,' I reply. The absurdity of this exchange isn't lost on me: we greet each other like neighbours collecting the mail, not as strangers at dawn in one of the most dangerous cities in the world. The alcohol and the heat from dancing are now starting to wear off, and my senses make a bid for attention. What the hell am *I* doing here? I laugh at my stupidity and then pick up the pace; I'm nearly home.

I cross *Paseo de la Reforma*. At this hour, the city's busiest thoroughfare is void of traffic and humanity. The sun will come up soon and in this eerie silence I can no longer make sense of anything. I stop to look at the trees. Australian trees, I suddenly realise. The street is lined with eucalypts, incongruous and out of place, standing like impassive sentinels above me; emblematic representatives of my country. A touch of home, I think. Reminders that the past is here, everywhere, and inescapable; like them, my absence from Australia does not diminish its significance.

But what and where is home? Lately it's something I've been thinking about a lot. This place could so easily become home. As I gaze up at the naked branches their familiarity strikes a deeper chord. Perhaps that is what being here is all about: making real what is unreal and letting this country show me all I do not know.

Chapter Ten

Watching the World Go By

The following Sunday I wake at dawn to the sound of birds chirping. Rubbing my eyes, I notice sparrows on the window ledge. Arranged in a perfect row, they look like a chorus line minus tiny top hats and tails – their melodious song fills the room. In the distance I hear voices from the marketplace, a car horn, and the rubbish collector calling, '*¡Basura!*' Weekends in the city have a relaxed, lazy energy that I enjoy. I get up and head downstairs, where Jean and Sandrine are already waiting for me. We leave the apartment and walk the couple of blocks to the market, stopping for coffee on the way.

At Café Express we order coffee and donuts. The café is no more than a vendors' cart under an awning but it serves a delicious honey caffé latte in French-style coffee 'bowls'. We sit at a table in the shade, still half-asleep, and slowly drink the thick, heady brew. I tear a cinnamon donut in half and dunk it in my coffee. Although it looks stale, when I put it in my mouth it is milk-soaked and delicious. Jean looks as though he is about to fall asleep again when Sandrine leans over and shouts, '*¡Despiertaté!*' – wake up – in his ear. We both guffaw. 'Bloody women,' he grunts.

In front of us, teenage boys are playing soccer on a concrete quadrangle, underneath the Monument to the Mother, a colossal statue that for the time being is their goalpost. At its base an inscription reads: *For mothers – because they loved us before they knew us.* Because of its central location – one block from *Paseo de la Reforma* – this square attracts prostitutes, drug addicts and dealers. The Mother, who stands with her hands clasped demurely in front of her, would probably topple from her rest if she had eyes to see what was going on at her feet under the cover of darkness. But during the day, and especially on the weekends, the place is a hive of activity.

However, the crowds of shoppers haven't arrived yet and, with the exception of the young boys, the large square is empty. Even though it has only just turned seven, sunlight already fills the quadrangle, giving it a sleepy, romantic serenity. The sky is a clear and diaphanous blue. It's like Mexico as a stage, waiting for the performers to arrive. By midmorning the heat will be overwhelming and there will be people everywhere. Act one in full swing.

We finish our breakfast and walk back across the square and down the steps we climbed earlier. Having shed our early-morning stupor thanks to the strong coffee, we're ready to throw ourselves into the world of Sunday morning commerce. The narrow footpath is lined with one stall after another. Some vendors can afford *puestos*, metal contraptions with a display table, storage space underneath and a tarpaulin overhead just in case it rains – it hasn't rained in months but you never know. Whatever the set-up, everyone from the basket weavers to the guy selling artists' supplies seems happy to share this temporary space. Those without *puestos* have carefully laid out their *artesanías* on plastic sheets: woven cane baskets; painted tin ornaments such as bright pink butterflies and purple birds with lime-green tails; papier-mâché dolls; pottery; silver frames; and jewellery. Each stall is a splash of brilliant colour, right down to the bright orange sheeting on the ground. A rainbow kaleidoscope of products ready to be touched, bargained for, bought and enjoyed. I linger over a hand-painted drinks tray.

'Go on, buy it!' Sandrine says.

'Nah,' I reply, in a remarkable display of restraint.

The food market is five minutes from here, and the tendrils of an unidentifiable yet delicious smell wrap around us and waft under our noses. We are drawn towards its source. Music fills the air, competing with the singsong voices of vendor and customer, the sounds of a city coming to life. The air is teeming with a convivial clamour.

We enter the main market and I immediately lose sight of my flatmates as they are swallowed up by the chaos. Standing on tiptoes, I try to look out for them, instead stumbling over a chunk of rock. I'm saved from falling on my face by hands that grip me by the elbows and lift me so forcefully that my feet leave the ground and for a moment I'm suspended in midair. 'Careful!' a voice says, not unkindly. Two huge men are now standing next to me. 'Are you okay?' one asks, genuinely concerned. 'Yes, yes, I'm fine,' I reply, mortally embarrassed. 'Thank you again,' I say, more to the ground than the men. Pleased at having saved the day, the men nod in unison and disappear into the marketplace. I step off the grassy bank and back into this vibrant landscape that during the week is a dusty patch of gravel where rats come out at night to fight over fruit scraps.

Directly in front of me is a pyramid of lemons on green plastic; on the other side of the path are oranges in similar stacks. These impressive mountains are *en oferta*, on sale. Finally I spot Sandrine waiting for me next to a mound of avocados. We walk slowly through a sea of luscious, fragrant fruit: *plátanos machos*, black-skinned bananas; green papayas; melons; *guayabas* or guavas, a sweet fleshy fruit with a pale yellow skin; coconuts; and *zapotes*, a stone fruit with black flesh that is wonderful mixed with orange juice and eaten with ice cream. It's the same dilemma every Sunday. What to buy? And where to start?

You can buy any conceivable fruit or vegetable here. And if the *mercadero* doesn't have it on display, not to worry. He'll get it for you. I'm after lady finger bananas. '*Pérame señorita*,' the vendor says. He drops the '*es*' at the beginning of *espérame tantito* – the affectionate version of 'wait a moment' – as is habit among the Indians. In the same way, *pues* (well) becomes *pos*. I'm learning a language within a language, a secret code. A moment later he returns with my *plátanos*. I pay for them and keep moving.

A throaty voice calls out.

'*¡Mamacita! Pruebalo, es lo mejor.*' Try this, it's the best.

A man with a piece of melon skewered on the end of a knife is beckoning me over. He wears a green apron with a pocket at the front over a white singlet, and smiles broadly when he sees me approaching. *Mamacita*, little mother, he called me. The name and its amiable delivery make me smile. I try the melon. It is sweet and cool and slides down my throat easily. '*Muy sabroso*,' I say. Very tasty. The vendor seizes on this. 'Buy one,' he replies. But these are no ordinary melons: they're as big as a human head and probably as heavy. I don't want to lug one around the market. '*Regresaré*,' I say. I'll come back. 'Promise?' he asks. 'I promise.'

I catch up to Sandrine in the meat section. Before me rows of plucked chickens, with staring eyes and pink goose-pimply flesh, are laid on a bench. Men with enormous arms swing meat cleavers, chopping chicken, pork, beef and lamb on butchers' blocks as blood trickles down the sides of the wooden stumps. It is a brutal display of dexterity and skill. Further along, flies buzz around plastic trays of stomachs, intestines, wings, brains and tongues. Nothing is wasted. '¡Hígados, buen precio!' Livers, good price! I stop in front of a man wearing a long leather apron and gum-boots to order liver – something I haven't eaten in a while, but I'm feeling inspired, adventurous. My request is met with enthusiasm. The meat is wrapped in butcher's paper and handed over. Cooking advice is part of the service. 'Slice it in half,' the man says, 'and fry it with bacon, onion and butter.' He kisses his fingertips to his lips. 'Just don't burn the butter because the whole thing will then taste amargado, bitter.' Got it. Hígado con mantequilla, I'll soon discover, is surprisingly delicious.

We move from stall to stall, buying bags of black bananas, jícama – a turnip-shaped vegetable eaten raw with chile powder, tomatoes, guayabas, onions and potatoes, before returning to the melon stall. 'Ah, I knew you would come back,' the vendor says. I buy two of the melons. 'Gracias linda,' he says, handing me my change. Jean is now standing next to me, looking annoyed.

'You should tell him,' he says, making an emphatic gesture with his raised hands still holding the shopping bags, so that he looks like a weird version of 'I'm a little teapot'. I've obviously missed something.

'Tell him what?'

'That your name isn't Linda, it's Samantita.'

I laugh and give him a shove, a little harder than I had intended because he stumbles backwards and loses his grip on one of the grocery bags. A roma tomato flies out of the bag and makes its bid for freedom down a drain. When Jean recovers I address him again.

'Linda isn't a name, stupid,' I say with a smirk. 'It means sweetheart.' I tease him as if I'm an expert in Spanish, but part of my brain always hears the name Linda in *linda*, too. The only difference is that now I'm so used to being called sweetheart, I don't even notice. Jean grunts and walks off, struggling with the heavy bags of groceries, minus one valiant tomato.

Among the aromas of black beans cooking in coriander and garlic, chicken roasting in peanut oil and tortillas on a griddle, the smell of roasting pork reaches my nostrils. A vendor is selling long strips of *chicharrón* seasoned with lime, salt and chile *salsa*. I haven't eaten this delicacy since my previous trip but I still remember its exquisite taste. When you take a bite, the fried pork dissolves in your mouth, releasing a bacony flavour that mingles with the salt and cooking oil. I take in the aroma but move on. It's been a long time since I ate at a street stall, and for a very good reason: my feeble stomach can't cope with less than hygienic cooking practices. It's a shame really. Fried *everything* is one of my favourite food groups.

As if on cue, Jean walks past squeezing lime onto a piece of *chicharrón* as long as his arm. He must see my look of longing because he turns and employs a French word I'm familiar with: *bohf*, a word that can alternatively mean *bullshit*, *no way* or, as in this case, *what a shame you can't have any*.

Further along the path vendors are scooping powdered *mole* from plastic bins sitting in front of an endless display of chiles. *Mole poblano*, brown with flecks of red, sits next to mountains of green and red powder. The peppery scent of a dozen hot chiles fills the air. I ask for half a kilo of poblano. 'Si señorita,' the vendor says. It's while I'm waiting that I recall the first time I tried *mole poblano* at my grandmother's house. I was sure I had never tasted anything so disgusting in all my life. I'm crazy about it now, and I eat it at least once a week. Tonight I'll boil a chicken in garlic and salt. When it's cooked I'll take out the bird and spoon the *mole* powder into the *caldo*, the liquid remains, until it forms a thick paste, then the chicken is smothered with *mole* sauce and eaten with a side serve of white rice. While Jean and Sandrine eat spaghetti, I will eat *mole* – a feast of the senses, an earthy flavour without compare.

We leave the *mole* stall and head in the direction of our apartment. The crowds are growing, and it dawns upon me, as I move slowly through the sea of people, that I'm smiling with the joy of being here.

It is difficult for me to pinpoint what it is about the market that makes me so happy. Perhaps it is the interaction with strangers, walking among them and feeling part of their world. Or the excitement of being in a veritable wonderland where everything from the eggs still covered in downy feathers to the buckets of riotously coloured wild roses have been grown, nurtured and plucked by hand. This is the real Mexico in all its gritty, noisy glory. Maybe it's the bubbling energy in the air that is contagious. Whatever the reason, I love being in a market in Mexico City on a warm Sunday morning. There's no place I'd rather be. I think of home, wondering what I would be doing there on a weekend. My mind is a blank. Suddenly that life seems far away.

At Café Margarita overlooking Coyoacán Plaza, the scene is a lively one. The Sunday crowds – made up of locals and tourists – are milling; a man is selling pink fairy floss; another manoeuvres the legs of a marionette to walk with a clopping sound on the footpath. Children tug at their parents' sleeves as they stare open-mouthed at the *títer*, the dancing puppet. The vendor makes his pitch: '*Para los niños*.' For the little ones, he says.

I come here often, usually on weekends when study does not make demands on my time. Today Sandrine is giving French lessons at home. Jean disappears and I decide to do the same. I don't have to think hard about where I want to spend the afternoon. Coyoacán is one of my favourite places in Mexico City, not just for its quaint colonial charm but also for the chance to watch the world go by and absorb the energy of this vibrant *colonia*.

Now, from my terrace table, I watch as a man nearby buys a helium balloon and hands it to his child, who lets it slip from his grasp. The balloon floats away. The father chases after it, but it's too late. The red blip becomes smaller and smaller in the sky until it disappears from view. The picture-perfect sky of this morning has now turned grey, with clouds forming in threatening clusters, but it is still hot and humid. I've always loved rain, even just the idea of it. The air before rain starts has a magical, expectant quality. Here, the rare downpours are brief and refreshing, washing away the pollution so that, for a little while at least, the city is sparkling and new. This petulant sky reminds me of the afternoons of my teenage summers: floating in the water at Sorrento beach, looking up at the heavy clouds and waiting that fraction of a second for the uneven drops of rain to land on my face.

It's now early afternoon, and many hours have passed since my breakfast of caffé latte and a donut. It is time for more coffee. I should be eating *almuerzo*, the late lunch that is served between two and five, but the heat has robbed me of my appetite, and in any case I don't feel like eating a hearty meal by myself. That's the Mexican way, I muse. Food and company – an inseparable pair. A waiter comes over and places a cup of *café de olla* in front of me. 'Sure you don't want to eat?' he asks. I reassure him. He bows and glides away as I turn my gaze back to the square.

Behind me a man speaks to a woman. 'How do you say coffee again?' After a pause, the woman replies: 'Dunno.' It takes a second for their words to register, and then the penny drops. Australians! There's no doubting *that* accent. I'm strangely shocked. Although my countrymen are among the world's most intrepid travellers, somehow I hadn't expected to hear an Australian accent in a café in Mexico City. And just as I was thinking of home. It's a complete surprise, but a nice one at that. I put down my coffee and turn to speak to them when I'm struck by a mind-blowing realisation: *I can't speak English!* My opener was to be 'Where are you from?' But right now my brain is refusing to translate this basic question into my mother tongue and all I can think of is the Spanish equivalent, '*¿De dónde vienen?*' This can't be happening. I've been here just over three months and my own language has deserted me faster than the occupants of a burning building. I'm completely dismayed and sit back in my chair, silent.

The waiter goes over to the Australians. '*¿Qué gustan tomar?*' he asks.

I sit, looking over the plaza and listening.

The man speaks. '*Dos cafés,*' he says. His accent is passable and he gets the word for coffee right. I wonder if that's what I sound like when I speak Spanish. '*Sí señor,*' the waiter replies.

As I pay for my coffee, I turn to look at the Australians. Nice, friendly-looking people. Although they are strangers I find their presence comforting, their accents reassuring. I'd love to sit and chat with them but I fear my mouth will betray me. I'm trying to remember the last time I had a proper conversation in English. It's been a while. Nor have

I heard anyone speaking in English, let alone with an Australian accent. How could I? All my friends speak Spanish; even the French, Japanese and Irish have ditched their own languages in favour of this one. It's such a lovely language. But it is a practical consideration too. When in Rome. Still, to hear someone from my country brings up a well of nostalgia. This morning at the market I was thinking about how far away home seemed.

And now . . .

I leave the café, chuckling under my breath at the paradox. Just as I had thought the other night walking home from Mamá Rumba, being away from Australia does not diminish its significance. Quite the opposite. By embracing Mexico, I am recognising the importance of my own country. I can love both places because essentially they are both part of me. One is the country of my birth and family; the other an ancestral, spiritual home. And, I figure, there are worse dilemmas in life than loving two countries. Not that I think my mixed heritage is a curse, although I once did. I smile when I think of all the years I railed against being different. I should have given in a long time ago, though I understand that emotionally I wasn't ready. Now I'm older and better able to grasp a concept fundamental to my identity: *to have two homes is a gift.*

As I walk under an elaborate stone archway, my nostalgia turns to happy thoughts of home: swimming at Sorrento beach (again!) as pelicans bob in the turquoise waters of Port Phillip Bay, watching the bats at dusk in the Melbourne Botanic Gardens. Simple stuff too, like Twisties and Caramello Koalas. I sit down on a bench under the bough of an elm tree.

It is a little after two and the plaza is full of people strolling, eating and bartering with the Indian artisans. Mexican families drag children around the *artesanía* stalls;

others have lunch at Sanborn's, a restaurant and bar, chemist and variety store rolled into one. Tourists are attracted by the area's historical connection. Some are just passing through, others have come to 'find themselves'. I wonder what the appeal of Mexico City is to Westerners. Is it the savage and bloody history of this culture? The allure of something different from what they know? Or is it for the same reason that I'm here: that they too have fallen under the spell of this mad, enchanting and crazy city.

In the nearby *via pública*, a wide, cobbled walkway, a group performs the Aztec rain dance. A crowd forms a semi-circle around them and from where I'm sitting I have a perfect view. The dancers are dressed in traditional Aztec costume, complete with feathered headdress, loincloths, wrist bands, and bells on their ankles. Behind them, old men with ochre-red skin folded over their face like jagged, overlapping rock crevices pound on *tambor* drums. Faces that tell a thousand stories, I think. At the moment the performers are spinning and clapping; their ankle bells ring and the drums boom loud and sonorous across the plaza.

The scene then takes a surreal turn when a group of half a dozen new dancers join the performance. There are five men and one woman and all of them have blue eyes, white skin and dreadlocks. One of them speaks and the mystery is solved. They are German. I shouldn't be surprised. There is a large German community in Mexico – most have been seduced by the passionate, unrestrained lifestyle so contra-dictory to Teutonic culture. Yet watching them dance, I can't help feeling annoyed. Seeing these foreigners in Aztec dress seems to cheapen the significance of this tradition; it's a birthright that, to me at least, they have no claim to.

But maybe I shouldn't be too critical. They're not the only ones involved in a spot of cultural appropriation. The least I can do is try to consider things from their perspective

– and it's always good to see through someone else's eyes. If the Aztec rain dance can help them find their place in the world, then good for them. Perhaps the lesson here is that Mexico has many things to teach many people. And I'm not the only one looking for answers.

For the next hour I sit on the bench, captivated by the dancers and the people doing their own version of the *passeggiata*, the Italian late-afternoon stroll. The courtyard begins to empty as families and tourists alike move into the restaurants, bars and cafés for their *almuerzo*. I'm still not hungry and haven't changed my mind about eating alone, so I pull a book from my bag. But reading will have to wait, because I have barely opened the cover when the book goes flying.

'Uff, what a shot!' A teenager runs past me with his arms raised as if he had just kicked the winning goal in the World Cup. He comes back with the book in one hand and his soccer ball under the other arm. His friends are now hurling abuse at him: 'C'mon idiot, hurry up with the ball.' He ignores them.

'Are you all right?' he asks.

'Uh, sure,' I reply. I take the book from him. He looks at me intently.

'Chicana, right?'

Chicana. It was one of the first words I learned in Spanish and, without knowing why, it sounded vaguely offensive. That was until I found out what it meant and discovered it *was* vaguely offensive. A Mexican–American. Someone whose parents had gone to America and cut all ties with the motherland, only to come back now and then to lord it over the poor relatives down south in their new clothes and shiny shoes. I want to be offended but I'm not really that bothered. I see his point. With this face and a funny accent, he has to wonder.

'*Soy Australiana*,' I reply.

'No shit!'

He keeps staring and doesn't even turn when one of his friends comes over and filches the ball from under his arm. His lip is turned up in what looks like a smirk. I begin to feel awkward under his intense gaze, wondering what he is going to ask me next.

'Have lunch with me?' he finally blurts out.

I laugh. I wasn't expecting that. The attention is flattering, I explain, before declining his offer, citing my advanced age as a possible impediment. He steps back, then smiles. I smile back. 'Well, that's a shame,' he says, then he turns and runs back to the game. I get up and walk off smiling, enjoying the compliment of being asked out by someone nearly a decade my junior. For a moment I'm a Latin bombshell – all big hair and attitude – until I trip on a loose chunk of concrete on the footpath and stumble forward.

I walk across the plaza and look up at the street signs. I'm standing on a street called Allende, which I know isn't too far from the *Casa Azul*. The Blue House is the former home of Frida Kahlo; it is now the Kahlo museum. I'd made an abortive attempt to go there a few months earlier but was distracted by the bustle of the plaza. It's not too late so I decide to go now. The sky is still expectant with rain, even though it is hotter now than it was this morning. After walking for a few minutes I'm perspiring. I stop to catch my breath under a magnolia tree and find I'm at the intersection of Allende and Londres, across the road from the museum. The colonial building is painted royal blue with Mexican-pink window frames. It looks beautiful, like a gingerbread house with blue icing walls and marshmallow windows.

It is dark and airy inside the entrance to the museum. I buy a ticket from the *taquilla* and leave my bag in the cloakroom before walking towards the single turnstile at the end of the walkway. At first, coming from the darkened corridor, I can't see anything, but as my eyes adjust to the light, images swim into focus. On the far wall of this open courtyard, light is filtering through palm fronds, creating patterns of light and dark on the cobblestones below. The garden is filled with luscious tropical plants and pre-Hispanic artefacts: primitive faces that stare with wide eyes and impish grins. In front of me flowering cacti and ferns hang from bright pink stucco walls, along with life-size papier-mâché skeletons, arms and legs bent as if they were dancing.

Inside the thick walls of the museum it is eerily quiet, as though such beauty calls for complete silence. The frantic energy of the city has given way to the fragrance of frangipani and the rhythmic whirring of hummingbird wings. The effect on me is magical. On previous visits to Mexico City I'd come to the *Casa Azul* often. But the excitement of coming here still hasn't worn off, nor have I become blasé about the museum I know so well – far from it. Every visit leaves me spellbound, as though I have entered another realm: a secret fantasy world I never want to leave.

Directly opposite the turnstile is the first exhibition space. Inside the hushed *salón*, a middle-aged couple are seated on a bench in the middle of the room, talking in whispers. On the walls there are small canvases arranged in perfect rows. The paintings are extraordinary. Bold and bright, they are like a crazy dream brought to life: peasants and vendors, a lifeless woman lying on a footpath, monkeys and deer with human features, and intimate self-portraits of Kahlo. Images of countless calamities: the artist after a bus accident that left her impaled on an iron rod; an operation where her miscarried child, still attached by the umbilical cord, hovers above her naked and broken body; the amputation of her leg. They are gory, in-your-face and fantastic.

Until I got to Mexico I had never laid eyes on a Frida Kahlo painting. In high school I had loved studying art, but we learned about Renaissance painters, impressionists, cubists. I could talk confidently about Turner's *Hannibal Crossing the Alps*, but if asked about Mexican art I would have no idea. In class we never left Europe, and I never thought to step away from what I knew. So to see a Kahlo painting for the first time wasn't only a new experience, it was like being slapped in the face. Her paintings seemed to represent everything good and bad about Mexico: the proud faces of the Indians in the marketplace; the artist, arms out-stretched, straddling two nations – on one side the culture and warmth of Mexico, on the other, the industrialised might of her neighbour. Kahlo's work seemed to capture the suffering of her people, especially women, as if what she had been through gave her an insight into the pain, longing, loneliness and frustrations of those around her.

I stand in front of a sketch of a little girl with large eyes that seem to be looking right at me. These works are profoundly disturbing, but at the same time I feel fortunate, or perhaps humbled, to be able to immerse myself in the mystery of the life of a woman whose sorrow was told in brushstrokes.

Now the woman from the bench is standing next to me. She smiles. From her clothes I gather she is American. I venture a hello. I'm right. Her eyes light up and immediately we are beyond pleasantries.

'Aren't these paintings wonderful?' she says, engrossed in the study of the little girl. 'Look at how she has given life to this face.'

'They're amazing,' I say. The woman's husband, mean-while, is standing back from us, arms crossed and making it clear there's somewhere he'd rather be. There are so many museums in this area, even one for bread; I wonder if this guy is dreading an afternoon of being dragged around like a recalcitrant child. I lean over to my new friend.

'What's wrong with him?' I ask.

She laughs under her breath and raises her hand in a dismissive gesture common to those who have been married for a long time. 'Oh, don't mind him,' she says. Upon hearing this the husband snorts like an angry bull.

I leave the squabbling couple in the gallery and wander through the house, stopping behind a rope barrier to admire the kitchen. The room is exactly how it was when Kahlo lived here, decorated with the enormous earthenware pots called *cazuelas*, water jugs, and clay figurines of donkeys and pre-Hispanic warriors. It's like looking at a ghostly snapshot of the past; a home and a life frozen in time.

In Kahlo's bedroom on the second floor, a plaster back brace sits on the embroidered bedspread. The artist wore it for a year after the bus accident and it has been painted with green and pink butterflies, though there are darker brown stains around the neck and I wonder if this is dried blood. I would love to lean over and feel the coarse texture of the plaster, but this room is roped off. And it would be a bit like leaving a fingerprint on a Monet painting. As I contemplate the scene, the woman from downstairs comes and stands next to me. 'Hi again,' she says. She then turns and points at the cast on the bed.

'Can you imagine what she went through?' she says.

'Well, no . . . actually not at all,' I reply, eyeing the cumbersome contraption that has made a hollow in the middle of the bed. We begin a conversation. Diana is a retired school teacher from Colorado, enjoying a holiday with her husband now that the 'squatters' (their four grown children) have finally left home. But right now, Diana's husband is nowhere to be seen.

'Where is your husband?' I ask.

'He's in the café,' Diana replies. 'He said he couldn't cope. That all this blood and death was too weird for him.' She laughs. 'Actually I think he'd rather be fishing on a lake somewhere but I wanted to come here, so here we are.'

We talk some more. I tell her of a whirlwind trip to Rome many years ago where I took a tour of the Sistine Chapel. The father of a Midwest family had stood at an altar made of pure gold and announced in a loud voice, 'I'm sick of this religious crap. What's for lunch?' Meanwhile I had peered up at a marble statue of the Madonna, swathed in a flowing robe that looked to be made of silk. Some beauty has a way of stopping time. Like this place. We laugh in this tiny bedroom, anchored by the history all around us.

I ponder Diana's husband's reaction to the paintings by this extraordinary woman. *It's all too weird*. He's probably right. At first glance Kahlo's work is brutal and confronting, even morbid. But on closer inspection it reveals much about the nature of Mexican people. From childhood they are taught to get on with life, no matter what misfortune befalls them. They never give up. I'd seen this strength in my mother and my grandmother. In fact, in almost every Mexican I know. Kahlo, I muse, may have expressed her suffering on canvas but there was also an element of defiance in her work, an *I'm still here* resolve. Maybe that's why I love it here so much. Somehow Frida Kahlo has found a way to get under my skin. Her life is an inspiration to me: *be positive and never give up*. It's sound advice I'm quite happy to heed.

By the time I step into the courtyard another hour has passed.

In the garden I find a shady spot on a stone bench that is actually a rampart from a scaled-down pyramid. I think of all the trouble the Spaniards went to after the Conquest to destroy remnants of pre-Hispanic culture. Their plan was simple: find a pyramid and build over it. But it didn't work. All over Mexico, pyramids, ruins and statues have been excavated, cordoned off, preserved and housed in museums. Here in the Kahlo museum, the rampart I sit on is a small-scale replica of Teotihuacán's Pyramid of the Sun, surrounded by artefacts and Aztec totems.

I'm tired now, and my head is swimming with everything I have seen. In a daze, I look over at the cacti and succulents blossoming in a nearby garden bed. The late-afternoon light is moving in shafts across the emerald-green foliage. The courtyard is empty and quiet. I close my eyes.

'Excuse me, miss, are you all right?'

I open my eyes to see a security guard standing in front of me. He is framed by a tropical fern that seems to be sprouting from his head. 'Are you unwell?' he asks. I'd fallen asleep without even realising it. 'Yes, I'm fine thank you,' I reply. The guard smiles and walks off. A grey cat is now weaving his tail across my legs. He purrs loudly. I scratch his back and then gather my things.

On my way out I buy a postcard of the painting of the little girl in the first gallery. A reminder not only of Kahlo's artwork but of the beauty she saw in the people around her. I leave the museum, making a mental note not to wait another three months before I come here again. As I step into the street my senses are momentarily jarred by the noise. A truck rattles past trailing a cloud of diesel smoke and the ground below my feet rumbles with its aftershocks. Cars, buses and pedestrians whiz past. I turn down *Calle Allende* and walk to the metro, leaving behind the charming and genteel streets of Coyoacán, and a museum that has touched my soul.

Chapter Eleven

Where is the Grasshopper?

It is now early February. Spring has arrived. The days are sunny and crisp and a lethargic calm descends on the city like a fine mist. The languor is catching. Instead of going to the library to study after class, I catch the bus to Chapultepec Park. As we speed along *Paseo de la Reforma*, I turn to look at the *avenida* carpeted creamy ochre by the sun; grand trees spool past in a blur of green and grey. I glimpse a spectre of metallic light – the Angel of Independence, *el Ángel*, the golden monument looking down at the surrounding boulevard. Then we arrive at the park.

I walk under an iron archway and along the path that leads to the lake. The scent of magnolia blossoms lingers under my nose. Eucalypt trees, imposing and luxuriant, shade the pavement with their silver foliage and drop pods that crunch underfoot. Afternoon sunlight filters through their leaves as an unseen peacock calls to its mate. Its sweet song floats in the air. A perfect note. A moment of bliss. Out beyond the canopy of trees, the path meanders over a bridge and up a hill to Chapultepec Castle, the former weekender of the Austrian Archduke Maximilian who briefly ruled in the 1800s, now a museum and café.

On this weekday afternoon the park is dotted with people. Every time I come here to walk around, or just to sit, I like it a little more. Although to me it cannot compare to the luscious parks of Melbourne, Chapultepec does have its own picturesque charm. Trees lean in like old men; children play *canicas*, marbles, in the dirt; men play a chess game in the shade. It has become one of my favourite places in the city. An oasis among the madness. Here I can connect with the simple delights of the outdoors.

I stop on the bridge. A bench has been placed at its high point, taking advantage of an expansive view of the lake that was once part of the *Lagos de Anáhuac*, the lakes and their tributaries that bordered the great Aztec city of Tenochtitlan. In other words, a living reminder of the past. I sit down, prop my feet on the stone balustrade and watch as ducks and couples in rowboats send ripples across the glassy surface. Above me the sky is a white haze, the sun just peeking through the *contaminación*. A soft wind – *una brisa fresca* – whistles in my ears. A glorious, languid afternoon. This is my idea of heaven.

Nearby, voices interrupt my quiet contemplation. *Americanos*. In this setting their accents sound harsh and extreme. Or maybe I'm just more used to Spanish. The gentle lapping of water against the bridge competes with the voices behind me.

'You should ask her.'

'Why do I have to do everything? *You* ask her.'

'Fine. I'll ask her then. *Por favor, señorita.*'

I feel a gentle tap on my shoulder and turn around to see

a large man and a tiny woman, both with ruddy complexions and dressed in matching synthetic tracksuits. They are a middle-aged couple and have camcorders dangling from their necks. The woman smiles sweetly. Before I can speak the man addresses me.

'¿Dónde . . . es . . .?'

He's now making motions with his hands as if to say *be patient*. He fumbles nervously with a dictionary, probably thinking I'm going to get fed up and walk away. I smile, reassuring. Mexicans are infinitely patient and it seems by osmosis I've adopted this trait. I have time to give. I stand up and wait; it hasn't yet occurred to me to speak English.

'¿Dónde . . . es . . . chapulin?' he says.

I think he wants directions to the *castillo*, the castle, but I can't be sure. In any case he's just asked me, 'Where is the grasshopper?' I stifle a giggle. At this rate we could be here all afternoon. I feel sorry for him, imagining that my own Spanish once resembled this tortured, bumbling attempt. Do I still sound like this? I hope not. I'm reminded of *Mind Your Language*, a television program about a bunch of language students that I used to watch as a child, where the Spaniard would say, 'Lookee see teacher, it's one foot . . . two foots.' My mother would sit with me and cry tears of mirth, obviously getting the joke. I decide to help this guy out.

'I speak English,' I finally say.

I hear myself speak and am completely thrown by the sound of my voice – in English! The words have stumbled from my mouth like rugby players looking for the ball in heavy fog. My accent is deep and throaty. This heavy pitch rings in my ears and sounds monstrous when compared to the sweet, lilting *lengua de romance* I've been speaking for the past few months. I instinctively put my hand to my mouth. What's going on? This is *my* language. Sure, it's an improvement from the other day when I couldn't even recall a simple sentence, but right now I feel like a complete idiot.

If I'm freaked out, the couple don't notice at all.

'Oh, wonderful,' the man says. 'We are looking for the castle. Can you help us?'

'Yes, of course. It's at the top of the hill,' I say, pointing in the right direction. That's more like it. A perfectly executed sentence, Admittedly, I'm amused by this lapse of English. My own language has become the dance partner waiting patiently for his turn as I glide around the floor with another *amor*. It's funny how my mind has shaped itself to the contours of a new *lengua*; to the rhythms of another culture. And in a sense, it's only natural. A shift has occurred within me, though I didn't see it happening. The language is a perfect example. Many words are now as familiar as their counterparts in English – *árbol, mariposa, hoja* – tree, butterfly, leaf. A whole new world of names.

As it happens, the man turns to me.

'I must say, you speak beautiful English.'

'Oh, thank you,' I reply.

The couple walk away, and I watch them disappear from view, feeling as though I've just had a conversation in Martian, but gripped by an irrational desire to follow them, keep talking, anything to get this forgotten language flowing again. The moment has such a surreal, fantastical aspect that I start to laugh. This incident, coupled with my experience with the Australians at the café in Coyoacán a few days earlier, gets me thinking about how foreign my life in Australia now seems. It's not an unhappy thought, more of a detached one, like trying to remember a dream in the full light of day. Just how far I've strayed from home – or adapted to life in Mexico, depending on which way you look at it – has been confirmed by an exchange with two American tourists.

Late in the afternoon I leave the park. I walk back under the old eucalypts and through the ornate gate into the street, where the traffic seems to greet me like an old friend. I'm on my way to *Zona Rosa*, the Pink Zone, in downtown Mexico, to meet a friend for coffee. Standing on the footpath, I watch a bus pull up across the road. I contemplate making a dash for it but quickly dismiss the idea, knowing I would get there as it drives away.

Though there will be another *colectivo* soon, I decide to walk. It's time I did some exercise – in Mexico City there's no such thing as an 'official' bus stop and having buses that arrive every thirty seconds and stop wherever you happen to be standing is making me incredibly lazy. And why walk when you can travel anywhere in the city for about twenty cents? No, today I'll walk the few blocks to *Calle Geneva*. The exercise will do me good.

But instead of the invigorating stroll I'd envisioned, the walk turns out to be a really bad idea. I hadn't factored in peak hour traffic; the roads are jammed with so many cars they form one continuous line of colour like a Christmas garland. I plough through clouds of diesel smoke and a cacophony of horns. Three different *taxistas* in their green and white cabs stop to ask me if I need a ride. '¡*Señorita!* ¿*Taxi?*' At one point, while trying to cross the road, I end up on a thin wedge of concrete on an overpass as cars thunder past inches from my ear, their downdraught so strong I have to hold on to the railing to keep from being blown onto the road.

I arrive at *Zona Rosa* in fifteen minutes, nose clogged, tongue grimy and ears ringing. But I made it! I'm feeling light-headed, although I suspect it has something to do with chemical intoxication. Next time, I'll catch the bus. For many Mexicans, exercise is an obscure concept, and I'm starting to understand why. You'd have to be crazy to *just do it* out there. In this city of twenty-five million inhabitants, it seems walking is what you do to get from your front door to the bus stop.

At Café Obregon, my friend Elizabeth is already waiting for me. I walk over to where she is sitting and lean against the edge of the table for a moment. She looks concerned. 'What happened to you?' she asks. I tell her about my walk and she looks at me with incomprehension. 'Why?' Like other decisions I later regretted – dyeing my hair purple, getting a tattoo, hurtling down the Geelong freeway in an old bomb the day after getting my driver's licence – I can only offer a feeble reply: *it seemed like a good idea.*

A teacher from the Mexico Academy, Elizabeth also happens to be the niece of my *profesor* Rogerio. A few months earlier I had suggested we get together for coffee so I could practise my Spanish with a local. Elizabeth readily agreed. At first I was slightly intimidated by her articulate, measured language but, listening to her, I soon grew to love her rich idiom and particular regional accent that seems to me the essence of Mexico City. I knew this was what I needed to give my own Spanish a more layered authenticity.

We hit it off instantly and soon started meeting for coffee almost every day. As we got to know each other, our conversations became less formal, replaced by long, rambling yarns about everything and nothing. We have quickly become close friends. I've been lucky here; I have close female friends from France, Ireland and Japan. But with Elizabeth it's different. I can't really explain it. It's as though we have an unspoken understanding, a connection that stems from our shared *latinidad.*

And under Elizabeth's tutelage, my Spanish gets bite. I pick up Mexico City words: '¡*Órale pues!*' – all right, okay, let's go (my grandmother spits out her coffee when she hears me say this, telling me never to repeat it because only the *albañiles*, tradesmen, use such slang); *pendejo*, asshole (very useful); *güey*, literally a castrated bull but among men a blokey salutation; *lana*, money; *fachosa*, scruffy; *peda*, drunk (so rude).

I also find out how to answer the phone, *bueno*, which means good but in this context hello. I practise this word with its elongated final vowel: *buen-oooooo*. Elizabeth tells me I sound more like a *chilanga*, a Mexico City resident, every day, but when I visit my grandmother I respectfully use a more formal Spanish, leaving my street slang to conversations with my buddies.

A waiter now brings us two steaming cups of *café de olla* and a tray of butter biscuits: almond shortbread, macaroons, crescent-shaped cookies and chocolate-coated shortbread. The *biscocho* are still warm and smell delicious. We take big crumbly bites and sips of coffee, suddenly silent in our enjoyment of the food. After a while, Elizabeth breaks the silence. 'We've eaten all the biscuits.' I look over at the tray and see she's right, all that remains are crumbs. 'How did that happen?' I ask, genuinely shocked. We both laugh and then order more coffee.

I listen with fascination as Elizabeth tells me about her father, an educated man, a doctor, who shares the Mexican obsession with marrying daughters young so they don't bring shame to the family. Unfortunately for Elizabeth, a good job and a sharp mind count for nothing when you are twenty-six and single. At the moment she is spending nearly all her waking hours out of the house to avoid the steady stream of suitors – perfect replicas of each other: short, squat, bald and old – her father, Dr Meddlesome, has invited around for the *almuerzo*.

'*Me va a refar*. He wants to raffle me off,' she says, only half-joking.

'Can't you tell him to lay off?' I ask, somewhat naively.

'*Ojalá*,' she sighs. If only.

I'm frustrated on her behalf, this beautiful girl who has to put up with the weight of social expectation in a country where being married means everything. But I'm not shocked. I understand this way of thinking because my mother went through exactly the same thing with her father. *You're on the shelf now.* This my grandfather told her at the age of nineteen. I thought attitudes might have changed. But despite greater numbers in the workforce, Mexican women still live in a *machista* society where they are boxed in by centuries of tradition. In this country the wheels of change grind exceedingly slow.

'You should have seen the one he brought around the other day,' she says. '*Tuvo un piecito en la tumba.*' One foot in the grave. We dissolve into fits of laughter.

When I first heard these stories, I sympathised vaguely, unable to really understand. But now things are different. I too have come under scrutiny. I don't have to *imagine* what it's like any more. I might not exactly be in these women's shoes – after all, I can leave whenever I like – but I'm learning from experience.

Visiting my grandmother the other day, I walked into an inferno blazing in the hallway. Lining the window ledge were half a dozen *lux perpetua* candles. At the time I thought my grandmother might have lit these *ofrendas* for her sisters, Carmen, Soledad and Concepción. A decade older than my seventy-eight-year-old grandma, they've had their share of age-related health problems. '*¿Cómo están tus hermanas?*' I asked. How are your sisters? 'Good, good,' she replied. I thought I detected a hint of a smile. The mystery was solved by my uncle who was visiting at the time and who, I might add, found the whole thing very amusing. The candles were for me! My grandmother was praying for a husband for *la niña*, her little girl.

I relate this story to Elizabeth.

'My grandma is praying to the *Virgen* to find a husband for me,' I say. 'She lit so many candles the other day she nearly set fire to the curtains.'

Elizabeth bursts out laughing and the mouthful of coffee she just took spurts all over the table. Other patrons turn around to see where all the noise is coming from.

'No way!' she says.

'Yup,' I nod.

She contemplates her coffee for a moment and then brings her face up to me again.

'Actually I thought you might be safe because you're kind of a foreigner.'

She has a point. Foreigners are free of the constraints that rule Mexican society. Women from other countries do not raise eyebrows here when they profess no desire to marry or have children, preferring a career out of the home. *Asi son los gringos* is a common refrain. That's how it is with foreigners. But with me the cultural guidelines are a little blurry. I take another sip of my coffee.

It all seems rather amusing to me. For a start I'm a single girl. I've contemplated getting a house plant when I return to Australia, and if that works out then I might think about a boyfriend. But marriage? I've barely thought about it. It's harder for my grandmother. All her sisters are *bisabuelas*, great-grandmothers, and she's only an *abuelita*. She wants great-grandchildren. She told me so. 'Hurry up,' she said one day, 'I'm not getting any younger.' We both laughed, except she was serious.

Sitting here, I realise how hard it must be for Elizabeth to live with this pressure every day. Suddenly life in Australia seems far less complicated. As my mother always says, *do what makes you happy*. I know my grandmother just wants me to be happy too and I love her for it, but

I prefer to follow my mother's more liberal advice for living.

We stay on at Café Obregon until closing time, drinking copious cups of coffee and talking. It's after nine when we walk towards *Paseo de la Reforma*, where Elizabeth will catch her bus home. 'You can hang out at the flat if you don't want to go home yet,' I say. She shakes her head. 'Gotta go home eventually.' As the bus pulls up she turns to me. 'Maybe we should go away for the weekend?' I nod. 'Sounds like a great idea.' I watch the bus drive away until it disappears in a pall of black smoke.

Chapter Twelve

Happy as a Slug

The following weekend we are heading down the *carretera* towards Cuernavaca, a town known as 'the place of eternal spring' for its temperate weather. As it happens, Elizabeth's cousin had called during the week to invite her to a *bautizo*, a baptism. I'm invited too and, *a la mexicana*, Mexican-style, so are Sandrine and Jean. The invitation then extends to our Irish friends Patrick and Catherine. Now we are an excited posse crammed into Elizabeth's *yanqui* sedan and looking out the windows as the dusty landscape whizzes by. Finally we are getting out of Mexico City, even if only for a couple of days. We are all excited.

We arrive at the church halfway through the baptismal ceremony, after getting hopelessly lost and driving around the Cuernavaca ring road for half an hour looking for the turn-off. About a hundred people are sitting in the front pews, women fanning themselves in the extraordinary heat, men readjusting ties and collars – completely inappropriate attire for the weather but required for such an austere occasion. We find a seat, trying to make as little noise as possible – difficult when six people stumble into a deathly quiet room. At the altar a priest stands with a group of parents holding babies in a semicircle in front of him.

Amid much wailing, the priest begins to anoint the babies' heads with holy water. He's an imposing man standing well over six feet, solidly built and wearing a fierce expression. But when he speaks, his voice is surprisingly gentle. *He sounds like the angel Gabriel*, I think. And suddenly the six babies go quiet. Are they thinking the same thing? It's then I notice a man in a yellow shirt standing at the altar, moving in for a photo of a couple and their baby. He steps back and knocks over a tall candle holder with his bottom, and the babies are off again. The holder and the thick candle both go clattering to the floor, narrowly missing the altar cloth that's so starched it surely would have exploded in flames like a chemistry experiment gone wrong.

I try not to laugh. Sandrine snorts and I look away, knowing if I make eye contact I'll completely lose it. I sneak a glance at Elizabeth, whose face has crumpled and shoulders are shaking. The only ones who remain remarkably composed are Jean and Patrick. Good Catholic boys. None of us dare laugh. We don't want to get thrown out along with the yellow-shirted mook who is now trying to clean up the mess. Candle wax creeps across the marble floor and the wooden holder has rolled away. The man decides to cut his losses and returns to his seat.

The service ends with a choir of boys singing 'Ave Maria'. The stone church amplifies their pure voices and seems to lift them skywards towards the domed roof before fanning out through the open floor-to-ceiling windows, to rest on the luscious frangipani and hibiscus blooming in the sun. I close my eyes. The music travels down my spine, releasing me from the present so I'm floating, aware only of these voices that sound so holy and ethereal. I open my eyes to see that the others are moved too. Our souls have been touched by a song of bliss.

We drive to Elizabeth's cousin's house. En route, Elizabeth stops to buy wild roses from an old woman sitting by the side of the road in the middle of nowhere. Where did she come from? Where will she go? With her gnarled hands she wraps an enormous bunch of long-stemmed roses in newspaper and hands them to Elizabeth. The *rosas* are bursting with colour: orange, yellow, pink and red petals spill over their wrapping and fill the car with a heady, fragrant scent. We hang out the window and wave goodbye to the woman, who sits on her stool and laughs and waves at the same time. She's still waving as I watch her disappear in the distance, wondering if she's actually an angel in disguise, dropped from the sky. After the priest at the church, I'm fixated on angels. It's one of those days.

The afternoon is hot and perfect. The cousin's house is on the outskirts of Cuernavaca. The *casa* is in the concrete bunker style popular with many Mexicans. A massive two-storey edifice, still under construction, the house seems designed to withstand a nuclear blast but it also offers spectacular views of the surrounding countryside from the flat roof. Patchwork fields of green and brown, and wheat fields the colour of summer sand. Cows dot the landscape, black blobs like speckled paint on a watercolour. We are standing on the roof but after five minutes I make my excuses. '*Me da miedo las alturas*,' I tell our host, Elizabeth's cousin Ernesto. I'm scared of heights. '*Ah, comprendo*,' he replies. I inch my way towards the trapdoor and safety. Not even this beauty can convince me to linger.

I sit on the veranda and watch the waiters setting up tables under enormous umbrellas in the garden. The *fiesta de bautizo* is happening here. A dozen tables are scattered across the pristine lawn. Crisp tablecloths are laid with cutlery and glassware. As I'm watching the preparations Ernesto comes and stands next to me. 'Just a small party,' I say jokingly. He nods his head solemnly. 'Yeah, I know, a lot of people couldn't make it.' Nearly one hundred people turn up for the party.

At two in the afternoon, lunch is ready. I'm starving now. Breakfast was a *concha* – a shell-shaped pastry made from eggs, butter and cream – dipped in milky coffee at seven. We're offered Sol beer wedged with lime, and *totopos*, corn chips, to nibble on. The *cerveza* is cool and sweet, and it goes straight to my head. After drinks the main course is brought over from the gargantuan barbecue on the other side of the lawn. We are served octopus with chile sauce, grilled prawns dashed with lemon, strips of beef, black beans, blue and yellow corn tortillas, fried tomatoes, and Mexican rice cooked in onion, garlic and saffron. There are also *salsas* of red and green chiles, raw onion rings, tubs of *guacamole*, pureed kidney beans with *chorizo* sausage, and baskets of *bolillos*, crusty bread rolls.

Platters carried by waiters in bow ties and dinner jackets go back and forth across the lawn. Laden with seafood and steak, the platters are delivered with flourish only to be vacuumed clean in minutes by the hungry hordes. *Cazuelas* of rice and beans thud when they make contact with the table. I'm glad now I didn't eat earlier. I want to eat everything, although shamefully after one plate I'm already full. Jean and Patrick are across the table making toasts with beer bottles. 'Samantita,' Patrick calls out, '*pásame el pulpo porfa.*' Though he uses the slangy *porfa* for *por favor*, please, to ask me to pass the octopus, his accent is still subtly tinged with lilting Irish. The food is excellent and everyone is happy. I feel a rush of pleasure to be enjoying the good things in life: food, company and the brilliant sun.

'*Perfecto*,' I say to Sandrine.

'*Perfecto*,' she replies.

By five the sun is beginning to set. The guests dribble towards the gate where cars ring a barren patch of lawn, like a country football match without the players. A diehard group, consisting of about twenty people including us, are seated and sprawled on the grass near the barbecue. Ernesto and his lovely wife, Isabella, have asked us to hang around. Elizabeth mentions something about dinner and Jean and Patrick immediately shake off their torpor and sit up. 'Great idea,' they chorus. I'm so full I can't move, but the idea is garnering support. 'I suppose I could nibble on something,' adds Catherine. Elizabeth mentions a hole-in-the-wall restaurant nearby and everyone jumps to their feet.

We walk along the dirt road towards a corner where a big stone pillar marks our location like a medieval relic. The darkness above us is dotted with stars and away from the house the only noise to be heard is our voices. Catherine is telling us how Patrick accidentally ate a whole chile at lunch, mistaking it for a piece of tomato. 'Eh, I thought his head was going to blow off!' In a perfect imitation of Patrick's earlier 'local' speak, she uses the ubiquitous Mexican *eh*. I smile. It's happening to all of us; this *mexicanidad* is catching. The lonely laneway fills with raucous laughter.

At the corner, we cross the road and walk about ten steps to the restaurant. It's actually someone's house with a table out the front but nobody's complaining. We sit down at the long bench and order six bowls of *pozole*, a soup particular to this region. The skinny road is empty of cars. There's a serene feel to this landscape; an owl hoots in a nearby tree, a dog sniffs around the table and then walks away, the wind whispers and sighs. The restaurant owner's mother comes out with a pile of tortillas. She's wearing a sleeveless cotton dress and a floral apron – the unofficial uniform of the Mexican grandmother – and has kind, sparkling eyes. '*Riquísimo*,' she says, pointing to the tea-towel-wrapped bundle. I love it here. It's so peaceful. Yet, oddly, it doesn't seem real; perhaps the chaos and noise of Mexico City is so intense my senses need time to adjust.

The *pozole* arrives. The specialty is a broth of corn, chokoes, ham hocks, garlic, chile and lemon, infused in *huesos de puerco*, pig bones, over a low flame. It's delicious. In many restaurants in Mexico City it is served with vegetables, but here, where it originated, it still retains its earthy flavour. After one mouthful I've decided I'm hungry again. Only the rapidly emptied bowls get us moving back to the house again.

The party is now in full swing. In our absence the living room has been transformed – the sofas pushed against the walls and the rug rolled up and chucked under the stairs. The entertaining area is an enormous space that looks even larger because two giant archways on either side of the room – the doors haven't been hung yet – open directly onto the garden. A garland of star-shaped paper lanterns hangs crisscrossed from the ceiling and gives the room a soft, romantic glow. *Salsa* music blasts from the sound system and carries over to where we are standing in the doorway.

Everybody is dancing. It might sound like a cliché but for *Latinos* dancing is in their blood. And they are, almost without exception, wonderful dancers. Couples move in unison, their *salsa* steps natural, seamless and completely uninhibited. *Sexy* is the word that springs to mind. The scene is energetic, hot and exuberant. The music, soft lights and the *ritmo*, rhythm, are so at odds with parties back at home where *men don't dance*. I sigh. If only Australian men knew how appealing women find a man who can dance, they'd be on their feet faster than you could say *Strictly Ballroom*. Jean must read my mind. 'Disgusting,' he says. 'They've got more rhythm than should be allowed.' He should know. When I partner him I'm in danger of serious injury – which is a shame because he loves to dance. Our last pairing at Mamá Rumba was to a lively Celia Cruz song, during which Jean spun me with such force that I crashed headfirst into a pillar. From then on I left him with his girl-friend, an excellent mover, who turned to me and screamed over her shoulder, '*¡Qué frustración!*' Oh, the frustration!

When the song finishes a man comes over and gives Jean a blokey slap on the back. They had chatted earlier in the afternoon over a couple of beers followed by tequila chasers. By now they're old friends, laughing, backslapping and sharing a private joke. They come back to where we are gathered and Jean introduces his friend.

'This is Eric,' he says.

Eric shakes my hand and I'm too dumbstruck to reply. He's gorgeous. In fact, I think he's possibly the most beauti-ful man I've ever met. Tall, solid, with caramel-coloured skin, rich brown eyes, an expensive blue shirt (sleeves rolled up so I get a good look at his muscular forearms), tailored pants and my greatest weakness, beautiful shoes. *Always judge a man by his shoes* is one of my grandmother's favourite expressions. I'd first spotted Eric earlier in the afternoon playing with the baby – he's the *padrino*, the god-father – but when he looked up and smiled at me I com-pletely lost my cool and practically ran away. And now here he is again – still holding my hand, I notice with embarrassment.

'Samantita,' he says. Ah! How beautiful it sounds coming from his mouth.

'Would you like to dance?'

Overcome by apoplectic shyness, I blurt out the first words that pop into my head.

'Oh, no thank you. I don't like to dance.'

As usual in such cases, my words betray me. If I had been standing alone I might have convinced him with my outright lie, but as it is, I'm surrounded by my friends, who know otherwise.

'What are you talking about?' Jean says, looking at me as if I've lost my mind.

'You love dancing,' says Catherine.

'Yeah,' adds Sandrine. 'You love it.'

Having been exposed as a complete fraud, I utter a pathetic laugh and allow myself to be pushed towards the beautiful man. A strong hand leads me into the *baile*. Soon we are all dancing. Here, no-one is being a wallflower – the music is too brisk and the beat too infectious. In fact, it wouldn't occur to anyone to stop dancing for anything other than a power failure or an earthquake. Eric spins me around and with all the fun I'm having I soon forget my shyness. As with most Latin men – he's Panamanian – Eric is light on his feet, a strong lead but gentle at the same time. It seems to prove my theory that dancing is in the blood – there are no lessons over here, you just learn as you go. And nobody cares whether they look foolish, although that's pretty unlikely – it's all about having fun.

For hours we whirl around the floor; there's no break between songs. We are laughing and dripping with perspiration, and I notice with appreciation that Eric's shirt is plastered to his chest. Isabella then cuts in for a dance with her baby's godfather and I take the opportunity to go outside for some fresh air.

There is an enormous tree in the garden; obviously it's been here for a long time. Its branches seem to spread like tentacles across the black sky. I flop into the chair underneath its canopy. The cool breeze licks my face. My body and hair are hot, as though I'm sizzling on the surface. I feel alive, my senses tingling. I close my eyes and am stopped from falling asleep by the sound of music coming across the garden in irregular waves, and by falling leaves landing on my head. After a few more minutes I've cooled off and I'm ready to go back inside. Elizabeth is standing on the balcony peering into the indigo night. She spots me under the tree.

'What are you doing out here? Come inside,' she says.

When we finally get to bed it is after five am. The soft Cuernavaca sky will soon turn from night black to grey, and then to sunrise blue. I'm lying on a mattress on the floor looking at the star-dotted sky through the window frame – the panes haven't been put in yet either – and feeling utterly content. All around me bodies rise and fall with the rhythms of sleep. I'm in the girls' room, the *harem* as somebody calls it. Eric, I later find out, sleeps in the only room with a lockable door because over the course of the evening he'd been propositioned by a number of young ladies. How did I not notice any of this? It's like my grandmother's favourite soap opera, *Mirada de Mujer*, in real life. Except I've missed all the drama.

Outside I hear the croaking of cicadas. They provide a background song for my thoughts about the day: the moving ceremony, the warmth of our hosts, delicious food, dancing, friends, and Mexico's passionate nature that is so contagious. Sometimes being in this country is like a dream. A crazy dream. But today seems to encapsulate everything I love about this country. As I drift off to sleep I think of an expression Elizabeth taught me during one of our coffee chats, one that loses a little in the translation but in essence remains the same. It sums up my feelings perfectly: *feliz como lombriz.*

As happy as a slug.

Chapter Thirteen

The Dog Smokes a Cigarette on the Train

I wake with a start at quarter to eight on Monday morning. I'd dreamed Jean was yelling at me, but now as I stumble downstairs I realise it wasn't a dream. He was telling me to get up. In any case, I'm late and he's gone. I leave the apartment at eight, just as classes are starting at the Mexico Academy. On our second night in Cuernavaca, after a delicious dinner of *enchiladas* with our hosts, we settled in to talk and drink rough red wine, and as a result didn't return to Mexico City until after midnight. A weekend of excess and little sleep has left me in tatters. I'd love to go back to bed but instead settle for a quick fix – a large *café americano* and a raspberry donut – and then race for the bus. We speed through the *distrito* and arrive at the college in a matter of minutes.

When I arrive, Jean, Kumi, our *profesor* Rogerio, and the college director, Señor Avila, are squashed around the tiny desk in the middle of the classroom. As I enter the room, they all look up and smile. For a moment I think they might be annoyed because I'm late but then I remember that in this country time is relative. To get an idea of *tiempo mexicano*, Mexican time, you only have to turn up at a party at the specified hour. You'll probably be the only person there since the guests (and hosts) don't plan on arriving for another two hours. Kumi beckons me over and we squeeze together on her chair.

'*Les tengo una propuesta interesante*,' Señor Avila begins. I have an interesting proposal.

'We've been hearing wonderful things about your progress.'

Word of our high marks during the weekly tests has attracted the attention of the *deus ex machina* at the Mexico Academy. Now Rogerio is beaming like a proud parent, and so he should be. Much of the credit for our improvement belongs to him – our extraordinary teacher. But there is also another factor: we are swots. Although Jean does not join us because he attends business college, every afternoon Kumi and I go to the *biblioteca*, the public library nearby. It would be monotonous to confine ourselves solely to the study of verbs and nouns, but invariably Elizabeth and Sandrine arrive and the sessions end over coffee in the garden café. Now, it seems, our efforts are paying off.

Señor Avila continues. 'Are you interested in sitting the exam for the Department of Public Education?'

The idea of the exam is to give foreign students the chance to qualify as interpreters and translators – recognised by a government diploma – who can work anywhere in Mexico and, for that matter, Latin America. But there is a catch. Places are limited to three students from each of the Spanish-language colleges in the Federal District, and you have to be *invited* to sit the exam. It is left up to the directors of each college to choose who they want to represent them, and on this occasion we have been chosen.

'Really?' I ask, wondering if they actually meant to ask some other students.

'Yes, really,' he smiles.

I'm thrilled. This is wonderful news. Rogerio told me of the exam a couple of months ago and it sounded interesting, but it never occurred to me that I would be selected as a candidate. That honour, I thought, would go to someone else. The Asian students perhaps. They make model pupils – no lengthy discussions about what makes a perfect *margarita* or whether Javier Alatorre, the newsreader on *Esta Noche*, is gay or not. (I say yes. Jean, as any self-respecting Frenchman would, says lemon sweaters don't prove anything.) But in regard to the exam, the decision has been made. We are it. We are worthy.

Now, as the news slowly sinks in, I realise one thing: our teacher has been preparing us for this exam. In fact, I find out later that he was so confident of our abilities that he put our names forward after our first week of classes together. And I smile. It seems like only yesterday I was trying to order a roll, confusing *jamón*, ham, with the similar sounding *jabón*, soap, and asking for a cheese and soap sandwich, or asking a shop assistant to wallpaper herself, rather than gift-wrap a present. Such simple mistakes frustrated me enormously.

Jean speaks for all of us.

'We would love to do it,' he says. Kumi and I nod in agreement.

'It's settled then,' Señor Avila says. He rises from his seat and shakes hands all round.

But there is one problem to deal with. I have no money! The exam and the two weeks of intensive preparatory classes with Rogerio will cost five thousand pesos (then around one thousand dollars). And I have no idea where the money is going to come from. I'd arrived in Mexico with three thousand dollars and a credit card. Having stayed longer than I originally planned, the money is long gone and my credit card debt is spiralling out of control. I ignore the pile of threatening letters the bank has been sending. *Your account is seriously in arrears, please pay immediately.* To be honest, I'm not that worried, I know there's nothing they can do while I'm here. My mind is made up. I'm going to sit the exam. And the money? Well, as the Mexicans always say, *todo saldrá bien*: everything's gonna be all right. I believe it too.

My classes finish in four weeks and the exam seems like a fitting end to all these months of study. And being able to challenge myself in this way – the pass mark is ninety-two per cent – is something I look forward to. I'm excited, determined to pass with flying colours. What's more, success in the exam will be more than just an academic achievement. Just as I have always thought of Spanish as a way of embracing my heritage, a high score will be my way of saying to myself: *you've made it.* It doesn't mean I'll now consider myself a *bona fide* Mexican; that will never happen. I may be descended from this land but I'm shaped by another, even if I were to live here for the rest of my days. It's more a case of achieving what I set out to do, without even realising it, all those years ago when I first came to Mexico. That is, finding out who I am. Here, I've discovered my *soul* has a home in Mexico, and I am enriched by this feeling of connectedness. I know I will never be Mexican, but it is the Mexico that I carry in my heart that resonates. And my knowledge of Spanish has helped me achieve a connection to Mexico that I could never have otherwise felt.

Three hours later, the class finishes with a song. It will be a month and a half until we sit the exam but, just as we are getting ready to leave, Rogerio drops the final bombshell.

'Oh, I need you to prepare a fifty-minute speech,' he says casually. 'You can choose the topic. Anything you like, just as long as it goes for the required amount of time.'

I turn to Kumi and Jean. Both have turned translucent.

'Fifteen minutes?' Kumi asks.

'No *chiquita*,' Rogerio replies. '*Fifty* minutes.'

I can't breathe. I need air. Fifty minutes! The idea of standing in front of a room full of people and speaking in another language terrifies me. Actually, it's not the speech so much, but rather the thought of boring my audience with an uninspired performance. I think because of my Mexican blood, I have a sense of the dramatic, the desire to tell stories, and to entertain. On the other hand, I've inherited my father's introverted nature, which is why this news inspires in me conflicting emotions. But the awesome scariness of such a task makes me determined to succeed. And if I can pull this off, I tell myself, I can do anything. At least we get to choose our topic; I'll definitely pick something interesting.

There is another problem we must overcome. The three of us are still unable to master the evil rolling 'rr'. As the speech in Spanish will count for nearly forty per cent of the total mark, correct pronunciation is imperative. I am now reminded of an Australian friend who had lived in Mexico telling me how it took him two years to master this vocal technique. Two years! I hope it doesn't take me that long. I only have six weeks. Rogerio suggests voice exercises.

'Repeat after me,' he says merrily. '*El perro fuma un cigarrillo en el ferrocarril.*'

The dog smokes a cigarette on the train.

Oh, great. As delightful as this image may be, he's managed to put into one sentence the three words in the Spanish language that I *cannot* pronounce. When he sings this ditty it sounds poetic and rich; when I sing, it sounds like I'm being tortured under water. It's the revenge of the 'rr's.' Still, there's no escaping them.

'*Ándale*,' he says, go on, not at all put off by our dubious faces.

As I leave the *salón*, I hear myself singing, *the dog smokes a cigarette on the train*, my throat growling as it encounters the double consonants. The song lodges in my brain, which isn't such a bad thing considering it's the key to mastery of this difficult technique. I descend the stairs, my footsteps on the wooden floors keeping time with the soft words emanating from my mouth. I know with practice I will succeed; the six-week deadline serves as an impetus to try harder. I walk out the door feeling confident about the challenge ahead.

Now the bus is roaring down *Avenida Insurgentes* and, for the second time today, I think I'll kiss the ground Papal-style when I get off, thankful to God and *all* the saints for sparing my life once again. While other passengers stare calmly ahead, I practise the life-saving technique of holding onto the seat until my arms ache. The driver is racing another *colectivo*, his head out the window, gesticulating and shouting abuse as he steers with one hand.

As we hurtle towards San Ángel it occurs to me that I should be used to this maniacal driving that seems to be a Mexican birthright. But I'm not. It's strange really, considering the hundreds of buses I've caught since I arrived here. Maybe it takes a certain character to be blasé in the face of danger. Mexicans have it in bucketloads. It's the art of *tranquilidad*. At times I'm as calm as can be, embracing the

Latin approach to life – and road rules – with ease. On other occasions, like this one, I worry: *we're going to crash!* Two contradictory cultures live inside me. 'You think too much,' my mother would say. 'That's from the English.' And she's right. Will I ever be *really* Mexican? Not likely. It's true Mexico has changed me. But I'll always carry elements of another race. Reserve and analysis will always compete with *pasión*. And that's okay. In this country I've learned something about human nature: you don't have to be one or the other, you can just *be*.

After another ten minutes, we arrive at our destination. San Ángel is a genteel *colonia* where the Spaniards built glorious mansions, churches and plazas after colonising the surrounding areas in the 1600s. Self-congratulatory monuments still stand impressive and ornate in the blazing sun. I haven't been here in a while because the trip usually takes about forty minutes, an eternity in this city. Today, however, I have planned to have lunch here with my Irish friend, Catherine.

I wait outside La Fonda de San Ángel, a popular restaurant that serves delicious *bocaditos*, little mouthfuls. Looking over the plaza I watch a small boy playing with an insect that is crawling along a stone wall. The market in the middle of the plaza is surrounded by boutiques, cafés and restaurants. In spite of the obvious tourist pitch, the area still oozes an old-world charm that seeps from the charcoal cobbles underfoot. I move under the shade of a cedar tree, away from the passing crowds. The heat has forced a stray dog under the same tree. He sees me and wags his tail once but then, as though exhausted by the effort, he drops his head to his paws and promptly falls asleep.

The plaza is the centre of activity in San Ángel. On three sides there are charming stone houses with elaborate arched entrances and imposing façades. A short distance from here is a major road but, looking down the cobbled laneway, it is hard to imagine I'm in the middle of Mexico City. Cars don't come up here very often because tyres are easily punctured by the jagged cobbles, lending even more of an authenticity to the *colonia*. Now it is geared towards the visitors, bursting with souvenir shops selling silver jewellery, *artesanías* and traditional Mexican furniture. But a sense of age still remains. The original idea of houses facing the plaza was to bring people together as a community. Women discussed families; men did business. Now crowds congregate in the square to chat, shop, enjoy; I see more people entering through other laneways. It might be more international now but there is still a sense of community. The area is vibrant, teeming with life and commerce.

I spot Catherine walking towards me. A petite woman with red hair, pale skin and the bluest eyes, she often attracts open-mouthed stares when travelling on the bus, walking in the street, everywhere. Mexico is a very homogeneous society and immigration from anywhere outside Latin America is uncommon; with the exception of tourists, a white-skinned person in this city is a rare sight. Coming from a multicultural demographic I find this reversal of the norm odd to say the least. Here in San Ángel Plaza, however, Catherine blends with the crowd. Amid the din I recognise a multitude of accents: Mexican, English, American and German; all talking excitedly, buoyed by the heat of this dog day afternoon. I too have shaken off my earlier lethargy.

'Hello,' Catherine says, out of breath.

She looks paler than usual and I ask her if she is feeling unwell.

'Oh, I'm okay, bit of trouble breathing today, that's all.' Her answer is matter-of-fact. It's accepted among people in Mexico City that sooner or later you'll get sick because of the *contaminación*. Every night I wash my hands and face, watching in amazement as black water gurgles down the drain. On days of severe pollution parents are warned by news broadcasts to keep children inside – scientists have discovered the toxic air destroys their brain cells. Right now the sky is a thick haze that looks like the aftermath of a summer bushfire; it's time to go inside.

In the restaurant – a former home to aristocracy – my eyes are immediately drawn upwards. The ceilings are high, an enormous crystal chandelier hangs from a rose, and a stone staircase winds upwards, elegant and timeless. Like most buildings in the area, it was built as recompense for the Spanish conquerors who made it to the other side of the bloody defeat of the Aztecs in 1524. Some reward, I think. This place is incredible. Perhaps I hadn't noticed it before because all the edifices in this area are equally grandiose and breathtaking.

When the waiter asks us where we would like to sit, we choose a table on the covered terrace, slightly awed by the main room, which seems more suited to state affairs than something as plebeian as lunch. I'm thrilled with the idea that we are about to dine on the terrace of a three-hundred-year-old *casa de nobilidad*. Something else becomes clear to me. Although Mexicans take great pride in their Aztec history and monuments, and their artists – building statues everywhere, naming streets after historical figures, encouraging public murals and festivals – they can also be quite casual about history, because it is all around them: the stones under their feet are centuries old. So-and-so once lived there, a shopkeeper will tell you, or someone will point to a nearby church and say that Aztec cooking implements were found just over there. Perhaps familiarity produces respectful admiration rather than the *awe* inspired in tourists.

There is such a contradiction here: the people who would open a café in an aristocratic mansion, or let us slide across the floors in a museum, are the same people who would stop building work to excavate an ancient temple in the middle of the city, or donate their own house as a museum while they're still living in it, as Dolores Olmedo did.

We order *micheladas* – beer and lemonade, but *michelada* sounds more exotic than shandy – and scroll down the menu. Most restaurants in Mexico City cater to the more delicate tourist palate and this place has the American in mind: large servings smothered in cream, *guacamole* and mild chile sauce. The standard dishes appear first: *enchiladas rojas* and *verdes*, rolled tortillas filled with chicken and cheese, smothered in red or green chile sauce; *albondigas*, Mexican meatballs; *ensalada mixta*, mixed salad – a novel concept in a country of ardent meat eaters – with lettuce, tomato, egg, cheese and dressing; and *fajitas*, tortillas with beef strips. Further down, however, are the local delights – like another country, one the *extranjeros* wouldn't even contemplate visiting. But I'm there, passport and visa in hand.

I order *huitlacoche con chorizo y arroz rojo*. Real Mexican food. The waiter, having heard my accent, pauses for a moment.

'*¿Segura señorita?*'

'Yes, I'm sure,' I reply. Used to foreigners' disgust for the herbs, spices and plant extracts that form the basis for much Mexican cooking, he thinks I've inadvertently ordered the wrong dish. '*¡Órale pues!*' I add. Although my grandmother would be shocked at my use of slang, it's the magic word, as Mexican as cactus and tequila, and the effect is instantaneous. For the rest of lunch the waiter fusses over the *chicana*, the Mexican–American (me!) and her friend, *la güerita*, the white girl. I forgive him this slightly offensive term. There's no point explaining the difference between

America and Australia – to a Mexican it's all moot. I catch Catherine smiling at me. 'More Mexican every day,' she says with a wink.

Our lunch arrives. Catherine has ordered *enchiladas* served with lashings of sour cream. A basket of tortillas, crackers and corn chips is placed in the middle of the table. My *huitlacoche* is presented on a big plate, steaming and aromatic. This delicious dish is as intriguing as its name suggests. Once considered an Aztec delicacy, *huitlacoche* is a corn tortilla filled with sweet corn fungus – the grey spores produced by infected kernels in damp weather – plus Spanish sausage, red onion, tomato, fresh coriander and cheese. Fried until crispy, it is served with red rice infused with onion, garlic and saffron. Ah! A gastronomical delight. Every mouthful has me in raptures, although I can't convince Catherine to taste it. 'I think I'll give it a miss,' she says, unconvinced of the merits of a meal whose main ingredient is fungus. 'Oh, go on,' I reply, 'it tastes like mushroom.' It's a dubious comparison but Mexican flavours are so unique they often defy description. We order more *micheladas* and toast the afternoon.

Now utterly relaxed, we finish with a dessert of *churros con chocolate*, a recipe borrowed from the Spaniards – an appropriate choice given the colonial feel of the area. A plate is delivered with a flourish and on it are six long pastry fingers, deep-fried (a Mexican obsession), coated in sugar and eaten with melted chocolate served in a small jar. The *churros* are washed down with two cups each of rich *café de olla*. The afternoon could not have been more perfect. And it is, I muse, how Mexicans approach life: a languid *laissez faire*. In other words, let life happen.

After we have finished the *churros*, I turn to Catherine with a question. 'Why are you here?'

Just like Jean, Catherine had followed her scientist

partner rather than be separated from him. But Patrick's field study wrapped up months ago and they are now reluctant to leave. He is negotiating a new contract with a Mexican university. There is something about this city, as chaotic and dirty as it may be, that anchors people to it. I want to know what it is. I'm curious about why others stay. Catherine puts down her beer and leans back in her chair, not at all surprised by this question out of the blue.

'This place is so much like home,' she says. 'I don't mean outwardly but in its essence.'

She holds her hands up in a contemplative gesture.

'Mexican people are like the Irish, they're warm and patient and funny. It's hard to explain. Maybe it's because we're both nations of underdogs, but every day I wake up and feel so at home – it really is the strangest feeling.'

She laughs.

'I guess you know better than anyone what I'm talking about.'

I guess I do.

I like her answer. Perhaps it is because some of why I'm here is reflected in her simple statement. But there is more to my being here, and I think Catherine, judging by her last comment, senses that too. It occurs to me that she has never asked me the question I have just put to her. And it seems to be a pattern: whenever I explain my background people nod, as though they are saying without words: *we understand*. Just as Mexican author Octavio Paz proposed in his Nobel-prize winning book *El Laberinto de la Soledad* (*The Labyrinth of Solitude*) about what it means to be Mexican, when he said Mexico's children always come home. I think he might have been onto something. Other people see what I for the longest time could not: that Mexico was always waiting for me to return and claim my place in it. And that is why I feel so at home – because I belong here.

The lunch has revived Catherine and when she suggests we visit a famous attraction nearby I readily agree. The Convent of Carmen or, as it is known locally, the *iglesia de las momias*, the church of the mummies, contains the perfectly preserved remains of eighteenth-century Mexicans. It now serves as a museum, drawing huge numbers of visitors, from all over the world, who enjoy a morbid fascination for peering at dusty corpses seemingly plucked straight from Edvard Munch's painting *The Scream*.

The church was built in the early 1600s in the aftermath of the Spanish invasion as a way to convert the Indian masses to Christianity. Unfortunately the Spaniards didn't count on the fervour of the original inhabitants and, despite appearances, to this day Mexico remains fiercely pagan. The ritual of the Day of the Dead, for example, although it bears some resemblance to the Catholic All Souls' Day, is actually an Aztec tradition where human blood, and not *ofrendas*, was offered to the gods.

In a country obsessed with death you soon find yourself reeled in. I, for one, can't get enough of mummies, spirits, *velorios* and offerings. When I light a candle for one of the *difunta*, the dead, I'm part of this world; imagining the spirits looking down upon me, pleased at how far I've come. As a descendant of a long line of passionate Catholics – though my father is Church of England, 'Poor soul, not his fault,' my grandmother says – I think I have inherited some of their fervour for the fantastical, romantic, mystical and downright inexplicable. Either that, or I've been here too long.

We walk under a stone archway. The courtyard is bordered by sparse poplars and the ubiquitous cobblestone. The entrance gives a sense of foreboding; there's something oppressive about the thick air. I step into the darkness. Inside are stone floors and wooden pews so uncomfortable that only the Catholic Church could be responsible for their design.

'How creepy is this place?' I whisper to Catherine.

'God, yeah,' she replies. Realising what she's said, she looks at me and we both laugh.

After a long hallway, we come to an internal courtyard. The fountain has been rendered with beautiful Moroccan tiles (the Spanish influence) and I run my finger along its cool surface. It's empty of water, as though it has sprung a leak, because there is a dark stain spreading across the stones beneath my feet. Moving towards an arched doorway we descend a narrow stone staircase and come out in an open space just beyond the catacombs of the dead. The mummies await! A security guard is standing to my left.

'Hello ladies,' he says.

'*Buen día*,' we chorus.

'Sure you want to do this?' he asks.

As I nod, Catherine puts to him the obvious question. 'Yes. Why?'

At this the guard smiles. 'Well, some people get a bit freaked out.' To which we reply, 'Not us!' We spend the next ten minutes chatting with our new friend about general stuff, like whether his football team, Nexcaca, will win next Sunday at the Aztec Stadium. In this way I hope we brighten his day. I always feel sorry for people who work in museums – particularly Mexican ones. It's not natural having Mexicans not allowed to talk, deprived of what they do best. *¡Qué cruel!* We walk towards the catacombs, eager to get a look at the *momias* that everyone raves about.

The tomb is quiet – well, deathly quiet. Along one wall is a line of coffins and, even more extraordinary, along another wall are the standing (standing!) remains of women and children. They look like soldiers at parade and I half-expect one to reach out and tap me on the shoulder. I feel an involuntary shudder. Upon closer inspection I see that their faces are frozen in tortured yawls, hands clawed, though an attendant later reassures us that they all died of natural causes. It is the most incredible sight. Nothing is hidden behind glass and it would be quite easy to just lean over and touch them . . . Except the guard was right, I am kind of freaked out. I feel as though someone has stuck their hands in my chest and is now squeezing my heart – not a pleasant sensation. Maybe the spirits really are here – and they're not happy about people snooping around their resting places. I'm spooked, but the desire to see the old and mystical is stronger, and I stay.

I'm not really versed on the history of mummification in Mexico but I do know it was quite a common practice in earlier centuries; a way of keeping the dearly departed close at hand (literally). Little did those generations know that hundreds of years later their relatives would become a macabre spectacle of horror and fascination. We're now standing in front of a coffin on a slab which houses the remains of a baby, perfectly preserved right down to its tiny fingernails.

'Weird, huh?' Catherine says.

'Uh huh.'

As we approach the door where we came in, a couple enter and whisper a hello. We greet them and stop to take one last look at a male mummy. I'm convinced he's grinning at me. I peek at the couple, who have now moved into the middle of the dark, labyrinthine room. The man is peering intently into a coffin when his partner leans forward and screeches 'Boo!' in his ear. His reaction is priceless. Previously a picture of concentration, he now jumps out of his skin and narrowly avoids cracking his skull on the low roof. I choke back a laugh, my shoulders shaking and tears welling in my eyes. I'm torn between the need to behave like a respectable adult (who am I kidding?) and the desire to collapse helpless with laughter on the floor.

Catherine grabs my arm and we race into the corridor, where we giggle uncontrollably for the next five minutes. The incident dispels the spooky mummy vibes and we walk outside into the garden, relaxed and at peace with the world.

We find a shady spot underneath a row of trees that line a wall at the bottom of the garden. Interspersed between the trees are stone benches and it is on one of these that we now plonk ourselves. I've always thought the stone that appears everywhere in Mexico City a marvellous invention; even with the oppressive heat of this tropical country, it retains a coolness that I think lends a lot of the grandeur to the old buildings of the city. I run my hand along the smooth surface of the bench. In front of us is a small bridge we have just crossed, spanning a sun-dappled pond where water lilies grow. Hummingbirds flock to the nectar of a hibiscus. The garden does not seem real. Beyond the luscious ferns and the blooms of fragrant magnolia and frangipani is the hard city. A tiny oasis in the middle of the craziness; the capital is full of them. It's all part of the contradiction that is Mexico City.

We are sitting in silence when two girls walk past. Both look to be in their early twenties and have strong Aztec faces, long straight hair, hooked noses and copper-coloured skin. I notice they are wearing tracksuit pants, which strikes me as odd – Mexican women, even if they don't have much money, take great pride in their appearance, so tracksuits are a big no-no. They stop near us and comment on the pretty garden beds and it's then I catch two distinct Californian accents. Catherine turns to see me staring at them, open-mouthed.

'What's wrong?' she asks.

'Look at those girls,' I say. 'Such strong accents. Americans with Aztec faces.'

I'm genuinely shocked; somehow I wasn't expecting *those* voices to come from such Mexican bodies. I can't really explain my reaction. *Is that how people see me?* Catherine must be reading my mind.

'Just like you,' she says.

I laugh. She is right. Just like me. No matter how far we go, somehow we still belong to this place. I move around this city, going here and there, never getting 'historied out'. I'd thought it was just a curiosity for all that was different, and yet somehow familiar. Now a far more pleasing thought comes to mind. I go to museums, churches and old houses, and linger over dusty history books in the library and visits with my grandmother – a living treasure in my eyes – for another reason: I'm moving through the city picking up the essence of my ancestors who have left their spirits here. As though they were waiting for my return. It's hard not to imagine them looking down from above and smiling.

But I also now realise that I didn't need to travel all that way. I've been looking in museums, churches and history books for the essence of the Aztecs, but their spirits aren't just in places and books, they are in the *people*, like the Maya boy selling trinkets at Palenque, and the Mexican–American girls across the courtyard. I just need to look at the faces of those around me.

Chapter Fourteen

Floating Valley:
A Weekend in Paradise

I'm up before it's light. I throw open the kitchen shutters and sit at the window, wrapped in a woollen cardigan and cradling a steaming cup of coffee. The clock says five-thirty. It is Saturday morning but this early rising has become a ritual for me in Mexico. Today's pleasure, however, has a particular intent. In half an hour the *tamales* vendor will cycle past our building on his rickety *bicicleta*; an ancient man in the heart of this ancient city. Now I listen for the sound of his bell while the rest of the apartment sleeps.

Outside, the sky is still black. A breeze blows gently against my face. The flower blossoms lining the courtyard are indistinguishable in the darkness but their fragrance floats in the crisp air. I love this time of day; the rhythm of the *madrugada*, dawn, when the city hasn't begun to pulse and the morning seems to belong to me alone. It's so quiet the calm is palpable. Even the *palomas*, pigeons, are silent.

With the sleeping city beneath me, I sip the thick *café con leche* and look off into the distance at the veiled morning tinted charcoal grey. The street lamps are still on, and they leave pools of pink light along our street. When I finish the coffee I put the cup in the sink and wait by the window. It's nearly six am now and the chiming of the *tamales* vendor's bell tolls like clockwork. I fumble for change in a drawer and race out the door, thundering down the stairs so my footsteps reverberate through all five apartments in our building. I walk along the path to the gate where Roberto, our *portero*, is standing. There, like a sentry, the vendor has also stopped, to sell steaming *tamales* to people who seem to have appeared from nowhere.

A group of men are standing together, talking in loud, throaty voices. I recognise faces. They're here every week-end. The *residentes* – street sweepers, delivery men, taxi drivers. One greets another with a strong handshake. '*¿Qué tal cabrón?*' It's a common salutation among men. How's it going asshole? They warm their hands over the steam coming from the vat of boiling water where the *tamales* bubble away. This *desayuno* or breakfast smells to my untrained nose of fried zucchini, onion and sausages, and is a small square of *maíz*, ground corn wrapped in banana leaves and cooked until it takes on a glutinous consistency. As I get closer the aroma becomes stronger, lingering under my nose. The regulars see me approaching and nod a greeting; their coarse language ceases. They may be rough characters but they dare not swear in front of a woman. It's considered *muy patan*, very crude.

One of the men, knowing I've heard most of his rather colourful dialogue, turns to me.

'*Señorita*, I tell you, if I catch that swearing guy he'll be in big trouble.'

I laugh. When I moved into this apartment complex last

December I was confused by the ringing bell I heard at dawn every morning. I thought I was hearing things. When I asked the *portero* what the noise was, Roberto had smiled and said: 'It's the man selling *tamales*. You should try them, they're delicious.' A week later I did just that. And at first these men ignored me. But after three months, while they never actually converse with me, they *always* say hello. It's not that they're being unfriendly; rather, this is a man's world, and as a woman I'm viewed with suspicion. For me, what's more important is the sense of belonging I feel by way of their acknowledgement.

Now, the *tamales* man greets me with a smile that reveals two lonely teeth in a sea of gums. He is a diminutive man with chocolate-coloured skin, a smooth face and laughing eyes. He's also wearing a big straw hat pushed back to reveal a shock of white hair that makes him look a lot like a New Age Romantic. '*Buen día chiquita. ¿Algo de desayunar?*' Good morning little one, he says – a cheery soul at this ungodly hour. Something for breakfast? I turn to Roberto, who's still standing at the gate. '*¿Quieres?*' He nods. I order four *tamales rojos*.

Roberto comes over and I hand him his breakfast. The only way to eat this meal is with your fingers. We open the banana leaf wrapping and scoop out the *tamal* with thumb and forefinger. It is delicious. Fiery hot in the middle where the *salsa rojo*, red chile sauce, is found. And well worth the few hours of sacrificed sleep. As I eat, Roberto turns to me. '*Bonitas pantuflas,*' he says with a wink. I laugh and nearly choke on a mouthful of corn. Nice slippers. It's now dawn and I realise, rather belatedly, that I'm standing in the street with a group of tough-looking blokes – not that I'm in any danger – wearing fluffy pink slippers. In my rush to get downstairs I hadn't bothered changing them. There's even a Mexican expression to describe how I look: *voy por las tortillas*. I'm going for the tortillas. The equivalent of going to the corner shop for milk wearing your pyjamas.

The apartment is quiet when I go back inside. I tiptoe across the room. There is noise coming from the kitchen and I start. Jean is standing at the bench next to the telephone. I put my hand to my chest and chide him, 'You gave me a fright.'

He looks at me, a bemused expression crossing his face.

'I gave *you* a fright.'

He's got a point. Dishevelled and flushed, I must look quite a sight at this early hour.

I'm self-consciously patting down my hair when he asks me if I've made any plans for the day. 'None,' I reply. He tells me a friend of Sandrine's just called. A colleague from the university, Arturo, who I've met on a number of occasions, has invited us to join his family on an excursion to Valle de Bravo, a beautiful town nestled at the edge of a lake surrounded by luscious hills and known as 'the Switzerland of Mexico'.

At seven-thirty Arturo arrives with his wife, Maribel, and their two children. We pile into their car and drive to the corner of our street, *Sadi Carnot*, where we join a stream of traffic. Although it's only a day trip, I'm still excited. The place we are going is often described as a virtual *paraíso* and I'm eager to see it with my own eyes, to reacquaint myself with nature: clean air, light and green grass – scarce commodities in this city. For me, this spontaneous getaway trip has a special significance. It is a chance to connect with my past, to slot in another piece of the puzzle, because Valle de Bravo, long before it became the playground of the Mexican elite, is where my grandmother comes from. It is where my great-grandmother, Julia Guadaramma, lived in the 1920s.

Arturo explains how the people of this region are known

to live longer than their counterparts in the rest of the country. 'Why?' Sandrine asks. He pauses. '*Hay algo en el aire.*' There's something in the air.

It takes a while to negotiate the city traffic but Arturo is a *chilango*, a Mexico City resident, so he knows what he's doing. We zip in and out of lanes crammed with buses, delivery trucks, taxis and cars. He cruises through red lights – a nuisance rather than a deterrent – and pays no heed to road rules. No-one does. I can see Jean is impressed. I look out the window and it occurs to me that, in all my time here, I've never seen anyone crash. 'Why don't I ever see any crashes?' I ask.

'Oh, there aren't any,' Arturo replies. 'Well, now and then,' he adds. 'But usually it's a *colectivo* that loses a wheel or something driving down the freeway. That's bad. When that happens most of the passengers die.' As a regular *colectivo* traveller, do I need to hear this?

'Are there road rules?' I ask as an afterthought.

'The faster the better,' Arturo beams. Despite the danger, Mexicans – *men*, I should clarify – are passionate drivers. There's even an expression that encapsulates the experience: *hesitate and die.* An inspiring thought if ever there was one.

Finally we are on the *carretera*. The road to Valle de Bravo begins as a two-lane freeway cut through the surrounding mountain, modern and fast-moving, until we come to a point where it becomes a single road that dips and rises steeply. (Apparently the rich residents have lobbied against an upgrade, convinced the tortuous route will keep tourists away.) For the rest of the journey the road winds through ever-changing scenery: imposing pines sprout from the forest on one side; looking out the other side, we gulp at the severe drop to a lush valley below. All the windows are wound down and sweet pine-scented air fills the car. The sun begins to blaze higher in the sky, the midmorning heat as languid and assured as the February days are long.

The landscape is breathtaking and I loll my head out the window, allowing myself to be regenerated by nature. It feels like we have entered another world. This is Mexico in all its glory. Here there is little traffic and, apart from the occasional petrol station, few signs of life. We are just over an hour from the city but a world away from its pace. Trees disappear into the sky and green earth tumbles into the distance like a rolled-out carpet. The beauty of the scenery is almost jarring. Is it the purity of nature that surprises me? Or have I adapted too well to the grey and chaotic streets of Mexico City? I'd felt this way in Cuernavaca a couple of weeks earlier – the rhythm of the countryside throwing me off balance. Of course, I know it won't take me long to get comfortable in this new environment, even if we're only here for one short day. Right now I'm thrilled to swap the gritty reality of life in the *capital* for this heaven on earth.

Three hours after leaving Mexico City, we descend into a valley along a narrow, winding road that leads into the town. Arturo drives slowly so we can take in the *vista*. And then, from behind a dense cluster of trees, the lake comes into view. A deep blue expanse surrounded on all sides by green mountains and hills, the scene could – if not for the absence of a fairytale castle – be plucked straight from a Bavarian landscape. From our vantage point, the town nestled at the water's edge is a cluster of orange roofs set against a lush backdrop. Thick brushstrokes on a canvas, I think.

'*Ya llegamos*,' Arturo says. We've arrived at Valle de Bravo.

We drive to the marina, where we get out and walk the short distance to the dock. I sit on a ledge and listen to the water lapping against this sweeping curved wall of blond stones. There's a view of the gentle lake. Nearby pleasure craft bob lazily. The sky is pastel blue, the air still, and there is not a solitary cloud in sight. I turn my face towards an unseen sun and allow its heat to embrace me like an old friend. Around me other daytrippers from Mexico City are seated at the waterfront cafés, mostly families with broods of children. They drink from tall glasses of *limonada* with wedges of lemon, or battle with rainbow-coloured *gelati* that melts too quickly in the brilliant heat. We choose a nearby restaurant and squeeze under the shade of an umbrella.

It's too hot to eat so I order a *limonada* and turn my chair towards the lake. The heat robs us of conversation and we all sit in silent contemplation, except for the children, who have been made belligerent by the sun. Sandrine pipes up, telling us we cannot swim in the lake because it is full of leeches. We look at her, unconvinced. '*Se lo rujo,*' she says. I swear it. Actually she says *I roar it*, but we know what she means. No swimming today. White birds hover above the water and then veer away again. Behind us the cool streets of the town are waiting to be explored. But for now we are enchanted by this blue oasis, sipping sweet lemonade and nibbling on *grissini* sticks.

Leaving the café, we walk across the *muelle* or wharf towards a stand advertising boat trips around the lake. I'm lingering with Jean and Sandrine in front of a display of photographs of the lake – in full sun, its ghostly beauty on a foggy morning, a twilight scene – when a man's voice interrupts my contemplation. '*Buenos días señorita. ¿Bonito, no?*' Beautiful, isn't it? I look up to see a middle-aged man smiling at me. He is wearing a fisherman's hat and has his gnarled hands clasped in front of him. 'Good morning,' I reply. Having captured my attention, he now makes his pitch.

'A visit to Valle de Bravo isn't complete without a trip

around the lake. You'll be sorry if you don't go,' he says, still smiling. He makes quite a show of raising his arm to point out the lake. 'Just look at that *belleza.*'

The charming man now leans towards me, conspiratorially. 'Tell your friends to think about it,' he says, nodding towards where Jean and Sandrine are standing. 'Oh, you can tell them,' I reply. 'They speak Spanish.' He falters. 'It would sound better coming from you,' he says, still talking through me – the Mexican-looking intermediary. Immediately, I regret my thoughtlessness. The indigenous community are often tentative around white foreigners, a superstition that goes back to Aztec times. When the pale-skinned Spanish *conquistador,* Hernan Cortés, first arrived in Mexico in 1519, the natives mistook him for the Aztec serpent god, Quetzalcóatl, returned from the dead and who, according to legend, was fearsome, imposing and pale, with skin *as white as chalk.* (Many *gente indígena,* indigenous Mexicans, still believe those with white skin possess special powers.)

We chat some more. This total stranger now takes his wallet from his pocket to show me pictures of his children. This immediate intimacy is what I love about Mexican people. Sure, at times it can be a bit too personal: I'm often asked *why aren't you married?* But for the most part I love this friendliness and warmth. He now looks at me with an enigmatic expression and asks, '*Señorita,* you don't talk like a *mexicanita.* Where are you from?'

When I tell him I'm from Australia I inadvertently close the deal. '*Bueno,*' he says emphatically, 'you can't come all the way across the world and miss out on this experience.' His enthusiasm is contagious and we finally agree to take a trip around the lake. I reach for my purse but the man shakes his head; he will not allow me to pay for my ticket. I try to insist but he is firm in his refusal. 'Think of it as a prize,' he says. 'For coming so far.' He then takes both my hands in his, and shakes them. '*Que le vaya bien*,' he says. It's a warm expression, generally used among friends, meaning *go well* or *be well*, and *take care*. I'm touched by this gesture and the concern behind it.

Our entire party is crammed into a *lancha* that is little more than a dinghy. The driver, an affable man named José, starts the engine, and suddenly we are bouncing along the lake. A few minutes later the marina is far behind us. The waterfront is terraced with chalet-style hotels enclosed by iron fences and patrolled by security guards with machine guns. Along the way José points out mansions with palm trees and pristine lawns stretching to the water's edge. Sunbathers dot gardens and luxury yachts are moored at private jetties. 'Who lives in those houses?' Jean asks José. 'Mostly presidents of companies,' he replies.

The beauty of this area is unparalleled and it seems like a perfect spot to set up a home away from home: a sparkling lake surrounded by spectacular cliffs, luscious plants and tropical weather. The problem is, I'm uncomfortable with these ostentatious displays of wealth. These big houses. Shiny cars. It's an 'us and them' paradox, something my grandmother had tried to put into perspective for me when she said *the world is not a fair place*. Indeed it isn't. But here, the disparity is all the more acute. Somehow it seems obscene, this privilege. Especially when I think of the 'other' locals: Indians who live in *casitas* with dirt floors, whose corrugated iron roofs glistened in the sun as we drove past on our way to the village.

But just as I begin to tire of this Mexican version of Millionaires' Row, the *lancha* rounds a rocky outcrop and idles to a stop in front of an inlet of stunning beauty. The small boat putters towards the shore, where the hill rises up in an almost vertical fashion. The sound of gulls on the lake punctuates the air. Because of its isolated location, no-one is around, although yachts bob nearby. Clear water laps against the shore. The *tierra*, earth, covered in dewy moss, surrounds clusters of pines and one enormous tree with drooping leaves like the folds of a ballgown. In the distance we can hear a waterfall. José drops the anchor. 'Let's go for a short walk,' he says. We all jump from the boat and follow our guide as he heads towards a path zigzagging up a steep incline.

This is more like it.

To get to the summit, José leads us uphill, past gnarled boughs and thick undergrowth. After a ten-minute walk the terrain becomes precipitous; the path narrows, we stumble over jutting rocks and hang on to tree roots for balance. 'Everybody okay?' José inquires. 'Just fine,' someone puffs. 'Where are we going?' Sandrine asks me. '*No importa*,' I reply, tasting the pure air. Doesn't matter. I'm in love with this place. Walking along this escarpment, I feel a sense of peace, even though one wrong step could be my last. I think it's the harmony of nature, its purity.

We reach a plateau. Dense foliage parts to reveal a roaring waterfall; foamy water cascades into a lake below. Nearby, elegant-looking birds, possibly egrets, stand with wings outstretched; there's a strong smell of pine and fresh earth. And something that smells a lot like rotten eggs. 'What's that smell?' I ask José. 'Oh, that's sulphur,' he replies. 'The thermal springs are nearby.'

At the library I'd read that this place, formerly known as *Temascaltepec* or Hill of the Hot Baths, was once a native spiritual purification site. But which natives? I wonder if the Aztecs ever came here to purify themselves in the thermal springs. What other tribes were regenerated here? Today we don't have time to visit the springs but there is a sense of purification in this communion with nature. When I read of these rituals I'd imagined a place like this. I stand breathing in the sulphur-scented mountain air and thinking of the tribes of this ancient land. They could have stood on this very spot.

And then with a new burst of energy we are skidding down the path under a canopy of pines, back towards the boat. As I often do in this country, I have the feeling of having stepped back in time. Perhaps it's because so much of my history – and who I am – is tied to Mexico that every new discovery seems astonishing; to experience the mysteries and delights of this eternal country makes me feel so fortunate. I cast one final glance over my shoulder as we climb back into the boat.

In the afternoon we have lunch at an outdoor café near the *muelle*. We are protected from the heat by the adobe buildings and cobblestones in this street that seem to absorb the sun's fierce rays. These narrow laneways or *callejones* that crisscross the town are, to me, the epitome of Mexican charm. From here, I can see the lake glistening at the bottom of the incline. Sitting at a table under an umbrella, we watch people passing by. The street is alive. A man walks a fluffy white dog. Women in sleeveless dresses carry baskets sprouting bouquets of leafy vegetables, or string bags with parcels wrapped in butcher paper that, by their shape, I immediately recognise as a kilo of tortillas. There is a sense of community here. And it is, I realise, because the demographic here is almost entirely Mexican. I like the idea that some places still haven't become part of the international tourist trail. It gives this place an air of normalcy not present in, say, Palenque, where everything from food to souvenirs is designed with the *turista* in mind. Valle de Bravo is Mexico for Mexicans – and a trio of foreigners.

By the time lunch arrives we are all mellow. There are glasses of crisp white wine and strong, dark beer in earthenware mugs. Heavy meals have been ordered, along with the usual accompaniments. *Enchiladas*, *fajitas*, piles of tortillas and sliced avocado, *frijoles*, and *albondigas* for the children. No-one talks during the meal, each intent on their own culinary pleasure. For two hours we sit eating, talking, laughing and drinking. 'I could live here forever,' says Sandrine. We all nod in agreement. The sun is moving across the sky, creating shadows of light and dark on the wall opposite us. Finally Arturo speaks up.

'I think we should go now.'

But I'm not ready to leave. I want to explore this place further, to get a sense of this town where my grandmother spent the early years of her life. It might not be 'walking in her footsteps' as such but it is a chance to see her past with my own eyes. I've barely scratched the surface. In Valle de Bravo at this time of the year there are no crowds, only daytrippers like us. The streets are uncluttered and it seems the perfect opportunity to wander and discover. I have no agenda – except to *be* here just a little longer.

'I'm staying,' I tell them. 'I'll go back tomorrow.'

Arturo, who is now standing, looks horrified.

In Mexico, women rarely travel alone – apart from the intrepid *extranjeras*, foreign women, who travel with only a backpack and a map. Here, it is a fear of the unknown, imbued from an early age, and understandable in this *macho* society: *women need the protection of men*. But my mother – who came from the most traditional of Mexican families – never believed this, and instead instilled in me her adventurous spirit. If I haven't seen much of this country it's not because of fear; my concern is more fiscal – I simply don't have the money. Yet if I'm frugal I can stay the night and have money for a bus back to Mexico City, a *guajalotero*, or turkey bus, so named for the fowl often carried by the locals who travel on it. My mind is made up.

'I'll be fine,' I tell Arturo. Knowing that Mexican men feel an obligation to protect women, regardless of age, ethnicity or any other factors, I reassure him one more time. 'Don't worry about a thing,' I say, trying to lessen the sense of *responsabilidad* I see in his eyes.

By the time the others leave, the sun is beginning to set over the lake. As the car pulls out, Maribel leans out of the window. '*¡Mucho ojo!*' She taps her eyelid. Be careful. The gesture warms me inside. For the second time today I'm touched by somebody's concern. The children screech a noisy goodbye. '*¡Adios Samantita!*' I wave and watch until the car disappears from view.

After standing there for a few minutes, I turn and walk up the street, keeping my eyes open for shingles advertising *hoteles*. All along the street, shopkeepers are lighting the hurricane lamps that hang above doorways. '*Buenas tardes*,' they say as I pass. In the twilight the lamps give the street a soft, romantic glow. I find a modest (cheap!) hotel near the *zócalo*, the main square. Situated at the top of a winding laneway, the Fiesta Hotel commands a view of the lake. The room has seen better, and cleaner, days but it has one major compensation – the view. From my window I see the fading sun move across the tops of the trees lining the hills surrounding the *lago* and, beyond that, the mountains, already blanketed by dusk. I marvel at this lovely sight.

Since it's now too dark to go exploring I decide to have an early dinner. I leave the hotel and return to the *muelle* where earlier I had spotted a floating restaurant. It's six-thirty and way too early for Mexicans to be out for dinner. They won't be out until nine or ten, and then only for the *merienda*, coffee and snacks. As it is I'm the only person in the restaurant. The waiter smiles broadly when he sees me approaching. '*¿Estás sola?*' he asks. Are you alone? '*Si, si,*' I reply. This place is unique: the kitchen and reception are built on terra firma and the area where diners eat is a pontoon at the end of a long gangway. I walk out to a star-filled sky and sit at the table closest to the water.

I order *arroz*, a plate of rice and tortillas. The waiter walks away and I sit and listen to the sloshing of water beneath me. He soon returns with a huge platter of rice. I laugh. 'Is that all for me?' I ask. '*Si señorita. ¿Está bien?*' I'm going to be here a while. He leaves but returns again, this time with the tortillas. '*¿Todo bien?*' Is everything okay? 'Yes, yes,' I reply, but it's only half-true. Even though I chose to stay for the night, suddenly I'm feeling very lonely. As I sit eating slowly, I realise that since I arrived in Mexico, I have barely spent a moment alone. In this country, I'm always surrounded by other people. At our apartment, for example, lunch is a communal affair with at least five people sitting down for the *almuerzo* every afternoon – Jean, Sandrine, Kumi, Elizabeth, myself and other friends who drop in regularly. It's lunch Mexican-style: casual, no invitation necessary and as much food as you can eat. I've taken it for granted, this company, this way of life.

I suspect, however, my feelings tonight, the shock of finding myself without a companion, have more to do with *aloneness* than loneliness. But I do not want to give in to these emotions; it would seem wholly ungracious given my beautiful surrounds. *Enjoy the moment*, I tell myself. To combat my melancholy I ask for my favourite drink: a *margarita*. It is so good I end up having another.

Now I'm warm and happy and slightly tipsy. I order a *café de olla* to finish. When I get up I'm not sure if it's me swaying or the motion of the current moving the pontoon. As I pay the bill, the waiter says, 'If you like, I would be most happy to walk you back to your hotel.' This is not a come-on. On many occasions I've seen men – and not just the young ones – *run* across a room to open a door for a woman, or throw a jacket over a puddle just like in the old movies; others have carried my groceries and helped me from the bus. When it comes to chivalry, Mexican men have no equal. 'Thank you, but I'll be fine,' I say to the kind waiter. The offer does, however, earn him a larger tip.

It is only eight o'clock and the streets are deserted. The Mexican version of the Italian *passeggiata*, the late-evening stroll, won't begin for another hour at least. Perhaps later I'll come out for chocolate ice cream or one last *café*. I climb the hill to my hotel and fumble with the keys to the heavy gate before stepping inside. Back in the room I open the curtains and look out at the panorama; in the distance I can see the lights of the houses on the other side of the lake. I don't go out again because, still giddy from the *cocteles*, I lie down for a short nap, and pretty soon I'm fast asleep.

I wake as the first light of day fills the room. For a while I sit on the bed and look out the window. The pane is framed by condensation which evaporates slowly to reveal a view of foggy beauty. Below me, the sun rises over the lake. Motor boats create wakes of violent foam as they speed from the marina. A crusty man is unmooring a boat; he throws an anchor line to the skipper, but with too much force, and he almost topples into the water. Now more people begin to appear. I decide to get out there too. I dress quickly and leave the room, eager to be part of the unfolding day.

Outside, there is an invigorating chill in the air. My breath forms clouds of steam when I breathe out. Across the lawn, sheafs of hydrangeas are dewy and fragrant. I'm taking big gulps of the sweet aroma when a voice startles me.

'*¡Señorita!*'

I look up to see the owner of the hotel, an elderly American woman, waving at me from a balcony three floors up. The balustrade is covered in brilliant blooms of pink hibiscus so I can only see her head and shoulders, which seem to be growing from the blossoms. She invites me to join her for breakfast. But how do I get from down here, among the greenery, to up there? Reading my dubious expression, she gives me directions.

'Head towards the front gate and you'll find a narrow staircase. Follow it up.'

I follow her directions to no avail. Three times I retrace my steps and, just as I'm ready to take myself off for breakfast in town, I see the aforementioned staircase hidden behind a dense cluster of foliage. I climb the spiral stairs, looking out at the misty landscape, slightly awed by this place – the beautiful view, the smells of nature and the invigorating morning. All mine. A private pleasure. The woman is setting tables when I arrive at the *azotea*, the rooftop café.

'Ah, I was wondering where you got to.'

The terrace is enclosed by a vine-covered arbour dripping with purple oleander. I sit at a table near the edge of the balcony, where the building meets the sky. It's like eating breakfast at the top of the world. It has just turned six am and the day is already brilliant. Since I'm the only person here, the woman fusses over me. Would I like my coffee in a *jarra* (a clay mug) or a cup? Continental or Mexican breakfast? Mexican, of course. After ordering, I begin to chat with her, but she seems unsure which language to use with me. Eventually we settle on a *mezcla* of Spanish and English. Or, as it happens, she speaks English and I answer in Spanish.

She tells me she has lived here for twenty years and has no plans to return to America.

'Don't you miss home?' I ask.

'Yes, sometimes,' she replies. 'But I've been away so long it now seems like somebody else's life. And I've changed too . . . I don't know if I would fit in any more.'

'Will you ever go back?'

She smiles. 'How could I ever leave that?' she says, throwing her arm out in an arc towards the horizon. It is beautiful, but I can't help wondering if it isn't too much of a good thing, this place so close to perfection. I think after a week or so I might just start to yearn for the clamour and *vida* or life of Mexico City. Still, who am I to say that what doesn't suit me cannot be another person's paradise?

After ten minutes she brings me a plate of papaya, pastries, coffee and two hard-boiled eggs. These are a novelty. Eggs! I can't remember the last time I ate them. I'm not averse to eggs, it's just that beans and *bolillos*, or else *tamales*, have become my breakfast staple. They are my preferred choice. My soul food. I tap open an egg and scoop out the soft, delicious centre. Tearing apart a *concha*, I dip it into the runny *huevos*. The combination of sweet pastry with eggs seems odd, but on a morning like this, with a breeze blowing magically around me, it is just right.

A peacock alights from its perch on the balcony railing and lands at my feet. I throw a few crumbs and it happily pecks at them, oblivious of me and the woman approaching with a pot of coffee. She fills my cup slowly, chatting all the while. Figuring she is familiar with some of the history and the people of this town, I ask her about a matter that has special significance to me. Fragments of the past. I recall my grandmother telling me she has a cousin who owns a store in the town. *Of course, she's old now*, she had added, with a sly smirk.

'You wouldn't be able to tell me if there are any Guadarammas still in the area?'

The woman thinks for a while.

'You know, I'm sure there's a Guadaramma shop in one of the streets near the plaza.'

'I'll check it out,' I say, thanking her as I rise from the table. I can look for this *tienda Guadaramma* while I explore.

I leave the hotel and walk along the cobblestones, washed clean and glistening in the early-morning sun. Along both sides of the street, roller doors are coming up. Businesses are opening for the day. I glance into a shop selling handpainted clay wind chimes. I spot a lovely creation hanging in the doorway: chimes shaped like big-bottomed *mariachis*, complete with *guitarras*.

In the shop next door, a man is intent on sculpting a lantern. I linger inside the door and watch as he cuts diamond patterns into the clay with an ancient-looking instrument. The lanterns are painted in splashes of pastel blue, white and pink. I'd love to buy one but I don't have the money – or a house for that matter. Just then a tourist enters. 'How much is that?' he asks the woman behind the counter – in English. He points at a lantern near the door. But of course she doesn't understand him. The man becomes annoyed. 'How much is that?' he shouts. I want him to shut up. But the woman isn't bothered. She smiles and turns to me, amused. '*¿Por qué me grita?*' Why is he yelling at me? The man huffs out of the shop. *And stay out!* I want to scream at him. I'm often taken aback by the arrogance of some tourists. A shopkeeper who does not speak English! Oh, the outrage. The term 'armchair traveller' springs to mind. Some people really should stay at home.

When I arrive at the plaza, I stop to look around. The dusty main square is dominated by the St Francis of Assisi Cathedral. Like most places in Mexico, no matter how small, it is the focal point of the town – it seems enormous for a village as small as Valle de Bravo – and I watch as old, stooped women shuffle towards the entrance, devotional candles in hand to light their *veladoras*, blessings, for their loved ones. Lingering on the steps of the square, the air redolent with the smell of moist, fertile earth floating down from the mountains above, I take a deep breath before setting out to explore the streets.

As I look at the streets that climb steeply on both sides of the cathedral, I feel once again as though I've entered another world: a fairytale place that isn't quite real. I recall a trip I once took to another place frozen in time. The walled town of Rothenberg in West Germany, with its gingerbread houses and cobbled lanes unchanged since the sixteenth century, was so surreal I had to remind myself I wasn't dreaming. I feel the same in this place. I'm half-expecting to turn around and see a man in turn-of-the-century dress amble past on a donkey. Here, I can breathe in the essence of the past.

At the back of my mind is my desire to find the mysterious *tienda Guadaramma* but, since there's no sign of it, instead I leave the *centro* and walk up the hill to the very top, where there is a spectacular view of the surrounding countryside. I stop at a shaded lane high above the town and sit on a cool stone step. From here I can literally see forever. Walking the meandering route back to the plaza, I head in and out of hole-in-the-wall shops, bazaars, boutiques, galleries and bustling markets. Everything is for sale: *fruta y verduras* (fruit and vegetables), leather shoes, more lanterns and handglazed ceramics, delicate lace fabrics known as *deshilados*, and also earthenware pottery.

I can't resist splurging in a shop selling pottery, not wanting to return to Mexico City empty-handed. Along the shelves are all manner of *cazuelas*: plates, cups, jars, casserole dishes and pots for cooking beans, stews and sauces, and smaller ones for boiling milk and coffee. I recognise the function of each by its unique shape – my grandmother has an impressive collection of *cazuelas* and I've taken the time to learn what's what. A milk urn with handles, painted with elegant blue swirls, catches my attention. I end up buying two from the *mercadero*, one for me and the other for my grandmother. As he wraps them in newspaper he offers me cooking advice.

'Boil the milk over a low flame,' he says.

'With a dash of vanilla,' I add.

He looks impressed but I explain I'm merely repeating my grandmother's tips for perfect *leche hervido*, boiled milk. She's the expert. I've seen the mountains of *cazuelas* stacked on her kitchen shelves and, rather than regale her with tales of my visit to this place, I want to take her something tangible.

For the next two hours I walk up and down the streets of Valle de Bravo, passing open doorways with people sitting on the stoop, and under washing strung between windows on either side of the street – billowing *sábanas*, bedsheets, bleached brilliant white by the sun. Old women in sleeveless dresses and floral aprons call out to each other now and then, their rich voices filling the air. Dogs laze in the sun. I feel like joining them. Having given up on my search for the *tienda Guadaramma*, I plonk down on a bench to catch my breath.

After a moment, I look up. Sometimes discoveries come to us quite by accident. Here is the shop I was looking for, right in front of me. Perhaps I was meant to find it. Or it found me? Across the street, a convenience store, the Mexican version of the milk bar, is painted pastel pink, with wobbly black lettering above the door: *Tienda Guadaramma*. What do you know? And I begin to laugh. It's closed! What would I have found in there? The old cousin Guadaramma? I would have loved to say hello. Still, I'm satisfied. It is enough to know my grandmother once walked these streets, breathed this air, lived here. In this magical place.

I get up and step from the narrow footpath, crossing the street. I walk over to the shop that bears my grandmother's maiden name and gently put the *cazuelas* on the ground before pressing my cheek and both palms to the pink wall. Standing completely still and quiet, I rest for a moment against the building before moving away.

As I leave Valle de Bravo, walking towards the bus station, I pass the *panaderias,* where the smell of fresh bread and pastries seems to follow me down the street. I turn for one last look at the town nestled at the base of a mountain. Soon I've reached the station and I sit down on the steps outside to wait for the midday bus that will take me back to Mexico City.

Chapter Fifteen

Cooking for Beginners

In the foyer of my grandmother's building, the light coming through the open door is bouncing off the white floor tiles. It blinds me momentarily so that when my grandmother's neighbour, doña Esperanza, appears in the hallway, she looks almost celestial. I squint.

'Hello daughter,' she says, swimming into focus. She is wearing a sleeveless dress and an apron with a big pocket at the front. A tiny, stooped and pale woman of about seventy-five, with kind eyes, she reminds me a lot of my grandmother.

'*Buenas tardes,*' I reply.

'*¿Espérame tantito?*' she asks.

I wait at the foot of the stairs while she disappears inside her apartment. A moment later she returns, holding a foil-covered plate. She is looking at me and smiling. I smile back.

'Please, little one, take this to your grandmother.' And she hands me the plate.

Climbing the stairs slowly, I peek under the foil. It's chocolate cake – the enemy of the diabetic. What am I going to do? There's nowhere to stash it, and anyway, Esperanza would be asking my grandmother if she enjoyed the cake. I'm aware that if I give her this cake I'm contributing to her diabetes. I know she eats sweet things. In old age, she is defying the doctors. 'When they reach my age, *then* they can tell me what to do,' she often says. My only other option is to hide it in my backpack, but the *cazuela* I bought the other day is already in there. No room. I reach her apartment and stop on the landing. While I'm dithering she opens the door and sees me with the cake.

'Is that cake?' she asks.

'Uh,' I reply. I've been caught red-handed. 'Yes . . . it's from doña Esperanza.'

I can't win this battle. For months I have been hearing: 'What do those doctors know? Nothing, I tell you. You don't tell me what to eat, child, you're not even thirty – you can't have an opinion yet. I need sugar for energy. It's good for me. Just this piece here on the end. One piece won't do me any harm.'

I give her the plate.

'Well, we better eat it then.'

I take a seat at the dining table as she heads into the kitchen for a knife to cut the cake. When she comes back I've already pulled the *cazuela* from my bag.

'What have you got there?' My grandmother is eyeing the newspaper-wrapped parcel I'm cradling in my arms.

'It's something you'll like,' I reply, although I'm not sure if the gift I've hauled all the way from Valle de Bravo is still in one piece. I put the package on the table and watch as she lovingly runs her hands over it, before tearing aside the paper in one swift move. Her face splits into a delighted grin. The enormous *cazuela* I bought is a great hit.

'I love it,' she says, holding it up for inspection. 'Good clay makes all the difference.'

My grandmother disappears into the kitchen, telling me the dish has to be *curado* – cured for cooking – so it doesn't crack when you place it on the stove. I follow her and stand in the doorway, watching as she gently places it in the sink. On the bench nearby is an array of spices arranged in neat mounds. Earthy-coloured *hierbas*: brown and green and black and ochre. From the look of them, ingredients for *mole verde*, but I can't be sure. The thousands of varieties of herbs, the essence of Mexican cooking, are still unfamiliar to me. My grandma, however, can not only tell you their names and uses, but also how to slowly poison someone without leaving a trace. Women in this country have been practising this technique on abusive husbands for centuries; it doesn't kill them but merely renders them docile and dim after a few years.

Along the shelves next to the stove, more *cazuelas*. There has to be at least fifty of them. Every variation of size and shape. In Mexico, the dish is often as important as what you put in it. *La comida sabe mejor cocido en barro* – food tastes better cooked in a clay pot – is a common refrain. From the stove, my grandmother sees me studying the herbs on the bench.

'Is your recipe for *mole verde* a secret?' I ask. I'd love to know what goes on in this kitchen. 'It certainly looks like it.'

She laughs and turns back to the hotplate, where the base of the *cazuela* has turned black to signify it's now safe to use. I am left to ponder the mystery *ingredientes* before me.

The fact that I'm fascinated by herbs and can happily spend an hour choosing a good earthenware dish seems to suggest a significant change has occurred within me. Before arriving in Mexico, I hardly ever considered the importance of food, let alone the merits of anything other than a good can opener. For many years I lived on chocolate biscuits and coffee, ignoring the terrible stomach aches that plagued me as a result of my appalling eating habits. I was often guilty of eating a packet of Twisties for dinner while staring into an empty refrigerator. My mother went as far as buying me simple cookbooks to encourage an interest in cooking and, as a result, healthy eating. The recipe books, dubiously named *Cooking for Beginners* and *Introduction to the Kitchen*, gathered dust because I scorned the kitchen.

But Mexico has changed me.

The passion for food, an abundance of fresh produce from the marketplace, and the belief among Mexican people that eating is not just a physical necessity but one of life's great pleasures – *el sabor de vida*, the flavour of life – makes me believe that my transformation would have happened eventually, regardless of my apparent indifference. In fact, it would be almost impossible to resist change after taking a bite of a freshly sliced papaya drizzled with lime. Oranges here are sweet beyond compare. *Hongos*, wild mushrooms, sautéed with a little butter, are extraordinary.

Only last night I cooked a *consome de arroz*, rice soup, from the meagre ingredients in the kitchen: one onion, a lime and a cup of rice. Hovering over my bubbling *cazuela*, I tasted and added a pinch of salt, a dash of pepper, until the flavour was just right. Jean and Sandrine swallowed mouthfuls of the *sopa* and then stopped to look at me. 'This is delicious,' they said in unison. And it was. But I am no extraordinary cook. My grandma takes that honour. Indeed, *lucky* might be a better description for me. And, let's face it, I still don't know how to kill a man armed only with a handful of coriander!

For the women of my family, cooking is an inheritance. My grandmother inherited her mother Julia's skill, and in the evenings her neighbours, from doctors and lawyers to *albañiles*, tradesmen, would knock at the door and humbly ask, '*¿Señora Rodríguez, me puedes hacer unos sopitos?*' Can you make me some *sopes*? My mother had never even been in a kitchen before she married – it was my grandmother's domain and out of bounds to all but her – yet somehow she knew how to create a delicious lentil soup, roast potatoes, *pollo al horno*, oven-roasted chicken, and the perfect chocolate cake. And I have learned too. It is as if skills and *entendimiento*, understanding, have come to me by osmosis. A friend calls to tell me she saw the Mexican love-and-cooking movie, *Like Water for Chocolate*, and now she never cooks when angry because she does not want to pass her anger into the food and make it bitter.

My grandmother, who never finished primary school because of the Mexican Revolution, cannot write but has the ability to remember at least three hundred recipes on account of her extraordinary memory. These *recetas* are carefully guarded secrets, and rightfully so, but by stealth – asking when she is tired! – I've managed to acquire a handful. When I ask her about secrets to success, she always replies, with a slight smile, 'If you cook with love, you can't go wrong.'

And what to make of this new passion for food, I can only come to one conclusion: this is meant to be.

Chapter Sixteen

In Search of El Dorado

A week after returning from Valle de Bravo, I'm standing outside Atzcapotzalco station, on the north-western outskirts of Mexico City. Heat shimmers off the tin roofs of the food stalls and the air is still. Above me a few puffs of fairy floss cloud float across the clear sky. I'm daydreaming on the footpath when a stray dog begins to lick my hand. Nearby, a beggar is asleep, his chest rising and falling in time with the whistling snores emanating from under the blanket.

The footpath is crowded with people entering and leaving the station. The factory across the road has broken windows and graffiti on the wall that says *I love Ricky*. I've come to Atzcapotzalco because one of the consequences of my weekend away is a rekindling of my desire to ingratiate myself with the places I have a personal connection to. Of course, here I don't expect charming cobbled streets like those of Valle de Bravo, or an oasis of beauty. Rather, I want to delve into the real city beyond the tourist attractions. And although on the surface Atzcapotzalco might seem like any run-down suburb in Mexico City, it is much more than that. For me, it has one particular distinction: this is the neighbourhood where my mother grew up.

As a child my mother regaled me with stories of her extended family, all living together on an enormous *hacienda*, a homestead in Atzcapotzalco. Here, the Rodríguez made their living from farming and related industries, earning a fortune from livestock, produce – primarily beef and milk – and horsebreaking. The *familia* once owned vast tracts of land in this area where my mother spent the first twenty years of her life. But even though the large, successful family, and the farms for that matter, have long gone, being here feels *right*.

I came here during my first visit in 1996, when I was appalled by the pollution and poverty of Mexico City. I'd caught the train to a friend's place but got off at the wrong stop – Atzcapotzalco. I took one cursory look around and went back inside the station. It has taken a while but I've finally returned. On a deeper level, I think this new vigour comes from the realisation that time is running out; my visa expires at the end of April and I want to see as much of Mexico City as possible, *before it is too late*.

After leaving the station, I walk along the derelict streets. I'm unfamiliar with the area but I resisted the temptation to bring my *Mexico City: A to Z*. Atzcapotzalco might be part of the mesh of my history but it also signals adventure. I want to explore without marking out places of interest on a map; having a plan often takes away the excitement of the unknown. By the time I've walked one block I'm perspiring in the heat. I stop to catch my breath outside a *tienda*, a corner store, before walking inside to ask for directions to

Calle Claveria. It is my only fixed destination: my mother's old street. I know two things about this *calle*: it was wide and leafy, and it's around here somewhere!

The shopkeeper is an elderly man with a kind face and thick spectacles. Now that I'm standing in front of him, he squints through his glasses, and for a moment he looks just like Mole from *The Wind in the Willows*. When I ask him about *Calle Claveria* he winces and shakes his head in a gesture that could be a yes or a no.

'I haven't heard of that street. Are you sure it's in Atzcapotzalco?'

'Yes,' I reply. 'At least it was fifty years ago.'

The man may be old but his humour is still sharp. 'You carry your age well,' he says.

I laugh. His reply is deadpan, his wit so dry it crackles. Like most Mexicans, his face is etched with laugh lines. Perhaps it's a way of dealing with the hardship of life in this country, but it seems people here have an innate understanding of the need for humour. We now get back to business.

'Well, miss, I can't be sure. Wait here and I'll just check with my wife, she might know.' He disappears around a corner and I wait for him to return. When he comes back he proceeds to give me directions that sound like the way to *El Dorado*, the city of lost gold. I listen intently but my head is starting to swim with directions and I'm too embarrassed to admit that I lost the trail after the first left at the end of the street. Instead, I nod.

'*Mucho ojo*,' he says, and smiles. 'Keep your eyes open.'

I thank him and walk into the street.

It's dusty, hot and frantic. At the traffic lights I watch streams of cars speed past. I pass an empty lot where I spy many pairs of eyes watching me – dozens of stray cats peeking from behind tall clusters of grass. A couple come out to rub against my legs. In doorways, men in straw hats are smoking and chatting. Others have set up card tables on the footpath and are playing poker and dominoes. Women are also sitting outside, clustered together on plastic chairs, shelling *canastas*, baskets of beans, talking, laughing, sewing. The streets pound to the rhythmic thud of music coming from hotted-up cars (the passion of the Mexican man), the clanging of the rubbish vendors' bell and the call of a juice seller on the corner who's advertising *jugos* made with fresh oranges and papaya.

Atzcapotzalco is a seedy place but, even so, this area is teeming with energy and vibrancy. I'd seen a report on the evening news describing this suburb as being among the top ten danger spots in Mexico City but, if indeed this is true, it seems nobody bothered to tell the people who live here. They are relaxed and incredibly friendly. A man on a stoop looks up and wishes me *buenas tardes*. When I pass an open doorway, the woman inside stops sweeping with her broom and gives me a smile. More than anything, in the faces of the women shouting to each other from across the street or the old men savouring *tacos* outside a hole-in-the-wall restaurant, is the sense of community and life. The neighbourhood is thriving.

Wandering around the streets, however, I see the same scenes of poverty you can find most places in Mexico City: beggars asleep on the footpath; tin shacks in empty lots where blackened coals from campfires still smoulder. High above the petrol stations, the ubiquitous billboards advertise Avantel mobile phones and Palacio de Hierro, an exclusive department store. The days when Atzcapotzalco was tranquil farmland, where children played with chameleons picked from trees, are long gone. I doubt my mother would recognise her home town now.

After stopping again, this time for a *refresco*, a soft drink, I keep walking. From the main *avenida*, according to the myopic shopkeeper, another major thoroughfare leads to Claveria, the street I'm looking for. The problem is, I can't tell one road from another. I'm unable to distinguish between roads and other important geographical landmarks. Everything seems to look the same because of the uniformity of the grey concrete buildings that dot the city.

Still, as nice as it would be to find my mother's old street, it's not imperative. (I find out later the entire area was converted into factory space years ago.) Instead I decide to wander along the skinny streets. Even in this mad-dog heat it's still good to explore. For the next hour I just walk. I end up in a residential area away from the major roads. It's quiet along these narrow streets. Even the car horns in the distance sound muted. The streets are almost empty. Where is everyone? Of course, I realise, these are the hours of the *almuerzo* and everyone is inside having lunch. Now the lure of hunger stirs me to return to the station. I'll just have to retrace my steps.

With so many wrong turns, it takes me until late afternoon to reach my destination. At one point I turn into a street and spy a small park with concrete benches and skinny poplar trees. Here, on a patchy grass embankment, I sit down to catch my breath, leaning against a small ledge surrounding an empty pond. It is cool under the shade of the poplars. Above me sparrows hop among the branches of a lone cherry tree in blossom. On a bench nearby, two girls are talking and laughing; they smile at me when they see me approaching.

As I sit alone, resting, I can't help overhearing their conversation.

'Vicente's having an affair with Perla's sister,' one says to the other.

'*¿Qué?*' screeches the other.

I can't believe what I'm hearing. I've exchanged the spiritual pleasures of nature and solitude for more titillating subject matter. But I don't dare move because then it would seem obvious that I've heard everything they've said. I have to wait for a more opportune moment.

'And you won't believe what Perla did to him when she found out,' she adds.

What? At this point I'm tempted to turn around too. The girl who dropped this bombshell is now talking about something else but her friend won't give up the thread of the conversation.

'For all the saints in heaven! Tell me what happened to Vicente.'

Oh God, I think, just tell us.

'I'm not telling!' she teases, and they fall about laughing on the bench, which gives me the opportunity I need to move away, not wanting to eavesdrop any longer. My questions will remain unanswered. Who's Perla? How could her sister do such a thing? And what happened to Vicente? After a few minutes I realise as I walk that the girls in the park were talking about the soap opera, *La Perla* (The Pearl). Another fabulous melodramatic *telenovela* where your lover is actually your half-brother who was presumed dead after trying to save the family's prize thoroughbred from a suspicious blaze in the stables.

The rest perks me up. I walk to the end of the street, where a woman on a balcony waves. Around the corner, nestled in the middle of another narrow street, is a railway line that seems to have appeared from nowhere. A metal barrier, painted barbershop red and white, signals the end of the line. What's more amazing is that someone has tied a rope to the barrier, and at the end of it a cow is chewing its cud. It blinks in the sun, utterly content. Is it someone's pet? Cars cruise past, their drivers unfazed by the bovine blocking the road. Perhaps it's just an example of how the people of this city still hold fast to rural traditions; at the core of this sprawling metropolis, there is still a charming, country heart.

Atzcapotzalco seems magical on this stifling March afternoon. I shouldn't have been so quick to judge this place by first appearances. This morning I'd stood outside the train station, disappointed by what I saw. But no sooner had I decried the neglect and the grey sameness of the streets than I came across these quaint *calles*: planter boxes filled with hydrangeas, blooms of pink, the luminous sky, a big, happy cow, and a man asleep under a straw hat. These are the paradoxes that make Mexico City so fascinating: you just never know what to expect. And the very act of coming to Atzcapotzalco has deepened my sense of belonging. It is as though by seeing where my mother comes from, I have shared something very important with her, even though she's not physically here. The ties that bind. And somehow I have made it mine too. I'm standing in this place of my history.

When I return to the apartment in the early evening, my flatmates and their friend Jaime are all sitting in the lounge room talking and watching television. I sit down and fill them in on my afternoon in Atzcapotzalco. Jaime – he's actually a James but nobody could pronounce that name so he was given the Spanish equivalent – is a pale, blue-eyed American who lives in Mexico City with his Mexican wife, Isabel, who attends business college with Jean. He listens intently to my story.

'I can't believe you went there by yourself,' he says.

'*Estuvo bien*,' I reply, a tad defensively. It was okay.

But for James, it is definitely not okay. And he has good reason for concern. As an executive chef at the Hotel Nikko – an expensive hotel in Polanco – he often has to go to Atzcapotzalco to visit wholesale *carniceros*, butchers, to buy meat for the restaurant. He tells me, 'I've been going there for six months and they have robbed me six times.' He doesn't say who *they* are but it is something that doesn't need explanation. Almost without exception, it's the *pandillas*, gangs of men driving around in taxis, cruising for targets. The taxis are regulation green and white Volkswagens, but the driver is unlicensed (the Department of Transport estimates that only forty per cent of Mexico City's drivers own a driver's licence). The passenger is then driven to an unfamiliar location where the rest of the gang are waiting; their usual method of robbery is to drive the person to ATM machines all over the city, where their bank account is emptied.

Seeing that I'm genuinely troubled, he smiles and says, 'But they never hurt me. Not once.'

'These things happen,' he adds by way of understatement, and suddenly it is quiet in the room as we all look at him in amazement, not in an unbelieving way but as though it has just occurred to us how fortunate we all have been during our time here. (When I later relate this story to my friend Elizabeth she doesn't even blink. '*Uff,*' she says dismissively, 'my father has been robbed seventeen times.') But there's an odd twist to James's misfortune, because it appears the *ladrones*, the robbers, aren't interested in the contents of his wallet – far from it. They have their eyes on something else.

'They only ever want my watch,' he says. 'Well, actually, once they took my sneakers.'

'What did you do?' Jean asks.

He looks at us and replies with a smirk, 'I walked home in my socks.'

We drink beers in the lounge room and discuss this strange dilemma. James scratches his chin as though he can't quite comprehend his situation. I make a suggestion.

'Why wear a watch then?'

The effect of this question, which is dictated solely by common sense (or so I think), is amusing. James looks at me like an *araña fumigaga*, a fumigated spider: mouth wide open and stunned. After a short pause, he replies.

'How else will I tell the time?'

'Oh,' I reply.

In the morning the phone rings early. When I shuffle into the kitchen, Jean tells me we've been invited away again by the same friends who took us to Valle de Bravo the previous weekend. This time our destination is Tepoztlan, a town not far from Mexico City which is the supposed birthplace of the Aztec serpent god Quetzalcóatl, and home of the ruins of the Aztec pyramid Tepozteco. New-age travellers gather here every full moon in the hope of seeing *ovnis*, alien spaceships rumoured to land there. Apparently sightings go back to before the arrival of the *conquistadores*. I'm happy to be invited and excited by the prospect of visiting such a legendary place. I had been planning to spend today studying for the exam, which is now only a few weeks away, but what the hell. It can wait. Tomorrow I'll go to the library and stay there *all* day.

An hour later, the car pulls up at the gate and pretty soon we are speeding through the outskirts of Mexico City. We pass a collection of ramshackle buildings painted in bright colours: lavender, fuchsia pink, yellow, green, baby blue. There are billboards, fast food outlets, flower vendors and a million sets of traffic lights that, by way of good fortune, are all green. After an hour we climb the mountains south of the city and pass under the 'Thank you for visiting Mexico City' sign.

On the other side of the valley the landscape is dusty and sparse. It's an amazing contrast with Mexico City. Here there are more cacti than people. After another half an hour the landscape changes again. There are less cars. Pickups drive past, blocks of hay stacked in the back; dogs wobble atop pyramids of straw. We drive through a palette of ochre earth until the road begins to undulate and pine trees sprout from the roadside. Ah, nature. The world seems fresh, clean and perfect.

En route to Tepoztlan, Arturo suggests stopping for something to eat. The road is rimmed with clusters of *puestos*, roadside food stalls, and we pick one at random. A wooden shack, with four rickety posts holding up a thatched roof, has a few wooden tables and benches inside and light streams through gaps in the grass canopy. There are no adornments here, just a blackboard out the front that stands askew, advertising, in thick chalk letters, real Mexican fare: *tortillas azules*, tortillas made from blue corn; *nopales*, strips of cactus; *sincronizadas*, tortillas filled with stringy white cheese and slices of ham; and *pozole*, soup with corn, chokoes and ham.

A man in a singlet who looks to be in his forties is standing out the front of the *puesto* and he beckons us over. '*Paselen*,' he says. Come in. By way of further encouragement he pats his hands on his pot-belly and says, '*¡Rico, rico, rico!*' Yum, yum, yum. His voice is gravelly and he laughs heartily at his own joke. Who can resist such an enticement?

We sit at a long table set with a bright plastic tablecloth, serviettes and small clay dishes full of *chile serrano*. The stall owners remind me of the vendors I see at the market every weekend. Women in sleeveless dresses and aprons pick green-skinned oranges from cane baskets, chopping and squeezing them in 1950s juicers. At the back of the stall men in white singlets stand over steaming hotplates serving slivers of cooked beef into plastic bowls. Wafting in the air is the rich smell of frying onion. As we wait to order, a commotion ensues. The men are yelling at each other –

Mexicans are naturally loud; I've often mistaken a normal conversation for a fierce argument – but it seems there's no need for concern because as I listen I discover the cause of the ruckus. They're discussing a very Australian passion: who gets to be in charge of the barbecue.

This meal can't be called the *almuerzo* because it's too early – it has just turned eleven am. As Arturo now tells me, 'What would Mexicans do if they ate lunch at midday? They'd be starving by three o'clock. You need to give yourself plenty of opportunities to eat *all* day.' To me, this is fine logic. Very soon our 'snacks' arrive. Two enormous bowls of steaming meat, piles of blue-corn tortillas, a saucer of fried *chorizo* and a *cazuela* of green chile sauce.

Jean stabs at a slice of *chorizo* and asks a rhetorical question. 'Can you imagine being a vegetarian in Mexico?' Indeed I can't. There is a furrowing of brows and a murmur of disapproval from all assembled. '*¡Qué horror!*' As it is, the *vegetariano* is viewed with suspicion. '*¿Qué clase de cabrón no come carne?*' my grandmother often says. What kind of asshole doesn't eat meat? On cue, a young girl brings over a plate of deep-fried pork skin. Yum!

I eat the *chicharrón* with its million grams of fat. I know it's risky with my delicate stomach, but I eat it anyway. It is too good to resist. This is a lesson Mexico has taught me: to enjoy life and to do what makes me happy – within reason of course. And what makes me happy is *chicharrón*. I don't want to deny myself these pleasures. Furthermore, what's *un día en el campo*, a day in the country, without this Mexican delicacy?

Nearby, a woman is chopping oranges with a cleaver on a thick wooden cutting board. The knife glints in the sun as she raises it and brings it down with a hollow thud. She's been chopping since we arrived and I watch as she places the orange halves in the juicer, pushes down the handle and flicks the *cáscara*, the skin, into a bin. I'm fascinated by her dexterity. She could do this in her sleep. Then she comes over with a jug and pours orange juice into the tall glasses already on our table.

'*¿Dulce verdad?*' the woman says, wiping her hands on her apron. I smile.

'*Delicioso*,' I reply.

It is a chorus that travels down the table. '*Delicioso*.' And it's true. The food is wonderful. Each ingredient is a complement to the next. Flavours and textures combine to create heavenly *sabores*. Despite claims by Americans that Mexican food is heavy and tasteless, not for a second do I agree. This assertion stems, I think, from a couple of things. Firstly, foreigners attempt to recreate dishes with ingredients that are *regional* to Mexico, and thus don't travel well; the results are inevitably disappointing. And more importantly, many people don't have the patience required to create a dish from scratch: *mole*, for example, can often take up to three days to prepare. I may be biased but I believe the complexity of *la comida mexicana* is what makes it so extraordinary.

After a quick bite, we are back in the car driving along an open road with a clear blue sky above, past fields of grazing cows, towards our destination. On the horizon verdant mountains look as though they have been painted by God himself. The landscape around Tepoztlan is dotted with fields of nopals, a type of cactus that is prolific in these parts. Sparse though it may be, this countryside does have a poetic beauty. As it's still early, we decide we have time to look at the ruins of the Aztec pyramid at Tepozteco. From here it shouldn't be much of a drive to the town, and then only a short distance to the ruins.

And so we set off along a *nopal*-lined route, driving kilometres down a dirt road that looks suspiciously like a wrong turn. After another fifteen minutes of bumping in and out of potholes, Sandrine makes an observation.

'If we are going to the mountains, shouldn't we be heading towards them?'

'*Supongo que si*,' Arturo replies. 'I guess so.'

Sandrine's right. The mountains that loomed so large in the distance now seem to be getting smaller. A map is brought out, consultations are made and the car is turned back in the other direction.

We soon find ourselves bouncing along another unmade road somewhere near Tepoztlan. A few minutes later we come to a village. The streets are lined with adobe huts, small houses with clay walls and thatched roofs. As we drive, I see movement inside the doorless *casitas*, a dog sitting on a step, children playing at the side of the road. We come to a stop outside a hut where two *campesinos*, peasants in white shirts and straw hats, sit in a doorway, chewing on straw. An emaciated dog lies at their feet. Their coppery skin is creased and weather-worn, and their leather sandals covered in red dust. They look as though they've been plucked straight from the pages of *National Geographic*. Arturo winds down the window and leans out.

'*Buen día*,' he says. The men nod. As is common in Mexico when addressing an elder, Arturo now asks for directions to Tepoztlan using the respectful form of 'you', *ústed*. Whereas he would normally begin with a casual 'Can you tell me . . .', he now says, '*Ústed podría ser tan amable a decirme . . .*' It is long-winded but elegant: 'If you would be so kind as to tell me . . .' In a country where the older generation are revered, anything less would seem like *malas modales*, a lack of education.

The men smile back but they do not respond.

'Maybe they didn't hear you properly,' Jean says to Arturo.

'Hmm,' he says, and repeats himself.

As we sit waiting for a reply, I'm struck by a spark of inspiration.

'*Niltze, niltze,*' I say, leaning out the window.

Immediately their faces light up and they burst into rapid-fire conversation in a language I do not understand. '*Niltze,*' I say again, now excited, as though I can hold a conversation with one of the handful of words I know in this ancient tongue: *hello.* They are speaking Náhuatl, the language of the Aztecs. At the time of the Spanish conquest there were over four hundred *lenguas* spoken by the tribes of Mexico, but Náhuatl was the most common. It still is. Nearly all indigenous Mexicans speak two languages, their own dialect, of which there are still over two hundred throughout the country, and the official idiom, Spanish, which was introduced in 1519.

I have been reading about Náhuatl at the library. I understand very little of it but to my ears it sounds poetic: *teponaztle, molcajete, Popocatépetl, Tlamahuizoltica, Nezahualcóyotl, Teponaxcuícatl.* Some of this ancient tongue has even made its way into the English lexicon: *aguacatl* – avocado, *jitomatl* – tomato and *chocolatl* – chocolate. I love the melody of these words and the singsong nature of the language, so similar to Spanish in that respect. But looking at Náhuatl in a book is one thing; these convoluted *palabras* are way beyond my pronunciation abilities. *Tlamahuizoltica.* Sheesh! I wouldn't even know where to begin. Non-indigenous Mexicans also trip over these complex phonetics, so I don't feel too bad. The four words I know by heart – *niltze*, hello; *amo*, no; *cualli*, good, and one word I learned from a book, *potoni*, you smell bad – aren't much use in asking for directions.

Still, I'm elated that with my awkward attempt, I have been able to do what I never thought possible: communicate with a native Mexican in *their* language – albeit in a very,

very limited way, but it's something. Now it is clear why these men didn't respond to Arturo's earlier request – they do not speak Spanish. He asks them again, just to be sure: '¿Ústedes hablan español?' A short pause. This they understand. '*Amo*,' they reply, laughing. No. My other word!

For me, the exchange is a revelation. I feel as though I have stepped into another world, one where the Náhuatl-speaking descendants of the great tribes of Mexico still live alongside the progeny of the Spanish. It is another example of how the past lives in the present. And this endurance pleases me greatly. Perhaps it is because my own family can trace their ancestry back to the Aztecs. When I visited Mexico as a child my grandfather often used to say, 'Look at me, little one. *Soy Azteca.*' Back then I didn't know any of their history. But I can still see his face; a fierce expression, hooked nose, elongated forehead and rich copper skin. When I picture him in my mind, there can be no doubting the veracity of his claim.

As we drive away, the men are still talking and laughing.

'*Cualli, cualli*,' I say. Good. There is a nod of heads that I think may be approval of my attempt to bid them goodbye. I hope so. They say something else and one makes an emphatic hand gesture that could be the much sought after directions to Tepoztlan. We wave and then drive off.

Less than a mile down the road, Arturo turns onto a road that heads to the town. We follow the signs and ten minutes later we arrive in Tepoztlan. It is a *pueblo*, a small town typical of rural Mexico: dusty roads buttressed by whitewashed buildings and overrun with stray dogs and ragged children. The moment the car stops we clamber out, arranging to meet in a couple of hours. Sandrine shepherds me towards the commercial stalls.

'Let's go buy some *cazuelas*,' she says.

I laugh. 'Absolutely,' I reply.

It seems I'm not the only one with a fascination for Mexican pottery. Sandrine shares my love of Mexican handicrafts, but I can't claim to have influenced her in this regard. By the time I moved in with Jean and Sandrine they had been in Mexico for three months and Sandrine had already scoured the *artesanía* markets for *cazuelas*, pottery and ceramics. Our interests are uncannily similar. One weekend at our local market we wandered off separately and went home to show each other our purchases. We each excitedly pulled from its newspaper wadding exactly the same tin-framed mirror.

Along both sides of a narrow street is an awesome proliferation of shops. We pass fruit and vegetable stalls with enormous baskets bursting with squashes, chokoes, red, green and white onions, potatoes, green tomatoes and tall bunches of leafy celery, coriander and parsley. There are also plastic-lined *canastas*, baskets, of *mole* powder, and mounds of spices and herbs, chile and pepper seeds.

There are stalls with ready-prepared food: *tortas*, sandwiches with ham and cheese, stacks of tortillas waiting to be filled with black beans that bubble on an enormous *cazuela* like a witch's cauldron. Long strips of *pan dulce*, sweet bread, and ear-shaped pastries. Everything that is sweet and savoury, cold, hot, spicy and mild – and always delicious. We buy two Cokes and a bag of *nueces*, walnuts coated in caramel. This day is becoming a delightful artery-clogging exercise.

Sandrine and I wander from store to store, looking and lingering. There are handicraft and pottery shops selling *cazuelas* like the ones you find at the *tianguis* – the Indian markets in the city. Papier-mâché birds of paradise hang from doorways. Men in straw hats. A hot breeze hangs in the air, heavy and thick. I fan myself with my *abanico*, a fan that smells of sandalwood. I love the way the heat here slows down life, the *tranquilidad* of the people. A hummingbird hovers over the pink hydrangeas cascading down a wall.

A few minutes later, Sandrine ducks into a pottery store while I wait outside.

'I'll be back in a minute,' she says.

Ten minutes later she still hasn't appeared. 'What's taking so long?' I ask the shopkeeper. '*Vé a verla,*' she says, shaking her head. 'Go and see her. I don't know what she is doing.' Thinking she might not be feeling well, I rush to the back of the shop and find Sandrine sitting on the floor in front of a stack of cups, plates, jugs and tureens. 'Are you all right?' She looks up and smiles. 'I can't decide,' she says. 'I love everything.'

In the end we leave with armfuls of clay mugs, plates, enchilada dishes, and pots for cooking beans and boiling milk. We walk the short distance to the end of the street. Here, rising like a phoenix, is a tall stone wall painted stucco and egg cream. In the middle of this structure is a beautiful iron gate. I push against it and to my surprise it springs open. Sandrine's eyes widen and she turns to me, '*¿Atreve-mos?*' she says. Do we dare? '*Ándale.*' We climb three worn stone steps that lead to an overgrown path. Gnarled bougainvillea trees bursting with foliage form a canopy over the path and thickets of shrubs carpet the ground. I feel like we have entered Miss Havisham's neglected garden and at any moment we'll spy Estella peering from behind a tree.

Suddenly the path comes to an end in front of what might possibly be the most beautiful church I've ever seen. It's the same egg cream colour as the wall out front. All vaulted arches, spires and colonnades. A monument of stone and light.

'*¡Qué barbaridad!*' Sandrine says. That's incredible! And she's right. It is a breathtaking kind of place.

'Let's have a look inside,' I say.

As we approach the entrance, Sandrine stops in her tracks. A group of people are standing in the doorway. A wedding, *una boda*, is about to take place. On the threshold is a bride dressed – *swathed* – in layers of white satin. She must be roasting in this heat. We linger near the entrance.

A middle-aged man in a suit approaches. He has dark skin and expressive eyes and reminds me a lot of the *tamales* man who cycles past my apartment building every morning and who, like this man, looks to be of indigenous descent.

'*Bienvenidos*,' he says, smiling. Welcome. He invites us to enter the church, waving his hand in front of him in a sweeping motion. 'Please go in. You're most welcome to join us on our happy day.'

The pews are already full, so we take a seat at the back, feeling like clods in our jeans and T-shirts. All around us are women dressed in two-piece skirt suits and oversized hats. Little boys fidget in navy slacks, crisp shirts and patent leather shoes. From where we sit we see the bride's mother fussing with her daughter's veil. The poor girl must be ready to croak under the ten layers of tulle she's carting around. The congregation are now getting restless as they fan themselves with their programs. The heat is stifling.

'I don't believe it!' Sandrine suddenly exclaims.

'What?'

I turn to where she is pointing and see a group of *mariachis* walking – well they're kind of charging – up the aisle, decked out in white suits and skinny black ties and playing violins, trumpets and guitars. They are singing a *bolero*, a love song, and seem to be playing a game of musical 'race you to the end'. There is a singer but he has been drowned out by a soaring melody of sound that is *almost* in time. They are a particularly bad bunch of musicians but it doesn't matter – they mean well.

Sandrine speaks again.

'*Mariachis* at a wedding?'

'Oh yes,' I reply with a grin. 'What's a wedding without *mariachis*?'

Actually I've never been to a wedding in Mexico so I have no idea what goes on, but having these traditional musicians as a preamble to the bride's entrance seems only natural: music that in its *esencia* is a celebration of life at one of life's great celebrations. It makes perfect sense. The musicians are singing, 'I celebrate the day you arrived in my life, my beautiful white dove,' as the bride walks up the aisle. When she arrives at the altar they reach a crescendo: 'For you I will reach up and bring down a handful of stars.' The bride and groom are glowing. Everyone is smiling. Grannies dab at their eyes with embroidered handkerchiefs. What are they thinking, these other guests? Are they thinking of their own wedding days? Other happy days? The romance of it all tempts me to get up and shout, '*¡Bravo, bravo!*'

Before we step back into the garden, I stop in the nave to get one last look at the church. The act of entering a church always leaves me with a great sense of peace. It is something I have difficulty putting into words and if I were to attempt it I would say it *feels* like what Vivaldi's *Four Seasons sounds* like: pure bliss. I used to think it was just the familiarity of my Catholic upbringing, but now I see it is a communion with the creator – in this place, with its leadlight windows creating coloured prisms of light on the stone floor, the flickering devotional candles, an austere altar, in this loveliest of churches, I feel the strongest sense that God is *here*.

'*Vamos a casa*,' Sandrine says. Let's go home.

We slip out of the church. By now the sun is muted, creating shadows on the stucco stone wall and bathing the street outside in a soft pink glow. Sometimes what ties you to a place, or a country, are the simplest things. Like the colour of the late-afternoon light. Or two old men on a step, talking and laughing in an ancient language, out here in the *campo*. The melody of a *bolero*, a love song that represents more than just a sweet tune but a connection to the land that lives in my heart.

The next day, as I had promised myself, I go to the library. Inspired by my trip to Tepoztlan and the encounter with the Nahua-speaking Indians, I search the shelves for books on Australian history. Lately, I'd been mulling over what topic to choose for my speech for the Spanish exam, and finally I have come up with something. Why didn't I think of this before? I decide on a topic that greatly interests me: the history of the Australian Aborigines. I've always been fascinated by their wealth of tradition, their storytelling culture, particularly stories of the Dreamtime, the beauty of their languages and the people themselves.

When I return to the apartment in the afternoon, Sandrine and Kumi are sitting in the lounge room talking. I have a rough draft of my speech so I decide to do a trial run with them as my audience, to gauge their interest. And so my first speech in Spanish begins to come together. The girls listen and then ask lots of questions. Where did the Aborigines originally come from? How many inhabitants were there when white people arrived in Australia? How many languages do they speak? And so on. I realise I have a lot of work to do: checking facts, researching, reading. But one thing is obvious – I have succeeded in capturing their attention, and that is half the battle won.

Chapter Seventeen

Hombres Perdidos — The Lost Men

A few days later I'm in the garden of the Rufino Tamayo museum, a monument to Tamayo, the Zapotec Indian – 'the People of the Clouds', from the mountains of Oaxaca in southern Mexico – who became one of Mexico's most famous painters for his sensuous depictions of the flowers, fruits, sunsets and colours of his *tierra*, his land.

This place feels like another world. It is an early morning in March and the air is thick and sultry. Sitting on a bench under a cedar tree and looking across the deserted lawn, it is easy to imagine I'm in the country. Everything is dry: the grass that crackles beneath my sandals, the magnificent trees and the rasping chatter of the *pájaros* from the branches above. This is spring masquerading as summer.

I am here to meet Señora Urdaci, an artist who lives in the mountains above Mexico City. I'd first met her architect son in Melbourne two years earlier when I interviewed him for a newspaper article. He had passed on my number to his mother and last night, out of the blue, she called me.

Introducing herself in a crisp accent, Señora Julieta Urdaci dispensed with any further formalities, before holding forth: 'I just couldn't wait to meet you. Will you tell me all about Australia? I can't begin to imagine what it's like. Why don't we get together for lunch tomorrow? And what do you think about coming around for lunch during the week? Actually you should come every day. Yes, that's a good idea. Every day. That way I know you're eating properly.'

'Sounds great,' I said, feeling slightly faint as I tried to follow this breathless narrative. I had to laugh. She hadn't yet met me but as a mother – a Mexican one at that – she was already concerned about my eating habits. I already felt a bond with this woman. She talked without intermission and included me in the conversation, by asking my opinion about topics from cooking the perfect rice to who's the sexiest Latin man ever. (We both had to agree on *Fantasy Island*'s Ricardo Montalban, although Spanish tenor Plácido Domingo came a close second for his voice alone.) Finally, after twenty minutes, the conversation turned to art.

'When I need inspiration I go to museums and I always come out with new ideas,' she said. 'Which museums have you seen?'

'Oh, I've been to lots of different museums since I got here,' I replied confidently.

My answer was met with a short silence.

'You mean you haven't been to the Tamayo museum?'

'Er, no,' I said, feeling vaguely guilty.

'But you live so close to it!' She's got me there.

Another pause. 'Well, if you haven't seen Tamayo, we'll go tomorrow.'

'Okay,' I said.

So, bearing a box of Sanborn's chocolates, I wait in the garden for Señora Urdaci. Out beyond the *jardín*, a courtyard of terrazzo tiles leads up to the entrance of the museum. At the top of the stairs is a wall of glass windows, reflecting the sun's rays and separating the vast grey building from its surrounds. The *edificio* itself is an odd shape – a multi-layered pattern of diagonal slabs. It looks like giant concrete Lego.

Seeing an elegant woman in tailored pants and a starched blouse walking across the courtyard, my first thought is that she is a *turista* about to ask for directions. Tall and slim, with light brown hair, she doesn't look Mexican to me.

Clutching the chocolates, I get up, but find I have to sit down again. I'm feeling woozy. Yet I can't blame the stifling heat or the smog for my dizziness. I'm sporting a cut lip and a large bruise on my temple thanks to a silly accident two nights ago. Running across the darkened living room to answer the phone in the bedroom, I'd crashed headfirst into the door, knocking myself to the floor. At that moment, Sandrine had arrived home to find me on the floor and panicked. '¿*Qué pasó?*' she screeched, immediately thinking I'd been attacked by a burglar or had fallen violently ill. But when she heard me laughing she knew I was okay. The incident took an even more farcical turn when I stumbled getting up and banged my mouth on the coffee table – hence the lip. Now I look like I've been beaten up. I hope the *señora* isn't too alarmed.

The woman stops in front of me.

'¿*Ústed es Samanta?*'

I shake her outstretched hand. 'Yes,' I reply.

'I'm Señora Urdaci,' she says, smiling. 'Call me Julieta.'

And then she gets a look at my face and raises a hand to her chest.

'¡*Cielos! ¿Qué hiciste?*' Heavens above, what did you do?

'I ran into a door,' I tell her. A dubious line. I wonder what she is thinking? But she leans forward and gives me a big hug, patting me on the back and calling me *nena*, immediately putting me at ease. I've been in Mexico for six months and the warmth of its people, even almost perfect strangers, is something I can't get enough of. I hug her back.

'Ready to go in?' she says.

'Absolutely.' I have heard great things about this place and I'm ready to see it with my own eyes. As the heat of the day builds I'm also eager to find respite inside an air-conditioned building.

Inside, we find an enormous atrium and many rooms packed with Mexican art. On weekends I've heard the museum fills with visitors taking advantage of free admission; today, though, we are the only visitors. We enter a vast *salón* with equally enormous canvases. The paintings are extraordinary. Colourful and semi-abstract, depicting bright flowers and tropical fruits; a child in a big yellow hat with a posy of flowers, standing next to a watering can; a smiling man, arms outstretched, holding up a sheet full of pineapples, bananas and mangoes; thin standing figures surrounded by glowing haloes of colour.

In another gallery, I'm captivated by one *obra* in particular. Blues swim with yellows, white and black. It looks like a reclining woman, with two slender arms and flowing hair, although I can't be sure. The painting is a swirl of colour and suggestion. The title offers few clues: *Mystic Night*. I step back and move forward again. Nope. No idea. In a way it doesn't even matter what it's meant to be; it is how it makes me feel. And one word springs to mind. *Serene*. Julieta comes and stands next to me.

'I love this one,' she says. 'It's my favourite painting in the whole museum.'

'Why?' I ask.

'It feels right. That's all.' I smile. I have a feeling we are going to get along just fine.

As we stand in front of the canvas, sun spills down from a glass atrium above, bathing the room in light. I have fallen under the spell of Rufino Tamayo. As a Mexican art critic once said: Tamayo *is* Mexico. His paintings are sheer exuberance.

We are about to enter another gallery when Julieta stops and turns to me.

'Let's go and have some champagne,' she says. Her eyes sparkle with mischief.

'Oh, okay,' I reply. She takes my hand and leads me towards the exit; the tour of the rest of the museum is quickly forgotten.

I listen as Julieta talks non-stop on the way to her car. 'My family came from the Basque region of Spain. Up near the border of France,' she tells me. 'When they arrived here none of them spoke Spanish, only *castellano*. That's the language Spanish came from. Do you speak it? It's rather a barking *lengua* and very hard to learn. I can't say much, although I do know a few words.'

Many *vascos*, the fair-skinned inhabitants of the northern region of Spain known as the Basque country, migrated here at the turn of the last century, and now they help to make up the broad spectrum of Mexican society that ranges from the Zapotec Indians like Tamayo, with their copper-coloured skin, to Julieta, with her blue eyes, pale skin and almost blonde hair.

Julieta's driver, Enrique, leans over to open the back door and greets me with a strong handshake. On seeing the *chofer* I suddenly realise how wealthy Julieta must be. He pulls the four-wheel drive into the traffic, heading west along *Avenida Insurgentes*, and the rich voice of Plácido Domingo fills the car. Soon we are driving uphill towards Julieta's *colonia*.

Tecamachalco is an exclusive suburb which is home to dentists, television personalities, doctors, engineers and other very wealthy people. Palm trees tower above tall stone walls covered with hibiscus and frangipani, hinting at the hidden gardens beyond. A stream of luxury cars and open-top convertibles speed along the skinny roads. There is a lot of construction going on and Julieta tells me this is to keep up with the influx of *ricos* eager to get out of the grimy capital. This is partly true but there is also an element of fear involved. Mexico City has the second highest rate of kidnappings in the world after Colombia, and the rich are abandoning suburbs in the valley for the relative safety of places like Tecamachalco and Las Lomas.

Apart from security reasons, I can understand why so many people would want to live here. It is beautiful. There are no beat-up cars or people cramming the footpaths. No food stalls. I haven't seen a *colectivo* since we left Insurgentes. Even the sky seems a perfect blue. We drive slowly past a small park of manicured lawns and blooming flowers. In the middle is a life-size sculpture of three men who seem to be dancing around an imaginary maypole. Their entwined arms create a sense of movement that is fluid and beautiful. This *escultura* belongs in a museum. Except for one thing: the sculpture has been painted with ugly spray-on concrete. Julieta leans across me and points to the sculpture.

'It's called *Hombres Perdidos* – The Lost Men,' she says. 'I made it.'

'Oh,' I reply, wondering why she would use a concrete finish on such a beautiful piece. 'It's fabulous.'

'It was,' she grimaces. 'Until the council came here and painted it. But I'll fix them.'

Her face is a gesture of defiance. 'What are you going to do?' I ask, intrigued.

She smiles. 'I'm going to come back in the middle of the night and strip the concrete from them. I'll return my statues to their original glory.' I turn to see if she is joking. She isn't.

'When?' I ask.

'Soon. *Very* soon.' Her eyes are sparkling again.

I chuckle. This proposed act of vandalism-in-reverse seems at odds with the refined woman sitting next to me. And it amuses me to think of some stuffy council employee driving past on his way to work and doing a double-take when he sees this sculpture that he could have sworn was *grey*.

'Won't they know it's you?' I ask, reasoning that if someone was going to vandalise a piece of public art, they probably wouldn't leave it in better condition than it was before.

'*Seguramente*.' She shrugs. Surely. 'But I don't care. It has to be done.'

Julieta's defiance pleases me, not just as a case of aesthetics – although the colour *is* hideous – but because she reminds me of my mother: a strength of character that is unyielding. Dogmatic even. There is no compulsion to please others. As a child I was constantly embarrassed by my mother, who was always fighting with everybody: bank tellers, the telephone repairman, my teachers. *Why can't you be normal?* I implored. The reply was always the same. *All you have are your principles.* Not the answer I wanted to hear. But since I've been here, I have seen that certain character traits, like my mother's refusal to compromise, are not just personal, although she is very stubborn – they are cultural. As my grandmother often says, *Don't let the wind blow you where it will.* In other words, stick to your guns.

Finally we enter a gated compound and after several dizzying turns we arrive at Julieta's house, at the bottom of a cul-de-sac protected by a boom-gate and two security guards with machine guns. We turn down a driveway where another man paces with an even bigger gun. On my very first visit to Mexico this surfeit of weapons made me nervous, but today security patrols in Mexico City guard everything from department stores to donut shops and metro stations. There is even a security guard with a Rottweiler outside the pizza shop around the corner from my apartment. They are a fact of life and I'm used to seeing men with *armas*. I'm more worried about the dogs, a childhood phobia I cannot shake.

'Here we are,' Julieta says, pointing to a lovely two-storey house partly obscured from the street by a stone wall topped with razor wire and a thick wooden gate.

Julieta rings a bell-pull and a smaller door cut into the gate automatically opens. We cross the courtyard, to where a woman in a maid's uniform and white apron is waiting at the front door. She bows slightly and leads us through a marble foyer into the dining room. 'Welcome to my home,' Julieta says. She then disappears through a side door. 'I'll be back in a moment.'

It is quiet in here, although I can hear voices coming from somewhere nearby. Classical music pipes softly from speakers on the wall. In front of me there is a cabinet lined with crystal glassware and what looks like a Fabergé egg. Elegant chairs rim an oak table. Although the *señora* told me to make myself comfortable, I stand, terrified of breaking something. Julieta returns and rings another bell. Like magic, a steady stream of servants enter the room carrying large platters of chicken, rice and crusty bread.

'As I promised,' she says, gesturing towards a silver tray with two flutes of champagne.

I take a glass. '*Salud*,' I say.

I sit down with Julieta to an enormous breakfast. There are *huevos rancheros*, eggs with chile sauce, and baskets of pastries, jelly and orange juice and beans and tomatoes.

A little dog appears at my feet and I tear a croissant in half and hold it down by my side. He takes it from my fingers and disappears out a door that has been left ajar. A soft breeze licks against my feet.

I accept another glass of champagne even though the first one went straight to my head. After a few more mouthfuls, I stop eating. I'm done for. *Llena.* Full as a googy egg. Julieta looks concerned.

'Are you finished? Goodness, you've barely eaten anything!' Is she kidding? Have we been sitting at the same table?

'Oh no,' I lie. 'Just having a break.' Rather than offend her, I take a deep breath and eat up.

By ten the sun is spilling through the windows and bathing the room in golden light. We finish with cups of *café americano.* I can't help comparing this austere but elegant setting with the modest surrounds and convivial madness of mornings at my grandmother's house in *Colonia Narvarte.* The pet canary would be singing, the toaster has just flung a piece of bread clear across the kitchen, the children are screaming, the downstairs neighbour and my grandmother are talking and laughing at the front door, and I'm trying to concentrate on the television that's turned up to full blast as my cousins pull my ears. This is nice. *Very* nice. But throughout this decadent breakfast I'd felt a nagging sense of unease. And I've just realised why.

I miss noise!

This restrained atmosphere seems at odds with the Mexico I'm used to. Although I complain about car horns, police sirens, exhaust brakes and all manner of white noise that is a backdrop to my life, the reality is that I have grown accustomed to it. I seem to take comfort from the rhythms of this *ruidoso* city. I do not begrudge anyone what they have, especially this delightful woman with her effervescent charm. But her life is one of drivers, servants and a house guarded by men with machine guns. It's nice to see how the other half live, but I like it on my side of the fence. There's no question where I belong: I'm much more Narvarte than Tecamachalco.

As the plates are cleared from the table, the *señora* invites me to lunch.

'It's just something small with a few of the girls. I'd love it if you could come.'

What do I do? I cannot say no; it would seem rude. I feel like the diner from the *Monty Python's Meaning of Life* restaurant scene: full to bursting when the waiter tempts him with one more biscuit – *it's only wafer thin* – and he bursts, literally. Anywhere else I would have politely declined. But in Mexico the notion of 'food is love' is so strong that to refuse this invitation would be tantamount to a personal rejection. There's only one thing I can do.

'Sure,' I reply. 'What a magnificent idea.'

I want to make a joke about the exploding man, but I fear Julieta might think the blow to my head did more damage than she'd previously thought, and in any case I don't know how to say *wafer* in Spanish.

It is just after twelve when we leave Julieta's house. Half an hour later we pull into the car park of a Polanco restaurant, where we've arranged to meet Julieta's sisters and a few of their extended family who get together once a week for a long *almuerzo*.

The *restaurante* is a large room with terracotta tiles and adobe walls, in the style of the Spanish *haciendas* of the early 1900s. Long wooden tables line the room, and in the centre are round *mesas* that are actually converted wagon wheels with glass tops. In the corners squat enormous, dangerous-looking cacti. On the walls are planters spilling over with ferns, and the ceiling has exposed wooden beams. The design is a bit haphazard but it has a rustic charm. This place obviously has the tourist looking for *comida tradicional* in mind; but right now most of the diners seem to be locals.

'*Ahí están*,' there they are, Julieta says, gesturing to a large group of women seated at one of the wagon wheel tables.

Our arrival provokes much clamour as we give each of the women the traditional Mexican greeting – a kiss on the cheek. I'm met with a volley of, 'Hello, pleased to meet you,' and 'My goodness, aren't you tall,' while a few cluck sympathetically and ask: '*¡Pobrecita!* What on earth happened to your face?'

I concentrate on returning everyone's greetings but by now the chatter is deafening, the laughter so raucous, that I have to give up. This is quite a contrast to our conservative breakfast, although I'd suspected after Julieta's spontaneity this morning that under her polished exterior, Julieta is a lot of fun. Her older sister – a perfect facsimile of Julieta – comes over to take both of my hands in hers. '*Qué gusto conocerte*,' she says. A pleasure to meet you. There is joy all around me and I am swept up by the delight these women share in each other's company. I allow myself to be drawn into the maternal embrace of this noisy, jovial crowd.

Lunch is hearty fare. *Enchiladas*, chicken, beans, turkey, cold wine, beer, corn chips, salted tomatoes and bowls of chiles. The fans are whirring at full speed and cool air draughts in uneven gusts against napkins, faces and bare arms. I'm the only one who's not a member of the family: there's Julieta and her two sisters, two of their cousins, a daughter, three nieces, a daughter-in-law, and a great-aunt. A cheeky waiter calls us the *viejas*, literally meaning 'old women' but in this case meaning a large group of women.

One of the cousins is now telling an embarrassing story about her husband. '*No le da por uno*,' she cackles. He's no good for sex. The table is in uproar. 'What about Viagra?' someone says. 'It's the middle-age slump,' another adds. The nieces are looking mortified. '¡Tía!' the one on my left, Pilar, remonstrates. I am laughing so hard at the cousin's account that I almost choke on a mouthful of wine. She's on a roll now.

'I'm going to swap him for a younger model,' she declares.

There is more cackling and then, to everyone's amusement, she turns and points out a gorgeous young man in a suit at a nearby table who, judging by his horrified expression, has heard every word. 'Like that *papacito*.' Suddenly he finds the tablecloth *very* interesting. I can't stop giggling. It must be contagious because now the nieces start laughing too.

'I could offer you some advice if you want,' the great-aunt says with a wink.

We are momentarily stunned, before collapsing into hysterics. Then the conversation goes off on another tangent. The *papacito* is looking mighty relieved his bones aren't going to be jumped today; he's safe, for the moment at least.

We eat and laugh and talk in an easy manner. The warmth I feel with these practical strangers is tangible. I love these *viejas*. When Julieta invited me to lunch this morning I had initially felt anxious that I wouldn't fit in with these women – I'd assumed they would be all glammed up and I'd be sitting there with my black eye, not really dressed for the occasion – but they have made me feel so welcome in the group, as if I'm part of the family. Although I might be the only person here who isn't blood related, no distinction has been made between me and the other *nenas*.

The air is filled with laughter. We feast on *churros con chocolate*, as well as ice cream and chocolate cake. All that's missing is the party hats. The *viejas* are encouraging the younger ones to eat more. And more. '*Cóme. Si no, te vas a enfermar.*' An entreaty I've heard at least a million times since I arrived in Mexico. Eat, or you'll get sick. It's a novel concept. If I eat any more I *will* be sick. I try to wash down the mud cake with *café*. Oh, the effort! We all sip from big clay mugs of thick coffee. I concede defeat and pass the rest of my cake to one of the nieces, Gabriela, on my right, who then passes it to Julieta's lovely (and bawdy) great-aunt; and by the time it gets halfway around the table not a crumb remains on the plate.

All the same, I do feel a small pang of homesickness. Spending time with Julieta and her family makes me realise how much I miss my own mother. I think of the *cenas*, dinners, she had with her friends. Affectionately known as the Latin Mafia, they are a group of women from Argentina, Uruguay, Chile and Spain who, like my mother, arrived in Australia with nothing and worked hard to create new lives in a new country – so much so that when they returned to their homelands they felt like *extranjeras*. Will I feel that way when I go back home? I'm so immersed here; my other life seems distant.

Finally, lunch is over. Someone asks another diner to take our picture and he obliges. But as he steps back to get us all in the frame, the inevitable happens. He falls backwards into one of the cactus plants. 'I knew they were dangerous!' I say for my own benefit. He scrambles to his feet. 'I'm *okay*. Just *fine*,' he says, refusing all offers of help. (He's probably overheard our conversation too.)

By the time we get to the car park I have been invited to dinner by nearly everyone assembled. We bid noisy, protracted goodbyes. So many words, so little time! There are kisses and lots of hugs. Fifteen minutes later we get in Julieta's car. Enrique revs the engine of the *camión*, and drives Julieta and me downtown. We drive down *Paseo de la Reforma* as dusk begins to settle on the city. I'm exhausted, as though I've been in a whirlwind. After lunch with these wealthy women whose lives are so different from mine, I feel like I've been in an episode of a *telenovela*. Minus the glam duds and chisel-jawed boyfriend, of course.

'How would you like to come to lunch tomorrow?' Julieta says. 'I can get Enrique to come by and pick you up if you like.' I smile feebly. More food! How do Mexicans eat so much? I never want to eat again. This time I have to refuse her invitation.

'That would be wonderful but I have to study tomorrow,' I say.

'Well, that is a shame.'

We arrive at my apartment and I thank Julieta for the wonderful day and for letting me share it with her and her family.

'*Chiquita*,' she says, 'don't mention it. Maybe our next lunch can be in Australia.' And she gives me a wink. I watch her wave from the back window as the car drives away and is swallowed up by the traffic.

Chapter Eighteen

Rapunzel, Rapunzel

I've taken refuge inside my apartment from the oppressive heat. I am slumped on the sofa in the cool living room, dozing beneath the slow-moving fan, when the buzzer rings. My friend Elizabeth's voice crackles on the end of the line. 'I have to tell you something,' she pants. Minutes later she's standing at the door, positively beaming.

'I have great news.'

I think something wonderful must have happened since I last saw her – about an hour ago – and she can't wait until tomorrow to tell me. We sit on the stools in the kitchen and I open two bottles of beer.

'Wanna hear a brilliant idea?' she asks.

'Sure,' I reply. I'm dying to find out why she's so excited.

'I know how you can get the money for the exam.'

We've been discussing ways I could raise a thousand dollars to pay my *colegiatura*, the cost of the Department of

Public Education exam I hope to sit at the end of the month. The study for the exam is going well. I now have enough material for my speech, although at one hour and ten minutes I need to trim it down a little. I've been spending plenty of afternoons at the library and I'm feeling more confident about my language skills, although my progress with the verbal tongue twister, *El perro fuma un cigarrillo en el ferrocarril*, is limited. Will I ever master this? My pronunciation still lends no beauty to this phrase, only suffering to the ears of the listener. 'Be patient,' Rogerio tells me for the nth time. 'Time is all you need.'

But time is running out and, quite apart from my ongoing frustration with rolling my 'rr's', I still haven't come up with any real solutions to my financial crisis. Invariably, my brainstorming sessions with Elizabeth end over coffee downtown, where the topic of fund-raising is soon forgotten. Notwithstanding a major miracle – I'd lit *ofrendas* in the living room but the smoke stained the wall black and I had to extinguish them – I need to come up with something fast.

'Okay, are you ready?' Elizabeth asks.

'*Sip*,' I reply. Yup.

She lights a cigarette, holding it towards the open window and blowing the smoke above her head. She is keeping me in suspense. Her eyes are bright and happy. I can tell this is going to be good.

'You can sell something!' she finally says.

'Oh,' I reply.

She ignores my dubious expression.

'It's a great idea, and anyway, you have something really valuable.'

'I do?'

Actually, the thought of selling worldly goods had crossed my mind but I dismissed it after scanning my room and finding it devoid of valuables. But maybe I've been too hasty. *I could have missed something*, the voice of optimism tells me. I conjure a mental picture of all my belongings. I'd arrived in Mexico with a basic wardrobe of jeans, T-shirts and sneakers, an old suitcase and a couple of books. Nothing cash-worthy.

Then the penny drops. My hair! Why didn't I think of it before? Carmen, a teacher from the college, sold her hair for extra cash and was paid handsomely. There are shops in the old district that buy *pelo* by weight and length to make wigs – apparently Mexican hair is stronger, as there's a big demand for these wigs in the United States, mostly for cancer patients. But the *contaminación* in Mexico City hasn't been kind to my long and *very* thick hair, and my once glorious locks are now straggly, dull and brittle. Even my curls have disappeared in protest. Still, you never know.

'What, my hair, you mean?'

Elizabeth looks at me, stunned. Then she bursts out laughing.

'No! God, no. What are you talking about?'

Now I'm laughing. I have nothing of monetary value. I envision the apartment blazing with a thousand candles, just like the afternoon at my grandmother's place when I found her *ofrendas* lit to find me a husband. That didn't work, but this time I *really* need a miracle. I still haven't given up on the hair-selling idea. What have I got to lose? And it's not like it won't grow back.

'It's a *good* idea,' I say emphatically.

Elizabeth stops me with a wave of her hand.

'No, *tonta*, you'd have to sell ten kilometres of hair to get that much money. I'm talking about your camera.'

Of course! I bought my camera two years ago when I was cashed up, and paid more than two thousand dollars for it in a rare display of extravagance, or perhaps insanity.

It is sitting upstairs in the bottom of my suitcase, gathering dust after coming out briefly when I visited Cuernavaca with Elizabeth a few weeks ago.

'Darling, it's much better than *your* idea,' Elizabeth laughs.

Although I was willing to charge ahead with my dubious hair plan, I am secretly relieved. Elizabeth is absolutely right. My dearest Mexican friend, confidante, fashion consultant and cultural adviser, knows better than anyone what social suicide cutting my hair would be. Mexican women are *obsesionada* about their hair, spending a fortune on hair products and natural remedies, such as warm almond oil or a combination of egg and olive oil to encourage shine. As a result, most have thick, lustrous and bouncy curls. To cut my hair would invariably lead to criticism of being *no muy femenina*, not very feminine – a grave insult – in a country where big hair is an institution.

When Elizabeth leaves to teach a night class at the college, I walk with her to catch the bus downtown, armed with the address of a camera store. There's no time like the present. Now all I need is for someone to make me a reasonable offer. Although I don't expect to get the same price as I paid, I'm still confident of success. My only alternative is to pull out and not sit the exam, and that's something I don't even want to contemplate. I must find a way.

Fundamentally, I know I'm being pushed by more than just the desire to succeed. Yes, the *examen* represents a sense of achievement, but there is something else. I am seven again, determined to get the highest marks in class so I can prove to the other kids – who won't play with me because I'm a *wog* – that I'm good enough. For many migrant and mixed-race children, it is this motivation that pushes them to regularly outshine their Anglo-Saxon classmates at school and university. Put simply, we can't settle for being just as good, we have to be *better*. As an adult, I know it is crazy to still feel this way, but I do. No matter where I am, there will always be a little voice inside my head, telling me to try harder.

On another level, the language has always been the threshold I had to cross to understand Mexican culture and, as a result, myself. So passing the exam will be my way of saying to myself that I'm well and truly on the other side of the door.

But my hopes depend on the sale of a camera.

'*Qué tengas suerte*,' Elizabeth says, smiling and waving as I jump on the bus. Good luck. I bury any doubts under a cheery grin, and wave from the back window as the bus pulls into traffic and speeds along the avenue.

Half an hour later I'm on the smoggy streets of the old district with the camera hidden inside a *morales*, a bag the Indians use to carry tortillas. Now the hands of a child are on it. He is one of *los pobres*, the beggars who live in the *alcantarillas*, drains, in nearby Alameda Park. He has matted hair, a dusty face and hardly any teeth, but his eyes are bright and inquiring. The authorities warn against giving money to beggar children because many gangs of *niños* – some as young as four – are controlled by a Mafioso-type leader who takes all the profits and often leaves his charges to die of starvation. But this one isn't after pesos.

'What have you got there?' he asks me, tugging at my sleeve.

He doesn't give me time to answer.

'Do you have food in there?' he asks. '*Tengo hambre.*'

In a language that is poetic and meandering, I've always thought this expression so crisp and direct – it literally means, 'I have hunger.' Here, in the heart of the old district, and not far from the *alcantarillas*, it's something you hear often.

I usually carry a sandwich for the homeless guy who sleeps outside the front gates of our apartment, but today I was rushing out the door and my bag is empty. I still want to give the child something. Rustling around in the bottom of my bag, I come across some *glorias* – caramel and walnut sweets. I'd forgotten they were there.

'I've got *glorias*,' I answer.

His face lights up. 'They'll do.'

My little negotiator holds out his hands and I pull the wad of lollies from my bag and hand them to him. In an instant he's disappeared. I head for the *Zócalo*. Weaving through the buses, taxis and pedicabs, I walk down *Cinco de Mayo* avenue towards the jewellery district. It is the first time I've been here since our class excursion to *Templo Mayor* in early February. But this time it's not sightseeing on my mind – I am on a mission. I'm here to *regatear*, to make a deal.

Leaving the crowded footpath, I enter the Merced bazaar down a flight of stairs and am drawn into this web of commerce. My footsteps squeak on the marble floor as I make my way towards the counters where watch, camera and jewellery *mercaderos* do business. It is remarkably quiet, as though these negotiations require reverential tones. Inside glass cabinets are an array of pendants, earrings and necklaces, all made of gold. There are also tiny earrings for baby girls. Jewellery is a traditional gift in this country, and it is customary for the grandmother to present a pair of earrings for the *nena* at birth, which is why you'll rarely see a Mexican woman without pierced ears. Men also wear chains and bracelets with pride, a sign of both success and virility. The *joyas* are beautiful. An emerald necklace catches my eye and I stop to peer at it before moving on.

The vendors – nearly all men since *joyeria* is almost entirely a man's domain – call out as I pass, '*¿Señorita, buscas algo especial?*' Looking for anything special?

I walk past *puestos* with shelves stacked with gold ashtrays, Aztec calendars (round discs with markers like a sun dial), onyx statues of warriors and rows of jade and other precious stones. Necklaces made of silver, handwoven shawls in a rainbow of colours and more jewellery. The aisles are thick with people and I have to weave my way through. Many are tourists, drawn here by the reputation of the goods sold: *precio y calidad* – price and quality. With Elizabeth's directions in my hand, I finally come to the stall I'm looking for.

At the *equipaje de fotografía*, cameras sit on shelves; lenses, brushes, cables and other miscellany are arranged in a glass display cabinet. Mexicans are extraordinarily adept at recycling, and nowhere is this more evident than here. On a shelf I notice a camera crafted from an old powdered milk tin, the aperture shutter made from a rounded arc of tin that was once the lid. A tourist standing at the counter inquires about this particular invention in hesitant Spanish. 'Does that work?' he asks, pointing at the tin can. '*!Claro que si!*' – yes, of course – the vendor replies, bemused by the suggestion that he would sell something that doesn't work.

He is about sixty years old, dressed in a white Cuban shirt, short and stocky with white hair. After the tourist leaves, I address him in a manner appropriate to his age, using a formal greeting.

'*Buenas tardes señor, me gustaría preguntarle algo.*' Good afternoon sir, I would like to ask you something.

He smiles and replies in an equally respectful tone, '*A sus ordenes.*' At your service. I outline my request. Putting on his glasses, the man inspects the camera I've taken from my bag, holding it up and turning it over in his hands as though it were a precious artefact. I watch as he places it gently on the bench, his face still intent. He takes off his glasses again and rubs his eyes.

'Are you sure you want to sell this?' he asks.

'*Absolutamente,*' I reply.

He runs his finger over the camera. '*Ay, no sé.*' Well, I don't know.

In Mexico, it is considered bad manners to say no. *Probablemente, tal vez, quizás, ya veremos.* Probably, maybe, perhaps, we'll see. In Australia I would take these responses at face value, to think there is still a possibility of a yes. Here, I understand them to be the many varied *formas* of the negative response. '*Siempre queremos ser lindos,*' my teacher, Rogerio, often says. 'We always want to be nice.' In other words, saying no makes you look bad.

The vendor is still mulling. 'Maybe,' he sighs. This sounds a lot like a no. I think that I won't be doing my deal today. But then I remember where I am: in Mexico, *anything* is possible. I ask if he knows anyone who might be able to help me.

'You know, there is someone,' he replies. '*Espérame tantito.*' Wait a moment.

He disappears behind a curtain and returns moments later, smiling.

'Come with me,' the man says, beckoning me with a finger. He leads me through a maze of aisles in the bazaar and finally down a narrow laneway where the shop awnings meet to form a canopy over the footpath. Many of them could hardly be called shops – more like archways cut into stone walls, with dark interiors. At first I can see nothing but, as I linger, shapes begin to swim into focus. Inside these alcoves I see heads hunched over benches. I stop outside a *tiendita* where a cobbler runs his hands over a piece of shoe leather. My guide, now standing a few metres ahead, calls out to me. '*¡Señorita, ven!*' Come.

'This is the place,' he tells me. 'All you need to do is show them what you want to sell and you can work out a deal between yourselves. The owner is good value so you won't have any problems.' He indicates a basement shop at the bottom of a stone stairway, cleverly disguised below street level. If he hadn't pointed it out, I would have missed it. Not even a shingle announces its presence. I turn to the man and thank him.

Clutching my bag with the camera inside, I descend, confident that whoever I find at the bottom of the stairs will want to *regatear*.

As I wait for my eyes to adjust to the darkness, an unseen voice bids me *hola*. It's almost completely dark, except for a pool of light cast by an ornate lamp on a bench in the corner. In the lamplight I spot a tiny old man stooped over an antique clock which has its parts spread all over the counter.

I feel as though I've stepped back in time. I see a box brownie and an enormous early nineteenth-century camera on a tripod. On the back wall there is a fabulous collection of sepia photos that have a ghostly aspect in this dim light. One *foto* in particular catches my eye, a photograph of the old district, dated 1953. I step forward to get a closer look. The old man comes and stands next to me. '*Mi mujer y yo*,' he says, pointing at the photograph. My wife and me. And there, in the middle of the frame, is a young couple. The man in a sharp suit, his arm around his beautiful wife, smiles proudly. The cat that got the cream. He was twenty-eight and the world was a different place.

The old man – 'Alfonso,' he says as he shakes my hand – is one of a dying breed of *especialistas*, specialist jewellers, clock and camera repairers and watchmakers, who remember the glory days in *el centro* when this place was genteel. He recalls the movie star María Felix (Mexico's version of Elizabeth Taylor) strolling down *Cinco de Mayo* in the 1950s, wrapped in a fur coat and draped over the arm of the heart-throb of the moment, Jorge Negrete. Talking to Alfonso is like taking a guided trip through the history of the *Centro Historico*. His conversation is punctuated by a slow, rasping laugh that warms me inside.

I ask if he remembers the events of 2 October 1968, when ten thousand students gathered at the Plaza of Three Cultures in nearby Tlatelolco to peacefully protest Mexico's one-party government and lack of political freedom. That night, the police and the military bayoneted and shot dead an estimated 325 unarmed youths.

'Oh yes, I remember,' he says. 'From that night on we all stayed inside. You can't imagine how terrified we all were. The streets were lined with soldiers and nobody knew what would happen if they went outside.'

It's the only time during our conversation that I see his face contort into a grimace.

'They were only children,' he sighs. I'd read a similar comment by Mexican Nobel poet, Octavio Paz, who resigned his post as Ambassador to France when he heard of the massacre, saying he would not support a government that murdered its young people.

I would love to know if Alfonso was actually there, but I merely nod.

He removes his spectacles, wipes them on his apron and smiles wistfully. 'You've seen a lot,' I say. He rocks on his heels and puts his glasses back on. '*Si señorita*, I've seen it all,' he replies, laughing.

Alfonso clasps his hands in front of him. 'The world has changed while I stood still,' he says.

I smile. 'Maybe that's not such a bad thing.'

'*Quizás,*' he replies. Perhaps.

We talk some more about his family, his health, life in general. '*¿Y nietos?*' I ask. Have you any grandchildren? '*Quince,*' he smiles. Fifteen. I've been in this country long enough to know that any interaction requires a gentle approach. Whatever the occasion, inquiries about a person's family and wellbeing are expected.

By the time we get to talking about the camera, it is dark outside. 'Are you sure you want to sell this?' he asks, parroting exactly the other vendor's words. We agree on a price we are both happy with: five thousand pesos. I do the conversion in my head: exactly one thousand dollars. Half of what I paid, but in Mexican terms an absolute fortune. It is exactly the amount I need; now I will have enough money for my *colegiatura*. I'm thrilled.

Alfonso walks me to the door and squeezes my arm. 'Be well,' he says. '*Y tu también*,' I reply. And you also. I climb the steps into the black night and leave him behind in his cave full of memories.

Chapter Nineteen

Eat, My Little Professors

We are in a large *salón* on the third floor of the Mexico Academy. Finally, the day has arrived for Jean, Kumi and me to give our fifty-minute speeches as part of our Department of Public Education exam. I'm standing in front of a panel of examiners who are seated at a long desk. Our teacher, Rogerio, sits near the window, a comforting presence. On the other side of the room, Jean and Kumi wait for their turn. It's going to be a long morning.

'What are you going to talk about?'

The head examiner has his hands clasped in front of him on the desk. He is a thin, middle-aged man with spectacles at the end of his nose and looks so much like a stereotypical professor that I'm tempted to laugh. But, terrified by the task ahead, I can barely raise a smile. His colleagues on either side of him look serious. I take a deep breath. I can't remember the last time I was this nervous.

'My country,' I answer.

'Of course,' he replies, 'but what exactly?'

'The indigenous people of Australia – their role in our history.'

And so, after six weeks of preparation, I start talking – 'The indigenous people of Australia are known as . . .' – and the very first sentence passes without incident. I'm surprised at how confident I am. I thought I would find the whole experience excruciating. Not that this is the most fun I've ever had, but it isn't as bad as I'd expected. As long as I concentrate I should be right.

'*El hombre recibió un payaso en la pierna izquierda.*' The man received a clown in his right leg. Ten minutes into the speech and I've made my first mistake when I confuse *balazo*, bullet wound, with *payaso*, clown. What's wrong with me? These words aren't even that similar. My carefully practised speech, rehearsed in front of my friends and read over and over again, is falling apart. Don't panic, I tell myself. I look at the examiners but their faces betray nothing, not even a smirk.

Then, halfway through the speech, as I'm describing how the Aborigines used to hunt game, one of the examiners stops me. I wonder why. Is it like when you make a serious mistake in a driving test? Have I done something to warrant instant disqualification? Fortunately not. He has a request.

'Could you please draw us a kangaroo? I can't begin to imagine what they look like.'

A short silence follows.

'Oh,' I reply, a little surprised. 'Absolutely.'

I walk over to the whiteboard, where I start drawing my kangaroo. But my depiction looks nothing like any *canguro* I've ever seen. It's more like an alien from the Planet Zorg, completely out of proportion with massive legs, a tail twice as long as it should be, a pin-head and big paddle-hands instead of forelegs. Impressive. I turn back to the examiners. Perhaps because I'm too nervous or just because my picture is *so* appalling, I get the giggles.

'Um, it's not to scale,' I joke.

'That's the weirdest-looking kangaroo I've ever seen!' one of them says, not unkindly.

The room erupts into laugher, and even the most serious of the examiners manages a smile. This interlude also goes a long way towards dispelling my nerves.

Half an hour later and it's all over. The examiners gather in a huddle and whisper among themselves. I turn to Rogerio and he gives me the thumbs-up. When they sit up I ready myself for the worst. What are they going to say? A gentle let-down? An offer to pay me as long as I promise *never* to speak Spanish again? The bespectacled examiner speaks on behalf of the others.

'You have some problems with your pronunciation of the rolling "rr".'

Of course. I knew it! These dreaded consonants are going to be my downfall.

'However . . .' He pauses. 'We do take into consideration the difficulties Westerners have with this technique and we mark your presentation accordingly. On the whole, we were very impressed.'

It takes a moment for the enormity of his words to sink in. Then I realise I'm smiling from ear to ear.

In the evening, Jean, Sandrine and I drink *margaritas* to celebrate. I go to bed early so I'll be ready tomorrow for the second part of the exam: the written component. It's not over yet. Nevertheless, I'm feeling optimistic.

The next morning I get up at four to do some last-minute cramming. I creep across the bedroom and open the window; the blast of air that hits me is as strong as it is icy.

Invigorated, I head downstairs and take a stool from the kitchen before clambering back up the spiral staircase. The upstairs bathroom is the quietest place in the apartment so I set myself up at the sink.

As I open my books I see a shadow in the doorway and let out an involuntary shriek: '*¡Diablos!*' Sandrine is standing at the door.

'What are you doing?' she says. I can understand her annoyance. For the past few weeks Jean and I have been staying up till all hours studying and not wanting to have any fun. Having lights on all night and speaking in loud whispers probably hasn't helped either.

'Uh, studying,' I reply. 'What? Did you think it was a burglar?'

She grunts. 'Are you kidding? A burglar wouldn't make that much noise. I thought it was a bloody earthquake!' she says, before stomping back downstairs. So much for keeping quiet. When she's gone, I return my attention to the books in front of me.

Despite six weeks of intensive study, I look at my books full of complex conjugations and grammar and think: *I don't know anything*. I attribute this meltdown to last-minute nerves. Or is it information overload? Can you study *too* much? Crammed with the minutiae of this language, my brain has decided to go on strike. In just over an hour the city will waken from its slumber. In this ancient *ciudad* people will set up market stalls and sweep footpaths with brooms made from twigs and tied with twine. The next thing I know I've dozed off and it's six o'clock.

Through the open window I can see the first light of day stealing into the room. I get dressed, throw on a coat and head outside to buy breakfast from the *tamales* vendor, whose bell is now clanging loudly up and down the street.

At the entrance to our building I get another fright.

'*¡Tita!*'

Turning around, I *hear* Roberto calling me, but he's obscured by a giant elephant fern so it seems the voice is coming from the plant itself. He appears, smiling. 'I have to show you something. It's really important.' I wonder what is so important that it can't wait for later when I'm more awake and semi-coherent. 'Okay,' I reply, utterly compliant.

I watch in amazement as he takes off at a sprint. When he gets halfway to the front gate, he jumps in the air and clicks his heels together *a la* Gene Kelly in *Singin' in the Rain*. I'm momentarily stunned and then I start to giggle. Maybe it is because I'm so tired but I find this display absolutely hilarious. He comes back, laughing. '*That* was what you wanted to show me?' I tease. 'Uh huh,' he replies. 'Now it's your turn.' I have a go. My attempt is pitiful. I make a feeble jump, just making it off the ground and losing a shoe in the process. I walk back to Roberto, who is shaking his head.

'That was crap,' he says.

He's right. Faced with his disappointment, and earlier magnificent effort, I try again. This time I manage a very respectable jump – clicking my heels together midair – and a smooth landing. '*¡Órale!*' Roberto says. Way to go! I come back to the fern, where we stand laughing like a pair of idiots.

A few minutes later my appetite gets the better of me and I'm standing at the gate with the regulars.

'*Buenos días señorita*,' they say courteously. Their voices sound raspy on this brisk morning.

'Good morning,' I reply, hoping they didn't see Roberto and me running up and down the courtyard.

I order the specialty of the day, *tamales oaxaqueños*, a combination of white rice and *queso oaxaqueño*, a stringy white cheese that melts into a delicious gooey paste. I've tried the *tamales* with red chile sauce that burns your lips, the *pollo* – seasoned spicy chicken – and the fiery green chile variety, but these are my favourites. I open the parcel and watch as the aroma escapes in a cloud of steam.

'My wife made these,' the vendor says as he hands me my breakfast. Everything is homemade. And *bien sabroso*, delicious. 'Smells great,' I say. He smiles proudly before turning back to the other men, who are now asking for more of everything.

I head back inside. The kitchen is empty and it is with a sudden feeling of melancholy that I sit down to eat my breakfast. In a fortnight I will be leaving Mexico – my visa is about to expire, and I am about to run out of money. In any case, I sense it is time to go home. Although it will be great to be back in my country, I can't help feeling sad to be leaving this chaotic *ciudad* for serene, sunny Melbourne. I will be going back to embrace the rhythms of a different culture; one that is familiar and *safe*. There is much that I miss about home.

I sit in the lounge room and think of the colour of the Sorrento sky. In my mind the richness of the blue takes on almost mythic proportions. Occasionally I'll long for the sounds of magpies as I pass under the eucalypt trees in *Paseo de la Reforma*. I miss the beach or, more specifically, the joy of opening a window and being able to hear the sound of crashing waves in the near distance. Rich, strong coffee that's from a poky Italian café in a Melbourne lane-way and not from an American coffee chain. And of course, the people – my family and friends. My brother has returned to Australia after a two-year work posting in London. My family are together while I'm here. I feel left out, and want to be with them. I'm ready to return to my other life.

But my time in Mexico has changed the way I think about Australia too. I'm more appreciative of what I have.

Indeed, I would have to possess a heart of stone to not be affected deeply by the sight of children begging at traffic lights and gaunt Indian women holding tiny, malnourished babies. My grandmother's wonderful advice, *'The world is not a fair place'*, seems to make more sense now. Probably the most important lesson Mexico has taught me is to be grateful for the important things: health, family, food, friendship and life itself.

On my return to Australia I find myself getting upset with friends who throw leftovers away, thinking how precious (and scarce) food is to many people in Mexico. On another occasion a friend discards a brand new coffee table because the colour is wrong. 'At least you could have given it to charity!' I rage, surprising him with my anger. Walking down a street in Albert Park, I'm shocked by the sight of a thousand-dollar dog collar in an upmarket pet shop. I laugh. In Mexico, the very idea would send most people into hoots of laughter. Quite simply, when you go without, your priorities are different.

Looking out the window at the mottled sky, I feel a fondness for this city that never sleeps: the *regulares*, the men who appear from under a blanket of darkness to eat, talk and drink *atole*, the bitter strawberry concoction that goes with *tamales*; the *tamales* vendor, who's worried because I've been looking tired lately – this from a man who pedals the streets every day, regardless of the weather, and earns five hundred pesos or seventy dollars a month; and the market vendors, who are familiar with the intricacies of *mi vida cotidiana*, my daily life, and I with theirs. From them I learn whose son has a new job or daughter is getting married, who has a new granddaughter or has been unwell with *un mal de estomago*, a stomach bug, and how to treat diarrhoea with apple sauce and cinnamon (it really works!). And my Mexican friends, who only need a whiff of a pretext to have a party – any more than four people in a room is cause for celebration.

The sky is changing colour again and the building opposite is coming into sharp focus. When the *tamales* are finished I go back upstairs to retrieve my textbook from the bathroom before flopping onto my bed for more reading. Two hours later I am still lying on the bed, surrounded by books, when Jean calls up from the kitchen. '*¿Lista?*' he says. Ready? I grab my things and head downstairs.

Around eight-thirty, I'm getting off the bus and walking towards the Mexico Academy with Jean, who is uncharacteristically quiet. I have butterflies in my stomach and feel a sensation that is somewhere between excitement and dread. Logically I know that regardless of how I do in the exam, learning Spanish will always be one of the most rewarding things I have ever done, but I'm still nervous. '*No te preocupes Tita,*' Jean says. '*Todo saldrá bien.*' Don't worry, everything will be okay. I smile. 'I'm okay.' I am more worried about him – he has turned milky white and is chewing on his bottom lip.

Kumi has come from her house in *Colonia Narvarte* and is standing at the gate waiting for us. She smiles wanly.

'I don't feel well,' she says.

At this point, if I suggested we all go home, I'm pretty sure Jean and Kumi would agree.

We go inside and are directed downstairs to where Rogerio is waiting. Upon entering the *sala de examenes*, a basement room next to the cafeteria, we are also met by the director of the college, Señor Avila. I think he is here to wish us good luck. But no, he has something else in mind.

'I brought breakfast,' he says.

'Really?' we reply.

'Of course.' Señor Avila smiles, as if he regards our surprise whimsical. He puts two large brown paper bags on the table.

'*Cóme, mis profesoritos*,' he says. Eat, my little professors.

He wishes us luck and leaves the room, promising to return later. We sit down at the table with Rogerio. If this attention is designed to ease our nerves, it has worked. Already I'm more relaxed. This does feels strangely unlike an exam. Breakfast for the students? I like this reversal of the apple-for-the-teacher concept.

We are now sipping scalding *café con leche* and munching on sandwiches – thick slices of white bread with *canela*, a caramel-flavoured syrup with a gooey consistency, a local delicacy. Suddenly Rogerio sits up in his chair, as though he's just remembered why he is here, and pulls from his briefcase the all-important exam papers. He places them on the desk and grabs another sandwich. 'I'll be needing another one of these for the journey upstairs.' He walks towards the door. 'I'll be back later,' he says airily.

'Aren't they supposed to supervise us?' Jean asks, delighted by this unexpected turn of events. Kumi shrugs and reaches for another *canela* sandwich. 'Fine by me,' she says. I laugh, thinking of all the exams I sat at university where the giant auditorium was filled with rows of desks numbering in their thousands. Images of scowling lecturers pacing the aisles and the intermittent coughs and throat clearing of nervous students spring to mind. It's with a certain relish that I compare the supply of a *desayuno* by a teacher (the director no less!) with the 'pens down' approach of the past.

For the next four hours we are visited by a steady traffic of *profesores* and students from the other classes, who poke their heads in on the way to the cafeteria. Our friend Tadeshi, from the level below us, brings us a packet of cigarettes. 'Just in case you get stressed out,' he says. Not much chance of that happening.

With the constant interruptions from well-wishers and bearers of *more* food, the exam room takes on a party atmosphere. Mexicans, it seems, don't bother with such formalities as supervision, unless you count the encouraging *you can do it* comments. 'We trust you,' the director's wife, Matilde, explains when she comes in at ten o'clock with more coffee and a bag of cinnamon donuts. As it happens, her *fé*, her faith, is rewarded because it doesn't even occur to us to ask each other for the answers. It's not that we are all supremely confident of our abilities. More likely the relaxed atmosphere has removed the tension that is often an impediment to success in exam situations. Whatever the reason, the hours pass happily.

Just after *mediodía*, lunchtime, we finish the exam. Actually, Kumi finished half an hour earlier and has been quietly eating a sandwich, her exam paper sitting on the table in front of her. Meanwhile, Jean and I are madly checking and re-checking our answers and finishing the last exercise, which is a one-page letter to test our written abilities. The exam itself was straightforward and I'm feeling pleasantly surprised that all those months of studying grammar, syntax and conjugations have finally paid off. At six am everything I'd learned seemed to have flown out of my head – but when I started writing, it all came flooding back.

Señor Avila, Matilde and Rogerio return to the room. 'We have a little celebration organised,' Matilde says. 'You'll need to be upstairs in half an hour.' They do not tell us what they have planned.

When they are gone it is just Jean, Kumi and I sitting at the enormous wooden table; in front of us the detritus of this morning's proceedings: polystyrene coffee cups, empty donut boxes, sugar wrappers, blunt pencils and scrunched-up paper. We are silent, spent. My head is swimming but at the same time I feel an immense surge of relief. This *examen* has been the hardest thing I have done in a long time. Admittedly, exams are never easy, but this one was different to any others I've done. And not just for the *fiesta* atmosphere. This one was different because it meant so much to me. The whole process has been tied to a growing sense of belonging. The fact that I'm confident of a better than average passing grade only reinforces this feeling. I might never be truly Mexican, but talking like one certainly lends me validity, and that in itself pleases me immensely.

It slowly sinks in that we are free. No more classes. No more studying. It's over. Jean finally breaks the silence: 'Well, don't just sit there. Let's go outside.' We stumble into the courtyard where we light Tadeshi's celebratory cigarettes – even though Kumi and I don't smoke – and cram onto a bench, staring ahead, unmoving like the statues in the garden of the Rufino Tamayo museum. Now that our brains are well and truly fried, we sit in complete silence. For the next twenty minutes we do not move from the bench, before finally getting up and heading to the administration office where Matilde asked us to meet.

'¡SORPRESA!'

I'm standing at the top of the narrow staircase that climbs from the basement, when I hear a communal yell. Jean, who has stopped on the landing, steps back and almost causes a domino effect. I step backwards to avoid him and narrowly miss knocking Kumi down the stairs. 'What's going on?' I ask Jean. His face has split into a huge grin. Now we climb the last few steps and find out what all the commotion is about.

'¡Dios mio!' Kumi says.

Standing around a table set with all manner of goodies are the entire teaching staff and possibly every student in the college. Above them in big wonky letters, a banner reads 'FELICITACIONES', congratulations. This surprise party is a wonderful gesture. For the all-sharing Mexicans this must have been quite a secret to keep. Jean and Kumi are looking as stunned as I feel. Matilde comes over and gives us all a kiss, saying, 'I'm so proud.' To watch her, you would think we were her very own offspring on their wedding day and not *estudiantes* from far-flung corners of the globe.

We squeeze into the middle of a cluster of students and are given bottles of cola, and chips to nibble on while Matilde goes to get the cake. I can just make out Elizabeth's head across the room. She catches my eye and raises her bottle in the air. By the time Matilde returns, there are even more people in the room. Where are they all coming from? She carries the cake above her head and eventually makes it to the table with the *pastel* still in one piece. Several empty bottles stand in a semicircle around empty bowls that not long ago were filled with chips.

As the party gets louder, Matilde tries to get everyone's attention.

'It's time to cut the cake,' she yells above the din.

But this is no ordinary cake. It is a *Rosca de Reyes*. Three Kings Bread. In Mexico children do not receive Christmas presents on December 25 but instead on January 6, when it is believed the three wise men arrived at Jesus' manger. This celebration is known as *Día de los Magos*, the Day of the Kings. Traditionally Three Kings Bread is served in the first month of the new year to honour the kings. Today, however, someone has gone to extraordinary lengths to break with tradition for our celebration. Filled with dried fruit and an almost *panettone*-like flaky pastry, the bread is superb. There is also an added surprise. Inside each loaf are tiny plastic *muñecas* or dolls, the Mexican version of the penny in the pound cake. As tradition goes, whoever gets a doll will soon have children, a spin on the Western 'catching the bouquet' superstition.

'*Vé primero*,' Rogerio says. He is standing at my shoulder and gives me a gentle push. You go first. I cut a sliver of the cake, and am placing it on a paper plate when Lola, the college receptionist, points something out. 'You got a doll!' I look down. Oh no! She's right. On my plate is a *muñeca* peeking from behind a piece of glacé fruit. The cake cutting continues while I eat, and because it is so big, I get another turn. And what do you know? Another doll. This is getting spooky. Why am I the only one finding dolls? Elizabeth whispers in my ear.

'Your grandma's wishes are coming true,' she says.

I turn to her laughing. 'But she only lit candles to find me a husband, not *children*.'

She taps the end of her nose. 'That's what you think,' she replies with a smirk.

If I had heard such talk six months ago I most likely would have dismissed it as superstitious nonsense. But Mexico has changed me so fundamentally, in ways I can't explain. When I first arrived, around the time of Day of the Dead, I saw the candle-lighting rituals as quaint and charming, and thought nothing more of them. But months later when Sandrine fell seriously ill with a high fever that showed no signs of abating, my grandmother offered me one piece of advice: '*Pónle unas veladoras.*' Light some candles for her. I did, and the next day Sandrine recovered.

It is the Mexican *creencia*: believing in what you can't see, giving in to what is mystical and inexplicable. To believe in God and the power of prayer, to light *ofrendas* for everything from good health to husbands to much longed-for *nietos*, grandchildren. I cannot know with any certainty that the *veladoras* I light do anything other than fill the living room with thick smoke. But it doesn't matter. I have faith, and that is enough. I accept that I'm not in charge of my life; that *el destino* is what guides me – this in itself is a very Mexican way of thinking. I suspect I have always believed these things. But being in Mexico, with its *pasión* and *fé*, passion and faith, is what I needed to truly understand me and, as a result, to embrace life fully.

Ten minutes later the *rosca* is all gone. A tiny Japanese girl called Hatsuoki gets the last *muñeca* and she doesn't look at all happy about it. By three o' clock it's all over and we say our goodbyes. I embrace Matilde, and she hands both Kumi and me a newspaper-wrapped parcel.

'Can we open them?' Kumi asks.

'*Ándale*,' she replies. Go ahead.

Inside each parcel is a beautiful papier-mâché doll dressed in traditional costume and painted with swirls of colour. They are the dolls that have been sitting in the cabinet in our *salón* since we started here; and ones both Kumi and I have admired.

'Thank you,' I reply. When I imagined the final day of classes I imagined myself bounding joyfully through the gate, but now I am reluctant to leave. I hug Matilde again and head towards the exit with Kumi, clutching my *regalo* and knowing it is unlikely I will see again these *profesores* whose encouragement and enthusiasm made learning Spanish such a rewarding experience.

As we are leaving, Lola comes out to say goodbye.

'I'll send the exam results by post,' she says. 'You should get them soon.'

Almost a year later in Australia, the *tramites* arrive in the mail. Lola had sent me an email telling me I passed but my actual results are still a mystery. When I open the envelope I get the shock of my life. I scored ninety-four per cent which, apart from leaving me speechless, proves my theory that there is no such thing as too much study.

Immediately I send emails to Jean and Kumi telling them my news and, some days later, they reply with their marks.

Kumi outshines us with an amazing ninety-seven per cent. Jean is devastated to discover he has been outscored by Kumi, receiving, in his words, a 'measly' ninety-five per cent. I suspect, however, his disappointment has more to do with being beaten by a girl than his actual mark.

With these results I can choose to become a translator or interpreter – the latter is of great interest to me. Unfortunately these 'foreign' qualifications are not accepted by the Australian Interpreters and Translators Association, but I'm not deterred. I am inquiring about further study, eager to make the most of my Spanish skills. Whatever happens, this language has added a whole new dimension to my life.

Chapter Twenty

A Balcony Under the Stars

The next morning, after a breakfast of *flan* and instant coffee, I catch a kombi to the northern bus terminal, a hellish place on the outskirts of Mexico City. From the window I can see sprawling shanty towns on the nearby hills, beggars sleeping on the footpaths and dead animals on the road, and smell the acrid smoke coming from the land-fill where the shanty residents earn their living by buying and selling refuse. The bus screeches to a halt outside the station.

I enter the colossal *terminal de autobuses* and head for the ticket counter. I've been mulling over one final getaway trip for a while now and, with only a week before I leave, one destination keeps springing to mind: Taxco de Alarcón.

Nestled in the mountains two hours from Mexico City and surrounded by rolling hills, Taxco is a colonial village, with a winding maze of laneways full of stores famous for fine silver jewellery, and a magnificent cathedral overlooking a plaza of cool elms and stone benches. It is a picture of old-world charm; a place simply too beautiful to miss. And, as it happens, it is the *pueblo* where my parents spent the first night of their honeymoon, back in 1969.

I need to catch the cheapest bus I can find. I inquire at a few counters but the prices are for the air-conditioned Mercedes coaches and I'm a bit stretched for cash. I'll be quite happy to settle for a cheaper bus – the ones the Indians use. They are affordable, relatively clean and get from A to B with a minimum of fuss. Just then I spot the right ticket counter.

'I'd like a return ticket to Taxco.'

The woman stares at me. I try again, thinking she might not have understood my accent.

'*Un boleto ida y vuelta a Taxco. Por favor.*'

'*¿Segura?*' she says. Sure?

I nod and smile. She smiles back. She's probably wondering what I'm doing in this line. Now that I've been here for a while and done the exam, I feel more like a local and am a bit annoyed that she thinks I'm an *extranjera*. But I have to accept the truth. I could live here for the rest of my life, even succeed in mastering a Mexican accent, but I'll never *be* Mexican. I can speak fluent Spanish and I might look like a *mexicana*, but people somehow know I'm not Mexican, and not just because of my accent.

'When you first saw me at the college did you think I was Mexican?' I once asked my friend Elizabeth.

'Yes, I did,' she replied. 'I thought you were a new teacher.'

I mulled over her reply.

'So how did you find out I wasn't Mexican?'

'I was looking at you for a while and I thought there was something about you that was *distinto*.'

I thought about her answer, and of a question my mother asked me before my very first trip to Mexico: *Don't you want to know who you are?* I know now. I'm an Australian with a Mexican mother and an English father. That is my identity. That's who I am.

From here, I catch a rickety old bus. We drive for almost an hour before the landscape begins to change. The road to Taxco is chiselled from the side of a mountain and as the bus negotiates the winding road buttressed by moss-covered rock faces and plunging cliffs, I'm intrigued and terrified at the same time. With every dip, I worry we're going over the edge. My knuckles are white as I clutch the armrests. Seated next to me is an old man in a straw hat who is grumbling in his sleep. He has a piece of straw in his mouth and is sleep-chewing and snoring simultaneously. I'm impressed. The man wakes with a start and, catching my eye, acknowledges me. '*Buenos días*,' he says with the lilting cadence of the Indians for whom Spanish is a second language.

'Good day,' I reply.

I smile and turn back to the view. Outside, the spectacular mountains and valleys spool past in a blur of ochre and verdant green.

Soon we arrive in Taxco, pulling into the bus station, a precipitous block of concrete that seems suspended in midair over the cliff's edge. My eyes are struggling to keep up with the sights before me. Across the road, small white-washed buildings line a hill so sheer it is like a rock face. The cobbled streets are almost empty of cars, except for the kombi vans known as *burritos*, little donkeys, whose drivers seem to be the only ones game enough to tackle the steep slopes. I tip my head back and look almost straight up. Beyond the town, the majestic green peaks of the mountains blend with the haze of sunlight. Here the sky is a deeper shade of blue then white as it folds across the *montañas*.

I cross the street to the market, where the noise embraces me. The air is filled with the scents of sunny days and fresh produce. Beginning at the base of a hill, the market wends its way up. Tourists usually avoid walking through here, preferring a more meandering, quiet path up to the *zócalo*, the main square. But I love these *mercados*. They are the essence of Mexico with their organised chaos and crazy sense of community.

I walk up the street blocked to traffic. It is swarming. It seems market day in Taxco happens all week. The vendors arrive when it is still dark and by eight o'clock there are *puestos* with every variety of produce. And just like the markets of Mexico City, everything you could ever want or imagine is here to be bought and sold. I pass the *fruta* stand where a vendor is selling mangoes. Another stall displays a pyramid of artichokes. A woman in a floral apron is removing the thorns from thick pear-shaped *nopal* leaves with an enormous machete. There are aloe vera plants, bananas, oranges, apples, pears, potatoes, papaya, red, black and white beans, *mole verde*, *poblano* and *rojo*, and mounds of chiles. Besides food you can also buy horsehair wigs, kitchen utensils, picture frames, winter scarves, shoes and hair clips.

I weave through clusters of people before ducking into an alcove to catch my breath. It is a killer of a climb and I've lost my footing more than once on the cobblestones and slid downhill. The Indians pass me by with the sure-footed confidence of mountain goats on a Himalayan peak. But even on this impossible slope, the trek is worth it. Looking back down the hill I see a rainbow of colour spread out below me. And because Taxco is eighteen hundred metres above sea level I can see forever. It is an amazing sight. Soon I've come to the main square, and I take another breather.

The *zócalo* is dominated by the grand-looking Santa Prisca Cathedral. Crowds are bustling outside the perimeter fence, where Indian women lace together wicker baskets, their fingers working deftly as they talk and call out to passers-by. I've arrived on the hour and the sound of the ringing bells reverberates throughout the square. It is late morning and the courtyard is bathed in sunlight. At the *artesanía* market, men in white shirts and straw hats hawk their wares. They hold up woven baskets and shawls, embroidered blouses, brightly coloured vases and leather belts. On trestle tables there are vases, mugs, pottery, bags, boots, and a saddle resting on a chair. In the plaza people congregate around a rotunda. The bells have stopped chiming but their sweet sound still echoes inside my head.

Like so many Mexican towns, *el pasado*, the past, has not been left behind, but brought along with every new generation. The eighteenth-century baroque church still stands imposing against the skyline. The craftsmen of jewellery and pottery use the same age-old *técnica* as their fathers. I climb the few steps to the rotunda and sit down. Being here seems a bit surreal. My parents were here on their wedding day thirty years ago, an overnight stopover on their way to their honeymoon destination – Acapulco. They are long gone, but the *calles empedradas*, the paved streets they walked, still glisten in the sun.

It was a momentous time in both their lives. My mother was preparing to leave Mexico, my dad wondering about the woman he'd just married. I reflect on their adventurousness in leaving tradition and family for a brand new life in Australia. I'd asked both my parents at different times how they coped with being separated from their families, especially my mother, who said it was the most heartbreaking decision she'd ever made. Their answers were similar: 'We didn't think about what we were doing, we just did it.' I try to put myself in my mother's position. For me, the equivalent would be deciding to stay in Mexico, marrying a man I barely know and never returning to Australia, or at least only for short holidays once every fifteen years. Could I be that brave? I don't think so.

I have always admired my parents for the extraordinary people they are, but now even more so. My experiences in Mexico have shown me the tremendous courage it took for both of them to start a new life on another continent, the sacrifices they made and the hardships they endured. More importantly, being here has shown me my mother in the context of *her* culture and homeland. Mexico has put her in perspective. I understand more of where her strength of character comes from, and the history and influences that have shaped the person she is today.

I sit in the *Plaza Borda* and watch the people around me. Across the way a couple on a bench hold hands and kiss. Two old men sit talking, dressed in suits and straw hats, canes at their sides. Barefoot boys kick a ball around. And, as always, the singsong voices of the vendors continue. I watch a young woman approach. She is short, *morena*, dark-skinned, with a shock of black hair, and looks exactly like my mother in the photographs I had seen of her on her honeymoon. So strong is the resemblance, in fact, that I can almost picture my mother sitting on a bench under one of these grand old trees; my dad at her side, captivated then, as I am now, by this place that was so different from anywhere he had ever been.

Leaving the rotunda, I'm stopped by a vendor. In his arms he holds a papier-mâché bird. With its blue, yellow, green and pink crepe feathers fluttering in the soft breeze, the *ave* is a work of art – and patience. He tries to convince me to buy it.

'*Señorita, cómpreme este ave de paraíso.*'

It is beautiful. And I am tempted.

'I will give you a good price,' he says.

'Maybe later,' I tell him. I don't want to give him an outright no; it would be rude.

I walk across the plaza towards a *callejon*, a laneway hemmed by white buildings with red brick archways and names painted above lintels in a florid hand. Tables line the footpath, and atop them are white clay lanterns, candle holders, a handcarved wooden rooster. On the corner, a sign on a wall advertises a *pensión*. I haven't had to walk far to find somewhere to spend the night. This small hotel just around the corner from the cathedral looks charming. It is a colonial building with wrought-iron balustrades that wrap around skinny balconies, standing room only; wooden shutters are open to allow the *brisa* to flit from room to room. It is a little after lunchtime and there is only one couple lined up at the reception desk.

The man at the desk is amiable and relaxed.

'Are you alone?' he asks.

'Yes,' I reply.

'You are a very brave girl,' he says somewhat admiringly.

I smile: 'Oh, thank you.' I've given up explaining that solo travel for women in Australia is *de rigueur*; it is rarely understood in this macho country. Then again, I know it depends on which way you look at it. If I had grown up in Mexico I might have thought the idea of women travelling alone was some peculiar kind of madness.

'We have a lovely room upstairs,' the man says. 'Would you like to have a look at it?'

'I'd like that very much,' I reply.

When I have checked in, the man leads me up a stone staircase and down a darkened corridor. He unlocks a door and ushers me into the room with a wave of his arm. The windows of the *habitación* are open to reveal a wonderful view of the cathedral. It is a sun-filled room with two double beds, a sofa tucked beneath a gilt mirror and a very fancy coffee table. And it is huge. I turn back to the man.

'There must be a mistake,' I say. 'I only wanted a standard room.' The man *was* right. This is a lovely room, but I don't want to tell him I can't afford it. Already I can envision my panic on checking out tomorrow when I'm presented with a bill containing a telephone number amount of zeros. Oh well, *ataque cardiaco* here I come.

'Oh no, there's no mistake,' he says. 'We're kind of quiet at the moment so I gave you one of our superior rooms.' He must read my stricken expression. 'At no extra charge.'

Well, if you put it that way.

'Thank you. That's very kind of you.'

He leaves me with a slight bow. '*Si necesitas algo. Avísame.*' If you need anything, just let me know.

I drop my bag on the bed and walk out onto the balcony. The view caters to all different tastes. From here, I can look down at the bustle in the plaza below and, way beyond that, at the panorama of the Mexican countryside. In the middle distance there are white *casas* with red tiled roofs, perched on the steep hillside; a haphazard collection of topsy houses. Hydrangeas and something pink and showy spill from window boxes, cascading from balconies in a splash of colour and brilliance. The sky is postcard blue, the trees are a luminescent green and the early-afternoon sun sits high in the distant sky. Further out, the hills undulate into the distance, coloured from the same palette as the Australian landscape: ochre and burnt orange, chocolate brown and green.

After a short rest I leave the hotel and head back towards the cathedral. Inside the *iglesia* the only light is provided by the sun bursting through the stained glass windows high above. I take a seat near the main doors, where it is cool and dark. The large crowd stands as a priest walks down the aisle. He begins the service. 'Thank you for coming,' he says. But I lose him after that. I can't hear a word he is saying over the sounds from outside of screaming babies, car alarms, vendors, children playing soccer, shouting, laughing, dogs barking. The priest is wearing a small microphone on his vestment but it's no use, his sermon has been completely drowned out by the almighty clamour. What he needs is a mighty voice *and* a megaphone.

I look over at the other parishioners; they are completely unperturbed. Heads are bowed. Some women are fanning themselves, oblivious. Another crochets a doily. I don't think anyone can hear the priest. I start to laugh. What kind of madness is this? Don't they find the racket just a little distracting? No, it seems. The *ruido* doesn't bother them at all. This is something I've known for a long time: Mexicans love noise. In fact, they thrive on it. I have adapted in so many ways to life in Mexico but part of me will always think like a foreigner, an *extranjera*. Perhaps I was thinking that a church might be an oasis of silence. Not this one. Now I can hear a *mariachi* band and a squealing trumpet. I find myself laughing – quietly of course, although it doesn't really matter because it's not like anybody would hear me. Or care. How I love this country. Leaving them to it, I slip out of the church and buy myself a strawberry *gelati* from a cart on the other side of the square.

For the rest of the afternoon I explore Taxco, puffing as I climb up and down the narrow, steep streets. I potter in and out of stores and stop outside pretty houses with planter pots spilling with hibiscus, or turn to look at the view from different vantage points all over town.

When I return to the *pensión* the man at the counter calls

out a greeting. '*Bonita noche, señorita.*' I can only nod, still stunned by this place and its timeless beauty.

In the evening I have a shower in a technicolour bathroom. The walls and floor are covered in Spanish tiles: a frenzy of colour, each *mosaico* handpainted by local artisans who reproduce designs from the fifteenth century. The sink patterned with swirls of colour looks too beautiful to use. As I stand under the invigorating spray, allowing the water to massage my scalp, I think what a wonderful idea it was to come here. The beauty of Taxco and the surrounding area is an affirmation of everything I love about relaxed, happy, languid Mexico.

I dress and open the shutters to a sun setting like a fiery orb on the other side of the mountain peaks. From the balcony I can also see a garland of star-shaped lights hanging from the cathedral fence.

I walk to a café I had seen earlier in the day and take a table near one of the two arched doorways that serve as entrances. It has just turned eight-thirty pm – too early for Mexican stomachs after their late *almuerzo* – and it is quiet and almost empty inside. It is a small place with half a dozen tables covered in white tablecloths and tealight candles. I love it! With the light from a *veladora* on the wall, I study the menu. Everything sounds fabulous. The food is rustic: *enchiladas*, turkey *poblano*, stuffed chiles and soups. I order *pozole*. The waitress leaves and I sit silent, absolutely content.

She returns to ask if I would like blue or *masa* tortillas. Blue please. Just as she walks away I hear a little voice. Then I hear it again, this time louder, coming from behind me. It is a little boy crouching in the doorway. I'd seen him outside the cathedral a few minutes earlier.

'*¡Hola!*' he says.

'Hello,' I reply.

He seats himself on the doorstep and rearranges the clay lantern he holds in his arms. 'Do you like this?' he says, getting down to business.

'Yes,' I say. 'It's very nice.'

'Buy it then.'

'But I don't have a house.'

'So, hang it in the garden of the *patrón*.' (A word that literally means 'boss' but in this context means a husband; a wife is known as *la patrona*.)

I laugh. He's sharp.

But I still decline. Instead I find two bars of Carlos Kinter chocolate in my bag, and give them to him. It is real Mexican chocolate made from an Aztec recipe, a bitter, unrefined version of the stuff I'm used to. Sandrine had given them to me and they've been in my bag ever since. The lantern is now forgotten as the boy rips one bar open and takes a big bite. Spying the waitress, he picks up the lantern, stuffs the other bar in his pocket and disappears down the street.

The *pozole* is delivered in a big clay dish. I take a mouthful. It is delicious. So many flavours in one bowl! It tastes like bacon – the ham hocks that are added during cooking – with corn and chokoes, a much-derided vegetable back home in Australia, but which give the soup an indescribable depth of taste. Apparently it is all in the slow cooking, an essential technique in Mexican cuisine. The *cazuela* is also important. Time, ingredients and implements, the keys to success. I have my grandmother's recipe for *pozole*. Now all I need is the earthenware dish. Tomorrow before I leave I will buy one from the market. There's a chance I will return to Australia like a pack mule but I can't leave without these dishes; clay pots are hard to find in Melbourne.

'*¿Sabe bien?*' the waitress asks. Taste good?

'*Increíble*,' I reply.

I've eaten enough but can't resist the *churros* and one last coffee. What *is* incredible is that I haven't put on any weight since I've been in Mexico. Which goes to prove the theory that living in a tropical country does wonders for the figure; in this heat you burn energy just by walking to the bus stop. And it's a good thing too. I have been eating like a starving sumo wrestler. Of course eating has an entirely different significance in Mexico than it does in Australia. Here, it is a way of life, a sign of affection. At least that's what I tell myself as I dunk another *churro* into the jar of melted chocolate.

At ten o'clock I leave the restaurant. Outside the street is dark and quiet. My shoes clack softly on the cool cobblestones as I walk the short distance back to my hotel.

Back at the hotel I open the shutters again and step onto the balcony to breathe in the frangipani-scented air. Above me, the stars blink in the evening sky. I feel tired but I resist sleep. I only have a short time left and want to enjoy every single moment. At three in the morning I'm still at the window, wrapped in a blanket and watching the stars, because it is so quiet here that I can't sleep anyway.

In the morning I climb the stairs to the roof garden where breakfast is being served. It seems the right place for a *desayuno*: at the top of the world. And in this place where I am feeling on top of the world. Looking down from the terrace to the plaza below, I am reminded of the weekend I spent in Valle de Bravo, another town perched high in the mountains. Two men are standing at the buffet, talking excitedly in another language. They seem overwhelmed, as I once was, by the typically Mexican banquet-style proportions of the food in front of them. There is orange juice and papaya with sugar and lemon to begin with, red and black beans, tortillas, scrambled eggs, chile, sausages, ham and bread rolls. After that, *conchas* (my grandmother's favourite), donuts, croissants, bananas, and as much *café de olla* as you can possibly drink. I settle for juice, coffee, thick slices of papaya and a *concha*. I finish breakfast and linger over the view for a moment longer, before braving the walk back down the hill, stopping to look at different *artesanía* stalls along the way. I buy a *cazuela* for making *pozole* and carry it gently in my arms towards the bus station.

Back in Mexico City, it is time to say goodbye. Jean and Sandrine are leaving for a holiday in Cuba and by the time they return I will be gone. I get up at four am for a sleepy farewell. We all hug and then stand there, not sure what to do next. 'Okay then,' Jean says. 'We better go now. Write us a letter before you leave.' He pauses. 'And make it emotional.' (I do write them a *carta* telling them how much they mean to me, and it must be a bit over-the-top because when Sandrine reads it a week later she bursts into tears.) Watching them leave, I feel a lump in my throat, but I put on a brave face and wave from the doorway. After they are gone I schlep back up the stairs to my bedroom, feeling overwhelmed by sadness.

Saying goodbye to my grandmother is even more painful. Having already bid my farewells to my aunt and cousins earlier in the week, I kiss her on the cheek hoping it won't be too long before I see her again. '*Dios te bendiga*,' she says. God bless you. Then she makes the sign of the cross on my forehead. She turns away quickly, picks up a washing basket and goes outside, leaving me alone in the living room. I watch her walk away, strong and much improved since her health problems late last year. I've learned so much from this wise old woman. From her I embraced a faith that accepts what you can't see, an understanding of this land of myth and magic, history and tradition. And most of all, I love her for just being who she is. I walk from the apartment and along the streets of *Colonia*

Narvarte towards *Ángel de la Raza*, where I catch a downtown bus. From my window I see the bakery I'd gone to on my very first day here, six months ago. It seems like a lifetime ago. On my way home I stare ahead, clutching the seat in front of me.

Chapter Twenty-One

A Suitcase, a Backpack and a Canasta

Three days later and I'm on a mission. The man on the other end of the telephone is laughing. 'So you want to order a pizza?' he asks. It's the middle of the night and I'm trawling the phone book for a pizza place that delivers at three am. Now I think I'm in luck.

'Yes please. And I was wondering if you deliver?'

He is still laughing. 'I'm sorry, dear, I can't help you. I'm just the cleaner.'

I thank him and hang up, bemused. After six months in Mexico City, I've only just discovered that in the largest city in the world you can't order pizza in the middle of the night. On the eve of my departure, I have a sudden craving for it. It seems strange given that I haven't even thought about Western food since I arrived in Mexico, let alone eaten it. Perhaps it's a subconscious desire for the comforts of home.

It is the beginning of April and I am finally ready to leave for Australia. In true Mexican style, I have left everything to the last minute. It must be about an hour before dawn when I finally get around to packing my suitcase. I've barely had time to contemplate this task. In the past three days friends have been popping in to say goodbye, others invited me out for a quick meal, my mother's cousin dropped by, and our downstairs neighbours took me to our favourite Cuban bar, Mamá Rumba, for one last *mojito*. Even the lovely Señora Urdaci came over with her little dog and a box of goodies.

After too many days of *reventón*, socialising, and hardly any sleep, I'm ready to lie on the floor and sleep forever. Elizabeth, who insisted on keeping me company for my last night in Mexico, is sound asleep on the sofa. And I'm facing a scene of unmitigated disaster.

I have a supply of *cositas*, little things to take back to Australia with me, and I have no idea how I'm going to fit it all in. On the armchair is a pile of clothes I'm giving to Elizabeth – in fact, all except for the clothes I'll be wearing on the plane. I need room for *artesanías*. I have a pink tin butterfly with gold antennae; a big woven basket my grandmother bought me in the Indian markets; pottery – cups, plates and *cazuelas*; *alebrijes* – handpainted wooden figurines; and a papier-mâché doll for my mother, like the ones she played with as a child. Then there are many gifts and trinkets from friends, another example of overwhelming Mexican generosity. Looking at all this and wondering how on earth I'm going to get it in my luggage, I don't know if I want to laugh or cry.

Of course, there is also the food. Cans of *ate de guayaba* (jelly paste), about ten packets of tortillas because I can't buy them at home, cans of chiles, *glorias* and bags of *mole* powder. I have only one packing rule: if I can fit it, I'll take it. I discover more stuff under the coffee table. Beautiful *talavera* candle holders and two tin mirrors. I stuff everything into a suitcase, a backpack and a *canasta*, a wicker basket. Then I notice on the bench the bottle of *pulque*, a potent agave extract, my mother's cousin had given me. I have never tried it before. Do I dare? I'm resorting to hard liquor – how has it come to this? I crack it open. Elizabeth wakes to find me swigging from the bottle.

'*¡Qué barbaridad!*' she exclaims. 'What are you doing?'

'Well . . .' I start. And then I start coughing as the liquid goes down my throat. It is the strongest drink I have ever tasted – stronger even than the tequila I dislike immensely – and it is horrible. I feel my head spinning and I lie back against the suitcase.

'*¡Guacala!*' I say. 'That's awful!'

'Of course it is,' Elizabeth says, laughing. 'Why did you drink it in the first place?'

'I thought it would wake me up,' I reply, shaking my head to try to disperse the aftertaste.

It is nearly five and the dark sky outside still reveals nothing. In this eerie silence I take in the wonder of Mexico City. The street lights are still on and I can hear the faraway sounds of traffic. Soon dark shadows will dissipate and daylight will blossom in the sky, turning it from charcoal into a heavy grey-blue patchwork. I picture the morning rituals: street vendors setting up food stalls and newspaper and juice stands under the cover of darkness. Working solidly like the people of this ancient city who lived here centuries before them. And as I stand here, I realise I am just like them – another dot on the timeline of history; just passing through.

Elizabeth comes over to the window.

'Are you all right?' she asks.

'Yes,' I say. 'Just taking it all in.'

If there is one image of Mexico I want to record in my memory, it is the view from this window of the city at daybreak.

An hour later we are standing on the footpath waiting for the taxi. By this time it is light and the air is cool and fresh. The green and white Volkswagen Beetle turns the corner and stops outside the front gate. Roberto stands with us, silent. He loads my things into the car, then comes back and says, 'Don't forget me.' I promise I won't. I give him a hug and push an envelope of my remaining Mexican money, about twenty US dollars, into his pocket when he isn't looking.

Along the road to the airport I see vendors erecting stalls, chopping gladioli stems and arranging them in plastic buckets, sweeping rubbish into neat piles ready to be collected, shoe sellers arranging sheets of plastic on the ground, securing them with chunks of rock. In a couple of hours the roads will be jammed with traffic, police will take their places at intersections around the city and hordes of people will descend on the metro. Even at this early hour the road has already begun to fill with taxis and *colectivos*. They pass us as we wait at the traffic lights.

After the early-morning quietness of the city, I'm shocked by the number of people who are already at the airport. In the street a line of people are waiting for the official airport taxis. Everywhere there is noise. The place still looks like a construction site. Giant concrete pipes, tall enough to stand in, have been left near the entrance to the Hilton Hotel, as though someone forgot to move them. There are piles of rubble nearby. Cranes. Scaffolding. Cars. Trucks. An earth mover. Nothing has changed. Except me. Amid the car horns, rumble of graders, yelling voices and police whistles, I feel completely peaceful. It is a serenity that the chaos around me cannot disturb, even when the taxi driver dumps my luggage on the footpath and hoons off in a cloud of exhaust fumes.

Elizabeth is looking bleary-eyed and exhausted. We buy big cups of strong coffee and sit on the upper concourse waiting for my flight to be announced. I hug her. 'Take care,' she says. This is the worst part of leaving anywhere. The final moments. And then I turn and walk through the departure gates. I stop for one last glance and see her standing in the same spot with a hand on her forehead. Although I'd managed to be brave saying goodbye, now I'm on the verge of bursting into tears.

On the plane I look out my window at the sea of houses lining the hill outside the airport. Concrete shanty towns. Buildings that match the grey sky. Traffic streams along the arterial road. Tears are now running down my cheeks. Looking out at this urban wasteland, something occurs to me: this was a sight once so horrifying to me that *it* made me cry. And now I'm crying because I'm leaving it behind. I smile to myself. It is amazing to think that at one time I had detested this place with all my heart. Now I can hardly believe that was ever true. How incredible that hate can turn to love in what seems like the blink of an eye.

But I know I will return. As my grandmother said: *You cannot deny who you are.* And how right she was. My wise Mexican *abuelita* knew before I did that as a mixed-race child I would always feel a sense of dislocation; but she also knew that being here would go a long way towards diminishing that feeling and finding peace within myself. It just took me some time to understand. This country is such a big part of who I am, I could never turn my back on it. Mexico will always have a very special place in my heart; no matter where I choose to live.

The plane arrives in Los Angeles at lunchtime. I'm still thinking of Mexico so it is quite a shock to see this place so shiny and clean. Outside at the taxi ranks, drivers wait patiently for their turn. People buying transport tickets form orderly queues, not like across the border at Benito Juárez airport where the *fila* is a writhing mass of arms, legs and bodies like a box of newborn puppies.

I am resting my chin against the handle of my luggage trolley and watching the human traffic rushing to and fro when two men in jeans and pullovers approach me. They are swaggering as if tough, but to me look skinny, pale and vulnerable, so they inspire a feeling closer to pity than fear. I mentally name them Tweedledum and Tweedledee.

'We've come to harass you,' Tweedledum, the bigger one, says.

I don't respond. Upon arrival, I'd sailed through customs with the assistance of a number of Mexican–American men who did everything but carry me into the United States on a reclining sofa. One got me a trolley, another a pen and the right arrival documents to fill out, so that even after two hours in the United States I haven't actually spoken a word of English. I decide to try out a joke.

I look at them, poker-faced. '*No hablo Inglés.*'

'What?'

It's working!

'*No hablo Inglés,*' I say again. Of course the one flaw in this plan is that if I really didn't speak English I wouldn't be repeating myself when someone asked me a question. I suppress a laugh. The good thing is that I have the face to carry this off.

Tweedledum turns to Tweedledee. 'She said she doesn't speak English.'

Tweedledee is shaking his head. 'Nah man, she told us to fuck off.'

Now I just want to fall about laughing, but I remain composed. The Tweedles are now looking oddly embarrassed. 'Er, sorry,' they say in unison. They beat a hasty retreat and I go back inside.

Gripping my overflowing *canasta*, I approach the X-ray

machine and place the basket gently on the conveyor belt. I step through the metal detector and move to collect my things. But the attendant, another Mexican–American, wants to look at something odd inside my bag.

He smiles sweetly and asks: 'Do you mind emptying everything out?'

No, no, no! It is so full I won't be able to get everything back in. The entire contents of the bag are spilled onto the counter. *Glorias*, canned chiles, an exhibition poster from the Dolores Olmedo Museum, tortilla packets and *pingüinos* – little penguins, the chocolate and chantilly cream cakes that are to die for. And the mysterious object – a *cazuela* with a lid and two bags of *mole*, one brown, one green, stuffed inside.

'Is that *mole*?' he asks, incredulous.

'Er yes,' I reply, feeling slightly embarrassed.

'Why have you got that?'

'Well, I'm going to Australia and they don't sell it there and I can't live without the stuff so I had to bring it with me from Mexico, you see,' I say in almost one breath.

'Aaahh,' he says slowly. 'Now I understand.' And after all that I re-pack my bag and head to my gate.

Finally, the Qantas flight to Melbourne is announced, but I haven't eaten all day, so I wander off, *a la mexicana*, to buy something to eat. My last ten dollars is spent at McDonald's, a mistake. The burger is awful, plastic and flavourless, and the fries are cold. Only yesterday I was craving Western food, but now after this awful McDonald's experience I realise what I really miss is Mexican food. I have been away for less than half a day and I'm already craving tortillas with black beans and *chorizo*. At least I have supplies.

By the time I get back to the departure gate the final boarding call has been made. The crowd is made up of a sea of white faces. No proud Indian faces. No *mestizos* – half-

Spanish, half-Indian. No-one to remind me of my family. Nothing to remind me of Mexico. Just a lot of white people in varying shades of pink. And me.

It's funny to think how going home can mean so many things. I am no longer *linda* or *nena* or even *Samantita*. Now I'm Samantha. It is time to revert to the person I am when I am in Australia. But who is that person? Fundamentally I am the same person but I also feel so different. I am stronger now, and *calmer*, more comfortable with myself. Perhaps that is what this search for identity was all about – coming to terms with who I am.

The plane lands in Melbourne at seven o'clock on an April morning. As the passengers cluster in the aisle, a woman turns to me. '*Buenos días*,' she says. 'I saw you at the airport.' I return her greeting. She tells me she had been visiting family in El Salvador. 'It is good to be home.' We get off the plane and walk together towards customs. She helps me carry the basket that I'm now cursing for the painful welts it has left on my palms. I'm so grateful I could kiss her. At passport control she leans forward and kisses me on the cheek, her eyes glowing with genuine kindness. '*Que le vaya bien*,' she says. Be well. I focus on her big dark eyes and see a lot of myself in them. My passport is stamped and, just like that, I'm back in Australia.

I collect my bags and walk out into the bright air of a Melbourne morning.

Epilogue

It is a sunny afternoon as the car pulls up at the Sorrento shops, across the road from the foreshore. Two hours earlier my dad had picked me up from the airport, and now we are sitting under a canopy of tea-trees that sway in the breeze, allowing glimpses of the shimmering bay. When my dad goes for a newspaper I get out of the car and stand on the nature strip, breathing in the salty air. He comes back and I tell him to go on without me. 'I'll walk home,' I say.

It's a short walk to the beach, down a winding path past brightly painted boatsheds and upturned dinghies lying in the scrub. At the end of the walkway I kick off my shoes and sink my feet into the cool sand. It is a sensation I haven't felt for more than six months. Trudging down the beach, I find a beach hut in the shade and sit down on the ramp. Above me seagulls hover, picked up now and then by strong gusts of wind that carry them sideways through the air. A lone man is approaching with a dog. It stops to sniff at a blowfish that has washed up on the shore, and yelps when it is poked in the nose by a spine. The man smiles as he passes me.

I lean back against the shed and close my eyes, feeling the warmth of the sun on my face. There is a pelican on the sand, wings outstretched, catching expertly the morsels of fish thrown from the fishermen on the pier. Yachts with tall masts bob in the distance. High above me, puffs of cloud float by like the dissipating letters from a sky-writing plane.

I think of the contrast between this beauty, so apparent, and the *belleza* of Mexico. I will miss the sparkling eyes of the marketplace vendors – the women who sit cross-legged on the ground, weaving and talking and telling me to sit down too when I come over to buy a *canasta*, because *these things take time*. And Mexicans have a lot of that. *Tiempo*. An appreciation of life and how to live it, and a *pasión* for food, parties, folklore and dance. I'll miss the smell of *masa*, corn flour, cooking on a griddle. The colour of a pink flower on a stone wall. A blood-orange sunrise over a grey city. A brilliant mural in a museum, showing the peasants rising up against the ruling Spaniards. A crowd of thousands filling the *Zócalo* on New Year's Eve to listen to *mariachi* music.

And of course, I will miss my grandmother. I remember climbing the six flights of stairs to her apartment for the first time in 1996, and finding my grandmother standing in the hallway, tiny and stooped. And yet so familiar. Because even back then – in the midst of the horror and confusion Mexico inspired in me – I had looked in her eyes and saw so much of myself.

In Mexico I learned to speak another language, to open myself up to the spirit world with *veladoras* and offerings, and to appreciate the rituals and beliefs of this mystical country. Battling to understand this culture and my place within it has given me the most valuable gift any person can ever have: the strongest sense of peace. And I couldn't ask for anything more than that.

I walk home to my parents' house from the beach. The

street outside the shops is full of people. A new café has opened while I've been away and there is a crowd standing under canvas umbrellas drinking white wine. The sun is so bright it picks up the reflection from the glasses so they look like liquid gold. I look at them and smile. I'm back and so happy to be here, yet it feels unreal. Life here seems easy. I laugh as I see a dog sitting in the front passenger seat of a car. Even the dogs have it good. Life *is* easy. I walk under a tea-tree and along the path to the house, shaking the sand from my feet at the front door. I go inside and call out, 'I'm home!' From the other end of the house I hear my mother's voice and footsteps running down the hall.

Recipes

Sopas

Soups

CONSOME DE ARROZ
Rice broth

This is one of my favourite soups because it is so easy to make. The taste is all in the balance of ingredients so don't kill the flavour by adding too much salt, just a pinch when ready. Begin by washing rice under a tap until water runs clear, to get all the starch out. Lay rice on kitchen paper and leave until completely dry. Fry rice with a tablespoon of olive oil until golden brown – 2 minutes is usually enough. In a heavy-based pan add water, fried rice and stock cubes. Remove skin of onion and add it whole. In a separate pan, boil the chicken with the other onion. When chicken is cooked, shred into strips and add to *consome*. Discard onions. When the rice is *al dente* take pan from heat. Stir in juice from half a lemon, then season with salt and pepper.

1 cup white rice
4 cups water
2 cubes chicken stock
2 medium onions
50 grams chicken breast
$^1/_2$ lemon
salt and pepper

SOPA DE TORTILLA
Tortilla soup

This variation on the staple tortilla makes a great soup. To make tortilla chips, *totopos*, cut tortillas into small squares and bake in a moderate oven until crispy on both sides. In a large saucepan, bring chicken stock to a boil and simmer for 20 minutes. Grill corn cobs under the griller or on a barbecue, then remove kernels by slicing along the cob with a sharp knife. Add to chicken stock, along with the tomatoes, chile, onion and lime juice. Simmer for another 10 minutes before finally adding the *totopos*. Serve with parsley, cubed avocado and crumbled fetta.

10 corn tortillas
2 cups chicken stock
2 cobs corn, grilled
2 large tomatoes, finely diced
2 medium jalapeño chiles, finely chopped
1 large red onion, finely diced
juice of 1 lime
parsley, avocado and fetta to garnish

Platos Principales

Main meals

ENCHILADAS ROJAS CON POLLO
Chicken enchiladas with red chile sauce

A hearty sauce made from fresh tomatoes is the perfect complement to the chicken in this dish. The traditional *salsa* can be varied in strength, depending on the chiles used. All herbs must be fresh for maximum flavour. Place tomatoes in a pan of boiling water until skins begin to come away, then discard water and peel tomatoes. Sauté the chopped onion in a tablespoon of olive oil and, when translucent, add chiles and garlic (cook until soft). Finally add tomatoes and allow to simmer for 5 minutes to release the flavours. Puree ingredients in a blender with parsley. In a separate pan boil chicken in a litre of water with the whole onion and a dash of salt; when cooked, remove chicken and tear into strips, keeping the *caldo*, the broth it was cooked in. Return contents of blender to frypan and simmer in a teaspoon of olive oil for another 5 minutes, then add 1 cup of the *caldo*, chicken broth. Simmer for 10 minutes. If the sauce is too runny you can add a tablespoon of cornflour to thicken. Remove from heat. Place tortillas flat, and in the middle of each put a small amount of chicken, grated cheese and sauce. Roll lengthways. Arrange tortillas in a terracotta dish and cover with more sauce, sour cream and remaining cheese. Cook in a moderate oven until cheese is melted.

6 tomatoes
olive oil
1 whole garlic bulb (cooking kills the strength, but leaves the flavour)
2 onions, whole for chicken, chopped for sauce
3 red chiles, finely diced
parsley (handful to taste)
1 litre water
10 tortillas
6 chicken breasts
1 bag of grated cheese
sour cream

MOLE VERDE
Green mole

This variation on the *mole* trinity – *verde, rojo* and *poblano* – is probably the easiest to make and, for Australian palates, the gentlest. I used to buy bags of powder from the market until I found out how easy it was to make from scratch, despite its intricacy of flavours. Combine onion, garlic, chiles, parsley, coriander, mint, cinnamon, sesame seeds, pumpkin seeds, peanuts and cashews in a blender with ½ cup of the chicken stock. In an earthenware pot (this gives it a fuller flavour), add a tablespoon of olive oil and ingredients from the blender. Pour in the rest of chicken stock (careful not to make it too runny). Bring to boil and add chicken, then cook over medium flame until strips are cooked. Serve with rice and tortillas. Or as in the preceding *enchiladas* recipe, substitute the sauce to make chicken enchiladas with *mole verde* sauce.

1 cup chicken stock
1 medium onion, diced
1 clove garlic, chopped finely
2 green chiles, chopped finely
7 stalks of parsley
7 stalks of coriander
3 stalks of mint
1 stick of cinnamon
2 teaspoons each of sesame and pumpkin seeds,
peanuts and cashews
olive oil
6 chicken breasts, cut into strips

ALBONDIGAS
Meatballs

This dish, served with crusty bread and a glass of red wine, is the perfect winter meal. All the way from the tropics! In a bowl combine the mince, bread crumbs, the diced onion, and 2 parsley stalks, then add beaten egg yolk and season with salt and pepper. Mould mixture into small balls. In a heavy-based pan, warm the olive oil before adding the chopped onion and chile; add garlic when onion is translucent. Place tomatoes in a pot of boiling water to loosen skin, then peel. Add tomatoes, oregano, sage and rest of parsley to pan with onion mixture. Put a lid on ajar and allow to simmer for 30 to 40 minutes. Season with salt and pepper.

250g beef mince
2 medium onions, diced for mixture, chopped for pan
3 tablespoons bread crumbs
3 stalks parsley, chopped finely
1 egg yolk, beaten
4 tablespoons olive oil
1 clove garlic, chopped finely
2 red chiles chopped finely
6 medium tomatoes, peeled and diced
1 teaspoon each oregano and sage

CHILES RELLENOS DE PICADILLO
Stuffed chiles

The best substitute for *chiles grandes* (not available in Australia) are green capsicums. Place them under a griller, until skin begins to blister; remember to char them all over. Remove from grill and put in a plastic bag, cover with a damp tea towel and leave to cool for an hour. Meanwhile, place mince in a saucepan with chicken stock, onion and garlic. Cook until all liquid evaporates. Peel capsicums and slit open on one side (try not to break in half) to remove seeds. Fill with mince mixture. In a dish beat egg whites until they form soft peaks. Fry a tablespoon of olive oil in a pan and when hot add pureed tomatoes and oregano, and allow to simmer for 5 minutes. Finally, roll capsicums in egg white and place in an oven dish, cover with tomato *salsa* and cook in a moderate oven for 30 minutes.

5 large green capsicums
500g beef mince
1 litre chicken stock
1 large onion, chopped finely
2 cloves garlic, chopped finely
3 egg whites
1 tablespoon olive oil
5 medium tomatoes, pureed in blender
1 teaspoon oregano

CARNE DE PUERCO EN RAJAS

Pork in chile sauce

A traditional favourite with pork, instead of the ubiquitous chicken. The recipe can be spiced up by adding extra chiles (depending on your guests). You can also use turkey instead of pork. The sauce goes well with everything. In a pan boil pork fillets with a litre of water, a whole onion and a dash of salt. Meanwhile puree chiles, diced onion, garlic, and a teaspoon of water in a blender. When fillets are cooked, remove from broth (but don't throw broth out). Discard whole onion. In a frypan, warm olive oil and fry meat until golden brown on both sides. Pour ingredients from blender over the fillets and add the broth in which the pork was cooked. Simmer for twenty minutes. Serve with rice.

1 litre water
$^1/_2$ kilo pork fillets
2 medium onions, 1 whole, 1 diced
250 gram tin of jalapeño chiles
1 clove garlic
3 teaspoons olive oil
salt to taste

Arroz

Rice

ARROZ MEXICANO
Red 'Mexican' rice

Rice is so popular in Mexico, it is served with almost every main meal. Of course, there is great debate among Mexican women about what makes a perfect *arroz*. I still can't make my rice as fluffy as my grandmother's, but I keep trying. The saffron is what gives this dish its distinct flavour. Rinse rice under tap until water runs clear, then dry completely on absorbent paper. Sauté onion with oil and then add rice, stirring gently until light brown (usually 2 to 3 minutes). Add chicken stock, saffron and carrot and cook on medium flame until all liquid has evaporated. You can throw in some peas at the end to complement the carrots.

1 cup long grain rice
$\frac{1}{2}$ onion, diced
2 tablespoons vegetable oil
$1\frac{3}{4}$ cups chicken stock
pinch of saffron
2 carrots, diced
handful of frozen peas

Salsas

Sauces

GUACAMOLE
Avocado dip

Chicken sausages covered in lashings of *guacamole* is one of my favourite dishes. You can serve this sauce with salads and main meals, appetisers or sliced vegetables. The mistake many people make is to add too much lemon; its strong flavour tends to overpower the taste of the other ingredients. Combine tomatoes, garlic, onion, salt, green chiles and a teaspoon of water (more if too thick) in a blender. When ingredients are mixed add avocado and blend for another ten seconds. Finally, add a dash of lemon and Tabasco sauce (optional) for extra flavour.

3 large tomatoes, roughly chopped
1 clove of garlic
1 medium onion, finely sliced
2 green chiles (nice and hot!), finely sliced
3 large avocados, roughly chopped
$1/2$ teaspoon lemon juice
salt to taste
Tabasco sauce to taste

SALSA PICADA
Hot chile sauce

When made right this sauce will instantly clear your sinuses, and the key to success is the chiles. In Australia, chiles don't tend to be as hot as those in Mexico so the best thing to do is to buy them fresh from the Asian food stalls at the market. They pack quite a punch. A tip to choosing the right variety: *the smaller the better*. If you're after a milder flavour just slice the chiles open and scrape out the seeds before blending. The recipe itself is easy – just stick everything in a food processor and blend until smooth.

2 green chiles
1 large tomato, chopped
1 medium onion, chopped
$^{1}/_{2}$ teaspoon of parsley
1 avocado, chopped
salt to taste

Postres

Desserts

CHURROS CON CHOCOLATE

Fried pastry fingers with chocolate

A Spanish recipe, this dessert appears in every restaurant in Mexico. And it's popular as a snack for the *merienda*, supper. In a pan warm milk, water, brown sugar and butter and bring to the boil. In another bowl combine flour and salt. Transfer liquid into this bowl, then add egg. Combine until the mixture forms a thick, elastic paste. Check the batter is thick enough, otherwise the *churros* won't keep their shape. Leave until cool. Use a piping bag with a star nozzle to make 'finger' shapes. Heat oil in a deep pan until very hot. Fry *churros* until brown and crispy, then place on absorbent paper to drain excess oil. Roll in sugar. In a saucepan add cream and enough chocolate melts to form a thick sauce. Pour sauce into a jar and serve with *churros* and *café de olla*.

1 cup each milk and water
2 tablespoons brown sugar
2 tablespoons butter
2 cups plain flour
1 pinch salt
1 large egg
sunflower oil for frying
sugar for coating
chocolate melts
$^1/_2$ cup thickened cream

FLAN

Creme caramel

Simple recipes are often the best. This is another of my grandmother's delights. In a blender, mix together milk, condensed milk, eggs and vanilla. Pour sugar into a heavy-based pan in an even layer, allowing it to brown (without burning) over a slow flame. When the caramel is ready, pour into a flan mould and leave for five minutes, then add contents of the blender. Bake flan in a moderate oven for forty minutes or until the custard is wobbly. Leave in oven until completely cooled, then refrigerate for at least four hours.

1 cup milk
1 can condensed milk
6 eggs
1 teaspoon vanilla essence
1 cup sugar

GELATINA DE VAINILLA
Vanilla jelly

A family recipe, this dessert was my grandfather's favourite and it was his youngest sister, Elena, who often made it for him when he was a boy. Back then my great-aunt used fresh eggs, milk and cream from the family farm. This recipe still stands the test of time. But be sure to use full cream ingredients – low-fat just doesn't stack up. Bring to boil milk, vanilla and sugar. Beat egg yolks separately. Dissolve gelatine in two tablespoons of cold water. Allow milk mixture to cool until warm, then add egg yolks, gelatine and cream. With a hand-held blender beat for one minute before pouring into a dish and refrigerating overnight. This jelly is delicious served with syrup and fresh berries.

1 litre milk
2 teaspoons vanilla essence
400 grams of caster sugar
10 egg yolks
10 grams gelatine
250 millilitres thickened cream

Bebidas

Drinks

CHOCOLATE ESPESO
Mexican hot chocolate

This thick brew is a special love of Mexicans, even though the climate doesn't really suit it. Chocolate was first discovered by the Aztecs, called *chocolatl* in their native tongue, Náhuatl; and was served to the Spanish conqueror, Hernan Cortés, when he arrived at the city of Tenochtitlan (Mexico City). Of course, back then it didn't taste like this! Warm milk, chocolate and cream in a saucepan. Scrape the seeds from the vanilla bean and add both seeds and bean to the milk. Stir with a whisk until chocolate melts and slowly bring to a boil. Strain liquid into mugs. Add whipped cream to finish.

2 cups milk
1 tablet of Mexican chocolate
(125 grams/4 ounces dark chocolate)
1 vanilla bean, split lengthways
1/2 cup thickened cream
whipped cream to serve

CAFÉ DE OLLA
Pot-infused coffee

This coffee gets its name from the *cazuela* or clay pot it is 'infused' in. It can be made in a pan but often loses some of its flavour in the process. Put the *cazuela* on a medium flame, adding the water, cinnamon, sugar, chocolate and orange skins. Bring to the boil, remove from heat and add good quality instant coffee before straining into mugs. Stir and serve.

2 litres of water
1 stick of cinnamon
3 tablespoons of brown sugar
3 tablets of dark chocolate (couverture if possible)
4 orange skins
$1\frac{1}{2}$ tablespoons instant coffee

MARGARITAS
Lemon and tequila cocktail

For the best *margaritas* use fresh lemons, or for a variation try the juice of the fabulous blood orange. Combine tequila, lemon juice and plenty of ice in a blender. Dip rims of glasses in extra lemon juice before dipping in salt, then pour in tequila mixture. The salt balances the sweetness of the lemon.

$1^1/_2$ ounces (45 millilitres) tequila
$^1/_2$ ounce (15 millilitres) lemon juice, plus extra
$^1/_2$ ounce (15 millilitres) Triple Sec (lemon concentrate)
crushed ice
salt

MOJITOS
Rum and mint cocktail

There is a large Cuban population in Mexico City and just as their delicacies like *plantains* (a relative of the banana) have made it onto Mexican menus, so have other staples, namely rum, cigars and the *mojitos* cocktail. Before placing mint leaves in a glass, crush the stems with a teaspoon to release the flavour. Completely cover with lime and sugar before adding rum and soda water. Stir well and serve with a garnish of lime.

12 fresh spearmint leaves
$1/2$ lime, juiced
1 teaspoon sugar
$1^1/_2$ ounces (45 millilitres) rum
soda water

Thanks

I owe my first debt of thanks to my agent, Lyn Tranter, of Australian Literary Management, whose encouragement, faith and humour were everything to me whilst I was writing this book. There's no-one I'd rather have a martini with! I am especially grateful to my publisher Fiona Henderson, whose patience and unstinting enthusiasm kept me going. For their superb editing, I thank Kim Swivel and Zoe Walton.

Most of all I am indebted to my family – especially my mother, my greatest inspiration – who were with me every step of the way. A million thanks will never be enough. I am grateful, too, to my grandmother, who shared with me the stories of her life, but never expected to see them in a book.

The people and events in this book are real, although names have been changed and some characters are composite. I must confess this book is a 'portrait' rather than a family history, as my aim was to capture the essence of the Mexican people. I have also taken liberty with the chronology, quite simply because there are people with a mind for perfect recall, but I'm not one of them.

Finally, for Mexico: *En mi corazón siempre estás.*